Lord of Attention

Lord of Attention

GERALD STANLEY LEE
& THE CROWD METAPHOR IN
INDUSTRIALIZING AMERICA

Gregory W. Bush

The University of Massachusetts Press
Amherst

Copyright © 1991 by
The University of Massachusetts Press
All rights reserved
Printed in the United States of America
LC 90–37499
ISBN 0–87023–724–1
Designed by Edith Kearney
Set in Linotron Sabon by Keystone Typesetting, Inc.
Printed and bound by Thomson-Shore, Inc.

Library of Congress Cataloging-in-Publication Data

Bush, Gregory Wallace.
Lord of attention : Gerald Stanley Lee and the crowd metaphor in
industrializing America / Gregory W. Bush.
p. cm.
Includes bibliographical references and index.
ISBN 0–87023–724–1 (alk. paper)
1. Advertising—United States—History. 2. Lee, Gerald Stanley,
1862–1944. I. Title.
HF5813.U6B85 1991
659.1'0973'09041—dc20   90–37499
                                                      CIP

British Library Cataloguing in Publication data are available.

All photographs are from the Forbes Library, Northampton,
Massachusetts, and are used with permission.

To Carolina
and
my parents, William and Margaret Bush,
. . . for your patience and impatience

CONTENTS

ACKNOWLEDGMENTS

A scholar seldom receives tangible rewards. A quick comment here or there may be the only encouragement one gets about the project one has worked on for years. Thus it is a great pleasure not only to see the completion of this book but also to have the space to express my appreciation to some of the individuals who, in many different ways, helped me produce it.

My parents have not always understood why scholarship is such a slow and laborious process, but their support of my work has been strong and consistent and reflects a trust in me, for which I thank them very much.

My wife, Carolina, read several drafts of this book and became convinced that our scholarly interests were not in the same field. Nonetheless, through difficult times she worked hard to help me complete this—and assumed a disproportionate share of the time it takes to raise a child. Thank you.

Gerald Stanley Lee was originally going to be the focus of only one chapter in a book of portraits of men who wrote about crowds from 1830 to 1940. John O'Connor of the New Jersey Institute of Technology is largely responsible for suggesting that I concentrate entirely on Lee. John read much of this book and improved it significantly. His long-standing friendship, his creativity, and his overall support and encouragement are deeply appreciated.

James Shenton of Columbia University, my dissertation adviser, slogged through an amazing amount of barely readable material in the early stages of this work and survived. Others on the Columbia faculty whom I also want to thank are Eric Foner, Ann Douglas,

Walter Metzger, Joseph Ridgely, and Robert McCaughey. Thanks also to Leo Ribuffo and Bernard Mergen of George Washington University, both of whom whetted my appetite for American studies in the early 1970s.

Warren Susman leaves a beautiful and demanding legacy, as a scholar who cared passionately about life and about understanding the past. He aided me with lengthy comments of great value. Gene Leach, a close friend and colleague, encouraged me to rethink many aspects of our mutual interest in crowds, helped with extensive comments on an early draft, and was a constant source of encouragement over the past eight years. My uncle, Robert Bush, read a portion of this book and has provided me with insight into American social thought and literature over many years which I deeply appreciate.

Some early typing and editorial help was provided by Sonia Kahlill, Steve Samuels, and Jane Shumate. The director of the University of Massachusetts Press, Bruce Wilcox, was a strong supporter of this book, for which I want to thank him. Louis Bateman has also assisted me on numerous occasions. Others at the University of Massachusetts Press helped with many suggestions, including Marie Blanchard.

Friends I made at Columbia in the 1970s, a talented bunch who chose not to write Ph.D. dissertations (and who are probably the better for it) helped me formulate many ideas in the early stages of this book. These friends include Janine and Dick Perry, Tom Cook, Tom Nerney, and Bonnie Braine. Janine's assistance in reading an early draft was especially helpful.

The staffs of Butler Library at Columbia University and of the Otto G. Richter Library at the University of Miami were of enormous assistance in tracking down sources. Blaise Bisaillon of the Forbes Library in Northampton was very kind in allowing me wide access to the Lee papers, for which I am grateful.

The University of Miami generously funded several summers so that I could rewrite sections of this manuscript and also provided travel money. Thanks to Dean David Wilson for his overall support. Miami-area colleagues Walter Kamphoefner (now of Texas A & M), Daniel Pals, Michael Carlebach, Susan Curtis (now at Purdue), and Michael Krenn read sections of this manuscript and provided useful suggestions, for which I thank them. Others I want to thank are

Whittington Johnson, Janet Martin, Steve Stein, Zack Bowen, Ada Orlando, Andrew Handler, Lenny Del Granado, Raymond Mohl, John Kasson, Sybil Lipschultz, Hugh Thomas, Paul Boyer, Jackson Lears, Roland Marchand, Leslie Fishbein, Paul George, and Arva Parks.

Finally, to Victor and Consuelo Amram and "Mima," thanks for taking care of Paula on numerous occasions when deadlines loomed.

Chronology of the Life of
Gerald Stanley Lee

1862   October 4: Gerald Stanley Lee is born in Brockton, Mass. His parents, Samuel Lee (b. 1832) and Emma C. Carter Lee (b. 1835), had three more children: Christabel (b. 1865), Grace (b. 1867), and Theodore Storrs (b. 1873).

1866–72   Lee family lives in Greenfield, Mass., where Samuel is pastor of the Second Congregational Church.

1872–78   Lee family lives in Cleveland, Ohio, where Samuel is pastor of the First Congregational Church for seven years.

1878–84   Lee family lives in Oberlin, Ohio, where Samuel held the professorship of political economy at Oberlin College. GSL attends Oberlin College until 1883.

1884–85   GSL attends Middlebury College (near his father's parish in Brattleboro, Vt.), from which he graduates.

1885–88   GSL attends Yale Divinity School but does not graduate.

1888–89   GSL is pastor of the Congregational church of Princeton, Minn.

1890–93   GSL becomes pastor of Sharon Congregational Church, Sharon, Conn., after having studied vocal methods in New York City.

1891   *About an Old New England Church* is published by W. W. Knight.

1892   GSL visits Europe.

1893–96   GSL is pastor of Park Street Congregational Church in West Springfield, Mass.

1895–1907   GSL writes a series of columns and articles for such publications as *The Critic, The Chapbook, Putnam's Monthly,* and *Atlantic Monthly.* He lectures widely on literary and religious topics, mostly in the northeast, and lives near Smith College in Northampton, Mass.

1896   March 9: GSL resigns from the ministry.

June 25: GSL marries Jennette Barbour Perry. The Lees settle on High Street, in Northampton. Their daughter, Geraldine, is born on April 1, 1897. (Geraldine later married Maitland de Goroza, a sculptor, and died in childbirth.)

The Shadow Christ is published by Century. "Hullabaloo," an article on the Democratic National Convention, is published in *The Critic.*

1900–1901   *Atlantic Monthly* publishes Lee's articles on crowds and machines.

1903   *The Lost Art of Reading* is published by G. P. Putnam's.

1905–18   GSL publishes the bimonthly *Mt. Tom: An All Outdoors Magazine.*

1906   *The Voice of the Machine* is published by Mt. Tom Press.

1908   *Inspired Millionaires* is published by Mt. Tom Press.

1912   GSL and his wife visit England for a prolonged stay.

1913   *Crowds: A Moving Picture of Democracy* is published by Doubleday Page. It becomes the best-selling nonfiction book of the year.

1914   *Crowds, Jr.* is published by Doubleday Page.

1914–15   GSL has a weekly column in *New York World.*

1916   *We: A Confession of Faith for the American People* is published by Doubleday Page.

1918   *Air Line to Liberty* is published.

1919   "Super Advertising" is published in *Saturday Evening Post. The House of Twenty Seven Gardens* is published by Mt. Tom Press.

1920   *The Ghost in the White House* is published by E. P. Dutton.

1922   *Invisible Exercise* is published.

1925–33   GSL and his family live in New York and run Training School for Balance and Coordination (also called the Coordination Guild).

1931   *Heathen Rage* is published.

1933   *Recreating Oneself* is published.

1940   GSL publishes a promotional pamphlet: "What Living in Northampton Is Like."

1944   April 3: GSL dies in Northampton. He is survived by his wife.

Lord of Attention

Advertising and the Contours of a
Preaching Mentality

Most Americans in the 1920s probably considered advertising essential to an expanding economy and high wages. Advertisements informed consumers of new products and modern ways of living. The best-selling book in 1926, *The Man Nobody Knows,* characterized Jesus as a brilliant business organizer, outdoorsman, and advertising genius. That October, President Calvin Coolidge congratulated an audience of advertisers for stimulating the buying habits of Americans. "The uncivilized make little progress because they have few desires," he reassured them, joining the chorus of Americans who conceived of advertisers and other businessmen as cultural heroes whose authority should be left largely unfettered.[1]

Yet the president went further, concluding that "advertising ministers to the spiritual side of trade. It is a great power that has been entrusted to your keeping which charges you with the high responsibility of inspiring and ennobling the commercial world. It is all part of the greater work of the regeneration and redemption of mankind." The president saw advertising as a new "profession" or public service, fulfilling a quasi-religious role in American society.[2]

Thirty years earlier advertising had been considered on a par with working as a circus barker or a fast-talking salesman, not a calling for respectable middle-class youth. But vast cultural changes, a cathartic world war, and several presidents adept at manipulating public opinion all helped endow advertising with new spiritual and patriotic properties. The transformation was clear by June 1913, when leaders of the Associated Advertising Clubs met for a convention in Baltimore. At the high point of the convention, attendees dispersed throughout the city to preach from church pulpits about the spiritual service rendered to the public by advertising.[3]

This book will examine several facets of this transformation through the career of Gerald Stanley Lee, a fellow resident in Coolidge's hometown of Northampton, Massachusetts. A New England preacher who left his congregation in 1896 to "preach" through the print medium, Lee became an exuberant advocate of advertising in the 1910s. While his writings certainly do not represent the full sweep of American thought, they are symptomatic of significant tendencies in other intellectually inclined advertising men, publicity agents, business evangelists, and progressives in the early twentieth century. Lee saw himself as a son of Puritans and a prophet of the machine age, rationalizing the centralization of mass communication in conjunction with an ideal of elite stewardship performed by men of wealth. While other business or "New Thought" evangelists like Elbert Hubbard, Bruce Barton, Edward Bok, and Orison Swett Marden undoubtedly had larger audiences, Lee's books and magazine articles were widely read during the late years of the Progressive Era.[4]

Born in 1862, Lee was the son of old-line New Englanders. He attended Oberlin College, Middlebury College, and Yale Divinity School in the 1880s, then became a preacher in several pulpits in New England and Minnesota before resigning from his position in Springfield, Massachusetts, in 1896 to focus his attention on writing articles and books. First publishing on literary and religious subjects, Lee then increasingly wrote about the impact of what is now labeled mass culture and the need for a redefinition of business leadership in the United States. He published articles in the *Atlantic Monthly, The Outlook, The Critic*, and other magazines. By 1908, he had also published several books on the impact of machines, the problems of literacy, and the book that started him on his road to national recognition, *Inspired Millionaires* (1908).

By 1910, Lee became convinced that advertising could play a transformational or redemptive role in American life. He corresponded with prominent businessmen and advertisers, made tours of England in 1910 and 1912, and eventually pulled together much of his evolving thought in another book, entitled *Crowds: A Moving Picture of Democracy*, which became the best-selling nonfiction book of 1913. Lee's writings provide stark evidence about the legacy of an older Puritan tradition in the prewar period; the reception to his ideas is an overlooked touchstone concerning the changes taking place within American intellectual and cultural life.

In *Drift and Mastery* (1914), Walter Lippmann noted Lee's prominence as a business evangelist: "It is obvious that the trusts have created a demand for a new type of business man—for a man whose motives resemble those of the applied scientists and whose responsibility is that of a public servant. Nothing could be easier than to shout for joy, and say that everything is about to be fine: the businessmen are undergoing a change of heart. That is just what an endless number of American reformers are shouting, and their prophet is Gerald Stanley Lee."[5]

In *America's Coming of Age* (1915), Van Wyck Brooks wrote specifically of Lee's ideal that "has had such a vogue during these later years" and was such a "landmark and touchstone." Why? Because "it is in the direct line of the American tradition, it is the climax of our old Transcendental individualism. It springs like the flower of the century plant, right out of the apparent heart, right out of the apparent center, of American society." What that center was and how Lee acted to comprehend, express, and alter it for his own generation provides a unique window into American culture.[6]

By studying Lee's career we can learn something about how young Protestant males of the Gilded Age may have shifted their conceptions about preaching to church congregations onto wider audiences and ultimately onto a national public during the Progressive Era. Through Lee we can also get a clearer picture about the operation of cultural metaphors and emerging definitions of modern personality during the process of industrialization. Specifically, the example of Gerald Lee reflects how the residue of a "preaching mentality" interacted with shifting perceptions about collective behavior to help rationalize modern advertising and public relations.[7]

We shall see how Lee's early disdain toward advertising as a symptom of the degrading qualities of mass culture eventually shifted as he idealized the United States as a democratic market society and "attention engineers" as spiritual and cultural redeemers. Social Gospeller Charles Stelzle later expressed the emerging marketing ethos most clearly when he wrote that "the supreme duty of the modern church is to get new business. The church must realize that it is in exactly the same position as any other solicitor of custom, and it must advertise its goods." Yet, beyond merely selling products, or attracting congregations, many advertisers in effect defined social and political values. Advertisers and managers of public communications were thus increasingly seen as agents of the moral order, passing on models of progress, respectability, and conceptions of modernity to more secular spokesmen of the public will, such as businessmen and entertainers. Like so many of his contemporaries, Lee became fascinated with the techniques of mass persuasion, unabashedly exploiting the disorientation of a status-conscious public with increasingly emotional appeals.[8]

Few contemporaries were able to grasp the fact that advertising, marketing, and publicity were becoming big businesses in themselves, tied to a consumer culture and amalgamating psychology and scientific language with a mystical aura of knowing the public mind. Modern advertising, Raymond Williams relates, has become a system of organized magic obscuring important political and economic choices behind psychological facades. It is not simply a "way of selling goods, it is a true part of the culture of a confused society." The consequence for American culture was a profound failure to sustain adequate levels of public information affecting economic life. Ultimately Lee's writings reflect a variation of what Daniel Rogers has called the "rhetoric of social cohesion" in the Progressive Era. "The language of social bonds focused its users' anger on the irresponsible, antisocial act," Rogers writes, "but it directed its users' longings not to honesty but to a consciously contrived harmony." Lee joined a number of self-proclaimed idealists whose vague visions of harmony help account for the limited success of radical political challenges to the nation's economic structure.[9]

One who hinted at the perilous path that Lee traveled was the philosopher William James. In 1900 James was shocked by the prescient, "god like" quality of an article Lee had recently published. James commented to the publisher of the *Atlantic Monthly* that Lee "will be a force one day unless he degenerates into subjectivism and mannerism." Many others had long described Lee as the spiritual heir of Walt Whitman, Ralph Waldo Emerson, and Thomas Carlyle. It was to be Lee's fate that, even though he gained broad notoriety after 1910, he was to fulfill the latter part of James's prophecy by the outbreak of the war. By then he espoused a genial though coercive nationalism under the leadership of "attention engineers" which bears disturbing similarities to the rhetoric of European fascism. It is our fate to be living in an age wherein the outlines of the Progressive Era acceptance of "attention engineering"—tied to a belief in the United States as a democratic market society—remains largely un-challenged.[10]

The idea of the crowd is crucial to understanding the develop-ment of Lee's thought. As an ambiguous concept, sometimes con-noting fear of labor mobs or lower-class foreign-born hordes inhab-iting American cities, and at other times representing a more broadly conceived public, audience, or market, Lee's use of the crowd reflects its importance as a cultural metaphor in the period from 1890 to 1920. Many of his contemporaries who were attracted to literary realism or conceived of themselves as experimental, progressive, or modern, expressed ideas about crowds in ways that historians need to examine with greater precision. Through Lee, we can begin to appreciate the process in which the American public became vic-timized under a series of mistaken perceptions of crowd behavior fostered, in large part, by middle-class theorists.

I hope that this examination of Gerald Lee and the crowd meta-phor may make readers pause and reflect on the contemporary scope of "attention engineering," the pervasive trivialization of contempo-rary thought, the obsession with personality cults, and the power granted disproportionately to large corporations and the state in their attempts to channel public attention.

ONE

The Crowd Metaphor in Industrializing America

At the turn of the century Gerald Stanley Lee warned the readers of the *Atlantic Monthly* that a new tyranny had arisen in the United States, the tyranny of the crowd. Through the misuse of technology and the expansion of democracy, the United States had degenerated into a "civilization by numbers," Lee said, while individuality had largely dissolved into an irrational, crowdlike public. Modern heroes were needed to present spiritual visions to Americans. "A crowd can only be made beautiful by a man who defies it and delights in it at once," he wrote. Such a hero must be "a sharer and spectator at once; living above the crowd enough to lift it, and living in the midst of the crowd enough to be loved by it so that it will let him lift it." Lee conceived of such crowd consciousness as an emblem of a modern, well-guided democratic order. Derived largely from mid-century transcendentalists, Lee's vision led him on a desperate search for modern heroes; his was a religious quest to redefine and lead the public as its modern prophet.[1]

Lee's conceptions of crowds and publics were formed within the context of the late Victorian age when a communication revolution and fears of mob violence fueled both a patriotic awakening and a determination to understand and direct the behavior of crowds. Preachers, politicians, popular writers, businessmen, journalists, academics, cartoonists, and advertisers joined Lee in expressing opinions about crowd behavior that reflected the social tensions of the time. Spokesmen of culture reinforced the view of the American masses as fit to be ruled by either a self-styled "educated remnant" or by trained experts.

Four elements can be identified in assessing the changes in the prevalent conceptions of crowds that took place between the time when Lee left divinity school to become a preacher in the 1880s and the time when he wrote about the United States as a potentially "beautiful crowd" in the early twentieth century. First, the institutionally based republican tradition, informed by writers such as Abraham Lincoln and James Bryce, had long seen the need for a civil religion to bind the nation together, with mobs acting as the penultimate domestic hindrance toward that end. Second, the complex association of the city with mobs who were composed of the increasingly politicized working class was capped by national social dramas such as the Pullman Strike and, ironically, by the defeat of William Jennings Bryan, the leader of a predominantly rural revolt in 1896. Middle-class fear of the revolutionary intent of Bryan focused on the pivotal symbolic role played by the crowd. Informing these perceptions was a third element: a romantic view of the history of riots and heroic redemption from disorder that fueled a reawakened patriotic sentiment and the search for modern personalities in the 1890s. These, in turn, became linked to the efficacy of more efficient organizations, and an increasingly apolitical identity among the middle class. Fourth, by the turn of the century the sudden attraction of crowd psychology and the growth of a consumer culture helped solidify a highly organized culture of fads, fashion, and spectacle based on techniques of persuasion. Modernism, as an expression of an ostensibly democratic market society, thus became linked to manipulatable definitions of human nature. The "educated remnant" had helped usher in the consumer culture and the sense of inevitability through perceptions of collective behavior. This framework of diverse associations linked the public and the market to the mental contagion taking place within revolutionary mobs.[2]

Celebrating the machine age while fearing its consequences, conscious of the rising insurgency of Populists and the working class, and searching for new modes to evangelize the American public through mass persuasion, many northeastern Protestant intellectuals—especially clergymen, journalists, and academics—sought to learn about the function of crowd behavior as a way of understanding their own problematic social roles. Seeking strategies to create righteous forms of collective behavior and to uplift the nation, many joined Lee in projecting fantasies of their own fulfillment within what was increasingly seen to be a crowd-dominated society. By the onset of World War I sweeping explanations about the mentality of mobs had been advanced by social psychologists and journalists and projected onto other forms of collective behavior. Advertisers and "experts" on public opinion wrote in knowing terms about tapping the emotional roots of the "crowd mind." The boundaries of "mental epidemics," in fact, were being extended into countless arenas of American culture from the public reaction to the Spanish-American War to studies of lynchings, revivals, and the vicissitudes of women's fashion. What people meant by "crowds" or "crazes" or even "public opinion," however, was becoming confused with changing ideas about the social order, human personality, and political behavior.[3]

What is a crowd? The term *crowd* describes a group of people. It is a word with synonyms that vary to extremes of valence. On one side can be the fairly benignant *group, public, organization,* or *audience;* on the other is the more sinister *throng, pack,* or *mob.* Just as values of the word *crowd* vary, so do cultural responses to the image of the crowd. The associations of the crowd used as a symbol or metaphor are by nature ambiguous. Throughout history, the perceived goals of one type of "crowd" have often informed people's opinions about other forms of collective behavior. It is one aim of this book to explore how those associations developed—or were applied or manipulated—especially during the period from 1880 to 1920—when Americans were finding their lives more and more composed of "group" or "public" activity, and in which emerging technology made it more possible to reach larger, less localized audiences, beyond the harsh gaze of family or town elders.

"Myths and metaphors permit men to live in a world in which the causes are simple and neat and the remedies are apparent," according to Murray Edelman. Cultural metaphors are dynamic structures that evoke meaning in relation to institutional demands, patterns of language and behavior, or natural phenomena. Metaphors of crowd behavior can become insinuated into oral traditions, written language, and iconography, legitimizing particular political or economic forces while delegitimizing others. The crowd as metaphor can operate to extend racial or gender stereotypes, or confuse notions about mobs with the consuming public, an audience of listeners, or even flocks of birds. Forests, fields of wheat, darkness, the sea, and other natural phenomena possess similar visual and psychological properties to human collectivities. When contrasted to ideas and images relating to individuals, the crowd metaphor can conjure up powerful statements about the meaning of life in cultures undergoing vast social change. When amalgamated with implications about another metaphorical reference such as a machine, the crowd can become one of the touchstones of social thought.[4]

The linguistic and philosophical roots of ideas relating to the crowd metaphor go back to the ancient world of Greece and Rome when terms such as *mobile vulgas* (the unstable common people, a term later shortened to mob) often carried with them implicit hierarchical notions of the social order. While some writers, notably Thucydides, "adopted an attitude that precluded his confusing the people with the multitude or with the crowd," few of his contemporaries joined him, fearing, like Plato, that the collective mentality of the masses undermined the possibility for a successful democracy.[5]

By the seventeenth and eighteenth centuries, popular conceptions of crowds were largely drawn from nature or the Bible, and became entangled with the growing implications behind popular protests and revolutionary assemblies. Analogies dealing with packs of wolves, contagious diseases, the domestication of animals, brainless monsters, or hydraulic properties were especially prevalent in describing what the Third Earl of Shaftesbury labeled the excessive "enthusiasm" behind many public collective actions. As the theoretical debates over liberty, order, and the role of the state fed revolutionary fervor in the age of the Enlightenment, the rural and urban poor continued to riot in traditional ways against unjust economic policies by merchants; forms of power contradicting the Lockean social ideals witnessed what E. P. Thompson has labeled a "moral economy of the crowd" in which mob attacks against property became proto-political tools of bargaining. As recent research has uncovered, the American colonies and later the newly founded nation also experienced preindustrial mobs and mass assemblies, whose

targets so often involved economic malfeasance by merchants. The
definitions related to collective behavior, sovereignty, and economic
power were contested territory.[6]

Within the past thirty years long-held assumptions about episodes
of collective behavior have been demolished by social historians.
It has become increasingly clear that errors in characterizing the
social composition and political motivation of mobs had a profound
effect on nineteenth-century thought. The romantic rendering of the
French Revolution (and to a lesser extent the Gordon Riots of 1780)
became a recurrent reference for understanding the riotous behavior
engaged in by lower-class American crowds. A long-term process
stigmatized most rioters to have lacked an economic stake in society;
that judgment became linked to other implications about how "the
public" operated. Mobs that had been localized or considered of
small political consequence in preindustrial Europe and America
were changing; increasingly urban oriented, their members protested the conditions of the industrial order and were seen as antithetical to natural law, public safety, and the orderly expansion of
corporate capitalism. Yet far from being a simple linguistic plot by
the wealthy to perpetuate their economic and political power, the
crowd acted as a cultural metaphor—from political parades and
protesting workers to ethnic celebrations conjuring up threats to the
bourgeois social order from a wide array of collectivities.[7]

By 1838, when Abraham Lincoln delivered his Lyceum Address
in Springfield, Illinois (the speech that became a frequent reference
of later Progressives who adored him), the antiabolitionist riots,
threats to the banking system, and the ethnic violence that had
erupted in previous years produced in him deep fear for the erosion
of respect for law and civil authority. The Revolutionary generation
had all died and Lincoln's understanding of mobs was couched in
terms of his political fears of Jacksonian democracy, civil discord,
and potential Caesarism stalking the land—beyond community or
legal control. As an aspiring lawyer, Lincoln sought a civil religion to
bind the opinions of all Americans to legal institutions. These years,
in fact, saw symbols of union become powerful throughout the
North, while they were simultaneously threatened by disunionists.

Lincoln's rhetoric, stressing the "mystic chords of memory" in his Second Inaugural Address, provides growing evidence of the romanticism of the era that was affecting ideas about crowds and publics.[8]

Notions of civil religion similar to Lincoln's became music to the ears of northerners who continued to advance ideas—many derived from the thought of Edmund Burke—seeking to distinguish mob-inspired clamor from "real" public opinion. In an address to Columbia University alumni in 1842, the Reverend Hugh Peters warned that "the mere excitement of public attention or interest, in relation to any subject, must not be regarded as indicating fixed public opinion." Professionals in medicine, law, and political economy were needed to help educate the poor and elevate public sentiment away from private fancies. He hoped that "right reason, may gradually displace the visionary and unsettling theories, the disorganizing plans, the secret corruption . . . which have thrown their blighting influence over the fair face of the social heritage." To Peters, Lincoln, James Fenimore Cooper, and many other Whigs and conservative Democrats in the antebellum period, mobs were evidence of an unstable public opinion that had to be properly guided. By the time of the Civil War draft riots, they were also seen as more than a local phenomenon.[9]

With the exploding size of American cities, numerous middle-class writers joined Lincoln in trying to understand how to control mob behavior, although others—including writers Nathaniel Hawthorne, Ralph Waldo Emerson, James Fenimore Cooper, and Herman Melville—showed greater interest in ascertaining the social types attracted to urban crowds than in their political ramifications.

From the antebellum period through the Gilded Age most assessments of mobs were based on legal definitions of riot and naturalistic analogies set against contemporary moral standards. Accentuating the growing social distance within American culture, and the tensions relating to race, class, and gender, images of disease, tests of restraint in one's manhood, volcanic eruptions, analogies to Indians' tribalism or European mobs, the loss of one's personality from overuse of alcohol—even the bloodlust of unchained tigers—were used to explain the animating force behind American urban mobs. Charles Dickens, widely read in the United States, when characterizing England's 1780 Gordon Riots, found the mob to be "usually a creature of very mysterious existence particularly in a large city. Where it comes from and whither it goes few men can tell. Assembling and dispersing with equal suddenness, it is as difficult to follow to its various sources as the sea itself; nor does the parallel stop here, for the ocean is not more fickle and uncertain, the more terrible when roused, more unreasonable, or more cruel." Mysterious, able to become invisible and evaporate at a moment's notice or turn around and become part of an uncontrollable and catastrophic stream or flood, the image of a current remained a popular literary device to understand social types throughout the nineteenth century in America. The editors of the *Chicago Times* went no further than Dickens's definition, in seeking to understand the causes of the railroad riots in July 1877.[10]

The increasingly severe strictures of riot law, the professionalization of law enforcement, the funding for enlarged militia units and huge gothic armories, even the attempts at reform such as the creation of trade schools—all measures toward quelling urban labor disorders—provided tangible evidence that reinforced the illegitimacy of working-class collectivities. In addition, of no small importance in hardening attitudes toward rioters was the role played by the insurance industry, which lobbied state legislatures to tighten the procedures for liability.[11]

Popular usage of medical language underscored the pathology and the psychological contagion of mobs. As a regressive social form, mobs were considered to have analogous psychological properties with children or mentally debased men and women, unworthy of the normal sympathies one extended to friends or neighbors. Many riots revealed multiple fears, based on stereotypical behavioral patterns, condemning the loosening of Victorian social mores. The drunkard, lecher, prostitute, the diseased, and the violent criminal were all personality types sketched in hundreds of graphics, in short stories, novels, advice books, news articles, and textbooks; such people were pictured as set in "currents" beyond a well-ordered existence, cut loose from the moral order, always ready for the mindless revelry and moral holiday symbolized by a mob. Because they represented the penultimate form of degraded moral contagion, mobs acted as an overpowering force for all but those with the sternest character. The strength of Victorian society's language upholding "civilization," "culture," and orderly forms of collective behavior came in no small part from the frequent counterposition of "respectability" against moblike barbarism, or formless masses. Through such definitional power, attitudes toward mob violence— and working-class protests—stiffened in patterns that congealed hegemonic power and reinforced attitudes toward a well-ordered existence. The city was a frightening place.[12]

Outbreaks of mob violence were episodic. Few people thought about mobs unless they had personal experience with them or unless journalistic attention was focused on particular social dramas. Jane Addams, writing in the early twentieth century, noted the power accruing to the forces of law and order during riots. "At times of social disturbance the law-abiding citizen is naturally so anxious for peace and order, his sympathies are so justly and inevitably on the side making for the restoration of law, that it is difficult for him to see the situation fairly . . . He is completely side-tracked by the ugly phrases of a great moral movement." From the Civil War draft riots through the Haymarket affair, to the Pullman Strike and the Populist crusade, the mainstream literature and the press left little doubt that violence was caused by those who composed the mobs or mass assemblies. Lithographs and cartoons in such publications as *Puck* and *Harper's Weekly* provided visual evidence to back up the perceptions of reporters and editors. With few exceptions, however, no "respectable" American could simply ignore the rising political impact of the immigrant masses any longer; nor could genteel Americans so easily separate their own social and political ideals from those of European theorists.[13]

Cities became characterized as "nurseries of crime," breeding grounds of public opinion that looked to narrow self-interest instead of broader republican ideals and long-held traditions. By late in the century, such concerns deepened as apocalypticism and decadence were seen to be generated by the spirit of the mob, which, in turn, emanated from "dens of iniquity" and dark anonymous places. Naturalistic images were combined with references to the dissipated mobs of ancient Rome. In Joaquin Miller's *The Destruction of Gotham* (1886), New York was pictured as a cauldron in which mobs fought the rich, a city with "365 days of carnival, [where] people scarcely seem to sleep." Public modes of entertainment were widely attacked as breeding grounds of immorality. In Chicago, an 1893 investigation of the city's dark places chastised French plays and so-called "museums" that attracted people to bizarre phenomena through "specious and misleading advertisements." Quoting Thomas Carlyle's comment that "Riot cries aloud, and staggers and swaggers in his rank dens of shame," the report called for public controls over immoral establishments.[14]

Following the Paris Commune in 1871 and the 1877 railroad strikes, urban riots took on a more overtly revolutionary aura, widely pictured as weapons of European-born radicals. The specter of socialism, anarchism, communism, and the promotion of labor organizations—often directly associated with the use of bombs and mass violence as weapons—became linked to un-American behavior, bred from both urban-related decadence and the loss of moral distinctions.[15]

Yet recent research has revealed that the urban unemployed and the working class were not blank sheets of paper on which alien demagogues wrote their malevolent designs. The quest for political empowerment and social justice by those unaccustomed to their new society got violent at times; rudeness against the rich became an assertion of equal status. The need to create new forms of collective action—parades, strikes, boycotts, cooperatives, encampments, and various forms of assembly—took on a quasi-political character. Further, as Herbert Gutman and other social historians have said, public attitudes toward mobs were far more complex than the mainstream press led their readers to believe. Residents of small cities, in which corporate malfeasance was more clearly understood, or divergent regional interests sometimes supported strikers or mass political assemblies against the repressive action of government troops or company police. Altogether, the working class was not always passive in challenging the simplistic definitions of mob violence.[16]

"There are in fact no masses; there are only ways of seeing people as masses," Raymond Williams has written. Nowhere does this become more obvious than when examining Victorian perceptions about mobs that helped to channel notions about public opinion. From Edmund Burke's confidence in the bonds of tradition over the momentary passions in the 1790s, to Theodore Roosevelt's biography of *Gouverneur Morris* (1888), the descriptions of mobs in the French Revolution were used to cast doubt on broader forms of collective behavior. A nation that was built up in a slow steady manner was the best evidence that education, culture, and progress were tied to natural law. On the heels of Civil War and Reconstruction violence, the disdain many northerners felt toward the South and the fear they felt for the future of their own cities under pressure from the working class helped to animate the crowd metaphor through the gloss of an emerging organic nationalism.[17]

Thomas Carlyle's characterization of the mobs in the French Revolution continued to provide guidance during the Gilded Age. His books and articles acted as a powerful model of certainty and assertiveness in defining national purpose, and he simultaneously championed a writer's ability to externalize the dramatic character of a crowd from a set of faces. Along with the writings of the influential French historian Hippolyte Taine, Carlyle's *History of the French Revolution* was to be instrumental in informing the thought of numerous French and American social psychologists who, by the 1890s, were beginning to suggest that there were ascertainable laws of group behavior.[18]

Carlyle's *History* looked on the eighteenth century as a period of relative serenity, pierced only by the exceptional mobs of the Gordon Riots of 1780 and the mobs of the French Revolution. The sans culottes in the French Revolution were consistently made to appear less human than those with property to lose, even though recent studies show that the mobs included a large number of lower-middle-class people, small property owners who were rioting to express their political outrage. Carlyle's later work revealed his increasingly authoritarian tendencies, arguing that workers should unquestionably follow their leaders. As grasped by many young middle-class men of the Gilded Age like Gerald Lee, Carlyle's historical misperceptions spread to include working-class forms of collective behavior—which were optimally regimented as well. Only with firm social control and assertive leadership could the fate of the French be avoided.[19]

Similar notions about mobs became a mainstay of school textbooks, fiction, and popular historical accounts in the United States.

By the late nineteenth century, historians and public officials in the Northeast had, for example, recast much of the history of the American Revolution era so that Shays' Rebellion was dramatized as a test of national will against local insurrection. Honoring the rioters at the Boston Massacre and the Boston Tea Party even became problematic to New England intellectuals who were fearful that they might be sending the wrong message to the working class.[20]

Several articles recounting the history of the French Revolution and the Paris Commune were published in *Scribner's Magazine* in 1887. Drawn from the eyewitness perspective of the conservative American ministers to France, Gouverneur Morris and Elihu Washburn, the rioters were pictured as little less than animals in both instances.[21]

Other writers reinforced a more abstracted disdain toward collective behavior. Although his writings were not strictly historical in nature, Ralph Waldo Emerson had by the time of his death in 1883 become a godlike figure to his fellow Americans in defining culture. Nonetheless, throughout much of his work there was "a constant disparagement of men in the mass." By the mid 1830s, Emerson was lashing out at the social forces he disliked by using the rhetorical ambiguity attending the crowd metaphor. He called for individuals to shun the "intruding rabble of men and books and institutions," which he labeled "invaders." The reign of conformity was equated to the power of crowds. Emerson's views of the crowd emanated from a basic distrust of collective action as a remedy for social problems.[22]

The idea that either mobs or mass demonstrations beyond the control of the two-party system could be credible forms of political behavior became anathema to numerous northern Protestant and British writers after Reconstruction. Writing in 1885, Sir Henry Maine commented that "a mob was once a portion of society who for the time had broken loose from the ties which bind society together." The spirit behind them had been more like panics or mischief, he added. "But mobs have now come more and more to be the organs of definite opinions," using nitroglycerine bombs as a voice for their "irreconcilable opinions." It was Francis Lieber, however, an émigré from Germany and professor of political science at Columbia University, who expressed the most cogent response to democrats who called on legislators to hear a broad spectrum of public opinion—even the voices of demonstrators. "[The] true and staunch republican, wants . . . the real rule of the people, that is, the institutionally organized country, which distinguishes it from the mere mob. For a mob is an unorganic multitude, with a general impulse of action."[23]

An Episcopal minister from New Jersey and admirer of Hegel named Elisha Mulford posited that the nation "has the unity of an organism, not the aggregation of a mass; it is indivisible; its germ lies beyond analysis." The historical process operating through the nation as a moral organism possessed a "moral personality," he wrote. These notions fueled an increasingly virulent nationalism by the 1880s—along with the fear of republican decline and urban disorder. A mystical nationalism, erected on top of the organismic metaphor, further thwarted any sympathy toward mobs or coercive popular assemblies.[24]

Even more than in the 1830s and 1840s, when Lincoln and Peters had warned of the dire effects of public sentiment, the political and social reality of industrialization and urbanization made the need to control the masses a cultural imperative to "respectable" Americans. Rigorous standards propounded by American gentlemen were needed, British author Matthew Arnold told a New York audience. Don't be swayed by mere numbers, he warned them, but extend the tradition of high ideals and cultural discipline. " 'The remnant shall return'; shall 'convert and be healed' itself first, and shall then recover the unsound majority," he said. What the United States needed, Arnold argued, was a revival of the "Puritan discipline" to circumvent the selfish and power hungry masses.[25]

From 1886 through 1896 associations derived from the romantic republican conception of riots were employed by the mainstream press to thwart a national political revolution. Strikes, demonstrations of the unemployed, the Populist movement, the potential for cataclysmic class warfare—in sum, the fear that the capitalistic order might crash to its knees—fueled demands to control mob violence. National confidence and crusades for reform were thus actuated, in part, by middle-class insecurity concerning the widening associational arc of mob behavior. The nationwide attention that was focused on the Haymarket affair, the depression of 1893 with its "tramp armies" marching on Washington, the Pullman Strike in 1894, and then the climactic 1896 election, all revived the association of urban riots with immigrant hordes, criminal behavior, working-class anger, farmer revolts, and the cycle of revolution that had taken place in France. A cultural reaction of great magnitude was taking place. David Swing of Chicago warned shortly after the Haymarket bombing that "our nation must be held firmly to the ideas of our fathers or it will soon become a mere crowd of struggling men and not a Republic founded upon eternal law."[26]

In some cases, radicals fed the flames of association. Populist writer Ignatius Donnelly invoked images of a mob obedient to the will of radicals. His novel *Caesar's Column* sold hundreds of thousands of copies in the early 1890s and helped sustain the Populist movement. Donnelly warned in dire terms of a great terror that would convulse the United States if social justice and free silver were not soon extended to the lower classes. "The multitude are like the soldiers of an army," he warned, "they will obey when the time comes." Clearly, metaphorical implications of the crowd could be used by revolutionaries as well as by supporters of the social order. It was a time of fear and fantasy.[27]

It was an era of fear and fantasy when evangelists—notably W. T. Stead, Josiah Strong, and Kansas City minister Charles Sheldon—tried to create new forms of spiritual unity to circumvent social disorder. In 1893 Strong suggested propagandizing the poor with tracts distributed by young men. The result would be the creation of a "collective church of the community" so that "the Christian public opinion of the state could quickly and emphatically utter itself." Sheldon's book *In His Steps* manifests how the idea of the crowd was being transformed by evangelicals in their search for a new collective consciousness and control over the behavior of an entire community—from the harlot to the corrupt businessman. Sheldon had his characters ask each other "What would Jesus do?" as if such a question could transform the world. A central scene of Sheldon's novel has pure and virginal Rachel Winslow singing to a large disorderly crowd and taming it. As the local minister "raised his head and saw the transformed mob," Sheldon wrote, he "glimpsed something that Jesus would probably do with a voice like Rachel

Winslow's." A civic awakening and a series of reform movements that promoted everything from the playground movement to the Boy Scouts, from folk dancing to choral songs, were being created, intended to channel the frustrations of young men from gangs and potentially riotous behavior into healthy activities. The working class, it was hoped, could become respectable and goal-oriented patriots.[28]

Although politicians had already been awakened to the effectiveness of imagery surrounding mobs, the election of 1896 saw the crowd metaphor come into full power at a crucial transition in American life. The contrast between the two main presidential candidates was stark. Orderly assemblies of loyalists descended by train to Canton, Ohio, to listen to set speeches by the Republican candidate William McKinley. Surrogates fanned out throughout the country decrying the free silver craze and identifying Bryan with the Haymarket anarchists, the Pullman riots, and "radicals" like Debs, Altgeld, Marat, and Robespierre. Revolution seemed to be in the air, many Republicans were saying, while prosperity waited behind the corner by McKinley's victory. Meanwhile, the eloquent William Jennings Bryan attracted large crowds of avid listeners to his personality and program. This was not the personality that the educated remnant had had in mind. Theodore Roosevelt's rhetorical offensive on behalf of McKinley revealed long-standing elite predilections. To an audience in Utica, Roosevelt said that Bryan's objective was "a government of the mob." To an audience at the Chicago Coliseum, Roosevelt yelled, "It is not merely schoolgirls that have hysterics; very vicious mob-leaders have them at times, and so do well-meaning demagogues when their minds are turned by the applause of men of little intelligence."[29]

Americans were then in the midst of a communications revolution that involved the rise of the yellow press and cheap, mass-circulation magazines spreading information and advertising about politics and a host of cultural fads. The educated remnant saw disquieting signs that the public, as a collectivity, was easily deluded by fads and fashions. The impact of Pulitzer, then Hearst and their imitators further stimulated lurid fears and hopeful fantasies of sweeping cultural changes. "Our cheap press speaks today in tones never before heard out of Paris," wrote *Nation* editor E. L. Godkin in 1898. "It urges upon ignorant people schemes more savage, disregard of either policy, or justice, or experience more complete than the modern world has witnessed since the French Revolution."[30]

The guidance or even regimentation of the public mind was enhanced by attempts to adjust individual behavior within large organizations. In Stephen Crane's best-selling novel about the Civil War, *The Red Badge of Courage* (1895), a "common" man of the infantry was described in the following terms: "He suddenly lost concern for himself, and forgot to look at a menacing fate. He became not a man but a member. He felt that something of which he was a part—a regiment, an army, a cause, or a country was in a crisis. He was welded into a common personality which was dominated by a single desire. For some moments he could not flee, no more than a little finger can commit a revolution from a hand."[31]

Crane's realistic picture of an individual's fate also spoke to the contemporary wave of nostalgia for wartime heroics, evoking feelings as well for an earlier era when community and public life seemed less divided and heroism more conspicuous. Sometimes counterposed against happy family units, town meetings, church services, and patriotic celebrations, this nostalgia carried numerous associated implications that defined what were seen to be righteous congregations. Critic Bliss Perry wrote in his assessment of the American mind in 1912 that "the 'town meeting' . . . has become a symbol of American idealism . . . Sentiments of responsibility to the town, the political units, and to the Commonwealth, the group of units, were bred there . . . It remains a perpetual spring or feeding to the broader currents of our national life." A country parson writing in 1910 lamented that "no one hears more about the good old times than does the country parson." Those were the days when the church had been "crowded to the doors, when the prayer room was thronged with the old guard and new recruits, when family worship flourished in every room." More clearly defined social, civic, and religious bonds were seen to exist in the past as models for modern institutions. The numerous genealogical and patriotic societies—such as the Daughters of the American Revolution—that also grew up in that era were thus attempts to place participants in a historical continuum, loyal to an orderly republic.[32]

Not sentimental nostalgia alone, however, but a militance born from palpable fears of disorder stimulated the patriotic revival as well as many reform crusades by the late 1880s. It was a militance that fed upon the moral clarity pictured in popular tales of war, chivalry, or frontier conflict. One can see this in the galvanizing theatrics of Buffalo Bill's Wild West Show, the flamboyance of Carl Browne of Coxey's "Army," the popularity of biographies about Napoleon. One hears it in the speeches of Civil War veterans like Oliver Wendell Holmes. Theodore Roosevelt became such an over-whelming national presence in part because he implicitly under-stood many of these elements: he had an abiding hatred of the Haymarket anarchists and anyone who sought to show sympathy for their philosophy; he had co-authored a book with Henry Cabot Lodge entitled *Hero Tales of American History* (1895) which con-centrated on military leaders and another book which applauded the value of Gouverneur Morris's view of the French Revolution; he combatted the urban "dens" of crime as police commissioner; and he made himself a national military hero through his self-promoting conduct during the Spanish-American War.[33]

The heroic revival often represented individuals happily sub-merged in righteous currents in which the problematic quality of identity was negated by one's service to a patriotic organization. Edward Bellamy's *Looking Backward* and Crane's novel provide numerous examples of this quest for identity within an army. Elbert Hubbard's immensely popular tale "A Message to Garcia" (1898) affirmed that the successful man of business should imitate the example of a soldier following the orders of his commander in the Spanish-American War, a man fully in tune with the dictates of the modern organization. Not surprisingly, this short tale was widely reprinted in business publications seeking similar loyalty from their employees.[34]

The ideals of political leadership, military professionalism, and organizational efficiency increased as new images were drawn of group behavior, the forces that controlled it, and the psychology of individuals involved. Naturalistic descriptions by Jack London and Frank Norris highlighted the dominance of machine technology and corporate wealth over "herdlike" human collectivities reinforcing a sense of fatalism about power relationships. One character in Wil-liam Dean Howells's utopian novel *A Traveller from Altruria,* for example, commented that the mill hands in the factory towns had "all the individuality of a 'flock of sheep,' " adding that "if you have capital in America, you can have individuality; if you haven't, you can't."[35]

To at least some of the thousands of people attending the Camden, New Jersey, funeral of Walt Whitman in 1892, the "good gray poet" as he was later called was one who had fully addressed the problems of lost congregations, mob violence, and the disorientation of a mass society. Remembered for his poem on the death of Lincoln and his belief in an organic democratic culture, Whitman had questioned conventional social forms through the vitality and expressive quality of personality that resounded through his poetry and prose. His writings were to have a strong and subtle impact on an influential band of Americans in the early twentieth century—including writers William Allen White, Van Wyck Brooks, Vachel Lindsay, and Hart Crane, and architects Louis Sullivan and Frank Lloyd Wright. One overlooked dimension of Whitman's vision of a democratic order was the confused legacy of his descriptions—and ultimately his understanding—of crowds and publics, and the redeeming roles to be played by great poets.[36]

The legacy of Whitman's notions about crowds can be appreciated through the writings of William James, the most influential psychologist and philosopher at the turn of the century. Like his friend Godkin, James was disturbed by public opinion that had been so easily manipulated by the sensational press during the silver craze in 1896 and then its role in helping to stimulate war fever in 1898. James had also read with horror about the barbarous lynchings of blacks taking place throughout the South. Informing much of his thinking on these subjects were the books on crowd psychology, then a hot topic of intellectual discourse.[37]

In 1899 James gave a lecture at Harvard University entitled "On a Certain Blindness in Human Beings." The lecture so moved one student in the audience, the future sociologist Robert Park, that he resolved to study the sociology of crowds. James told the audience that it was the poet Walt Whitman who had "felt the human crowd as rapturously as Wordsworth felt the mountains, felt it as an overpoweringly significant presence, simply to absorb one's mind in which should be business sufficient and worthy to fill the days of a serious man."[38]

Whitman's professed ability to know the crowd, to reproduce in words the reality he observed and experienced, could, James felt, help define the social distance between people and augment human solidarity. To reproduce one's own vitality and to re-create one's soul throughout a national public by the expressiveness conveyed through poetic forms was the ultimate reward of human consciousness. Whitman's intuitive consciousness of the social roles and the shifting physical boundaries as part of ever changing city spectacles were the product of an ostensibly boundless personality, a man unafraid to sketch a scene in words that seemed to many readers akin to a gallery of photographs of the urban environment. The passengers on the sunny deck of a ferry boat, the individuals in street crowds laughing to each other, the occupants of a Broadway bus, haughty and humble, jumbled together on a cold winter's night, these were the people that Whitman captured fondly. Yet as more recent critics have charged, there was little depth to the individual characterizations; Whitman seldom personalized his urbanites. Though he believed himself a true spokesman for the latent possibilities of democracy, the masses made beautiful, his "relations with concrete persons were shaped by a demand for perfect understanding."[39]

It was Whitman's special language of reportage and immediacy and his visualization of people that was appreciated in the early twentieth century by those who also found William James's pragmatism and tolerance so modern. The aesthetics of Whitman's crowd consciousness easily became attached to broader forms of collective behavior. As James and others appropriated it, Whitman's vision of the crowd was different from the terror one reads in Edgar Allan Poe's "Man of the Crowd" or in most other romantic writers. Yet in the years after the Civil War, especially in *Democratic Vistas* (1871), Whitman had grown fearful of the future of American democracy under the sway of materialism and corruption. Like Emerson and Carlyle as they aged, Whitman showed an increasing interest in the potential for heroic personalities to redeem American culture. Far from being fearful of the masses, however, Whitman celebrated them, seeking to embody and capture them as particles of his own persona. Whitman's later writings were to be used by others to rationalize and contain the crowdlike public.[40]

His romantic vision was ultimately co-opted into the tentacles of a streamlined era of experts and commodification, or it easily rationalized a definition of the nation as a democratic marketplace. As a celebrator of urban fraternity and mystical notions of poetic personalities able to uplift the visions of the nation, Whitman's democratic ideal was music to the ears of many Progressives, feeding their optimism, their belief in the possibility of reviving national identity, mastering urban development, and the behavior of crowds. Whitman also fed the hopes of some in the younger generation who sought to become mass persuaders, hopes based on dangerously simplified views of human complexity that they saw when they looked at the faces within a crowd.[41]

Whitman's writings provide strong testimony that "personality became . . . the way to think about the meaning implicit in human life," as Richard Sennett writes. It mediated one's relationship to the modern city. Defining oneself in relation to certain associated properties of crowd behavior became an unconscious preoccupation with many up-and-coming young men. Urban Americans continually reinforced a paradoxical view of crowds by both observing them from a distance as spectators and being part of them through the design of urban space—in parks, office buildings, train stations, theatrical districts, and roadways.[42]

By the 1890s personality had also become the province of the newly professionalized field of psychology. Philosophers and psychologists such as Alfred Binet, Sigmund Freud, Gustave Le Bon, Henri Bergson, and James observed that the individual personality was increasingly split into distinct sides, in which the civilized (or orderly) part was often obliterated under a more primal, crowd-oriented, hallucinated, aggressive, and disorderly one. Although influenced by scientific experiments on hypnotism and hysteria, many of the assumptions used by writers on the subject of crowd psychology over the next two decades were continuous with earlier ideas about the behavior of mobs. This continuity becomes especially clear in examining the mind of Gustave Le Bon, who had witnessed the carnage of the Paris Commune and projected his horror of those crowds onto his "laws" covering all forms of collective behavior.[43]

In Le Bon's best-selling book *The Crowd,* read by Roosevelt, Godkin, James, Lee, and many contemporaries, Le Bon warned that in a crowd-dominated culture "the conscious personality has entirely vanished; will and discernment are lost." He saw the influence of a speaker on modern crowd-oriented men as possessing a similar mental relationship to that of a hypnotized individual in the hands of the hypnotizer. Visions of racial souls and mentally defective groups were easily bandied about in this context. There could be power in the systematic cultivation of disordered minds. In the United States, middle-class fears of riots became buttressed by the late 1890s with a growing body of postulates concerning similar "laws" of crowd psychology.[44]

Young American social scientists by the early twentieth century were frequently preoccupied with the loss of personality in an urban industrial age, the individual mind seemingly more collectivized, melting into what popular sociologist Edward Ross called a "mob mind." This he defined as "a vast public [that] shares the same rage, alarm, enthusiasm, or horror. Then, as each part of the mass becomes acquainted with the sentiment of all the rest, the feeling is generalized and intensified. In the end, the public swallows up the individuality of the ordinary man in much the same way the crowd swallows up the individuality of its members." The public's interest in crazes and fads could also only be described as an attribute of the mob mind. Ross thought it his job to ascribe to "organized society" some of the conditions that favored the "growth of strong, robust individualities" who could stand as proof "against mental contagion."[45]

Psychologists and philosophers such as James Mark Baldwin, Boris Sidis, Josiah Royce, Robert Park, even William James joined Ross in affirming the broad outlines of the psychology of crowds. From such sanction more popular writers projected "scientific" explanations about the psychology of play and amusement, fashion, sensationalism, the nature of theater audiences. The paradox of the Progressive Era saw the "public mind" elevated by democratic reforms, while denigrated through its frequent association to the mentality of mobs.[46]

Altogether, the fear of debased mobs, the belief in society as a set of knowable crowds, the hope for spiritual unity, and the growing

importance of nationalism and organized forms of collective behavior all helped stimulate the search for righteous or recreational
collectivities and a more expertly guided public opinion.

Crowds were becoming ever more aestheticized, celebratory, and
apolitical. The participatory, theatrical, and consumer oriented
crowd was often seen to be filled with exciting personalities; fashionable, modern, and fun to be with, the individuals composing
these crowds were perceived to be less serious than their parents and
more reliant on peer approval. After all it was P. T. Barnum's world
more than that of the educated remnants. By the 1890s Americans
lived more and more of their lives in commercialized crowds. Circuses, sports events, and revivals were becoming highly organized
and widely accepted as adjuncts to the social order. Merchants of
leisure and consumption were quick to find, channel, and capitalize
on these opportunities. Shoppers "flocked" to department stores
that officially featured consumer goods, but unofficially these stores
were attracting crowds who themselves acted as dramatic elements
in what Daniel Boorstin has labeled festivals of consumption. Millions of Americans went to amusement parks like Coney Island or
Atlantic City by the turn of the century because the attraction of
anonymous crowds and the disorientation of exotic and mechanical
thrills provided a feeling of liberation. People celebrated their association with crowds, their mutual entertainment, and their excitement with modernity.[47]

The commercialization of individual behavior was creating new
notes of moral urgency among "respectable" Americans. Those who
criticized the excessive individualism of the times or the lack of
deference to proper authority also believed that crowds needed
supervision, rules, and accountability. Dance halls, saloons, and
nickelodeons became the targets of censorious reformers. Yet more
importantly, public opinion was increasingly being influenced by
advertising and marketing experts, many of whom relied on the
prevalent conceptions of crowd psychology; metaphorical implications drawn from the understanding of mobs had not only informed
the field of crowd psychology but were also reinforcing images
dispensed to the public about itself.[48]

"More and more does the self appear a changeable and evanescent section of experience," sociologist Michael Davis wrote in 1904; "more and more are its boundaries continuous with other sections of experience. The 'individual' seems almost gone." The self as a person of character who stood for certain definable moral principles and was accountable to a specific community was giving way to a more desperate view of a potential self who sought to appear magnetic, attractive, and masterful; a dominating, charismatic personality who acted in relation to a dynamic series of groups, instead of in a world of face-to-face relationships. This modern personality, Warren Susman has illustrated, sought individual fulfillment against what was perceived to be the anonymity of modern mass culture. The obsession to cultivate a powerful and dramatic aura about oneself in order to become successful in business also functioned as an avenue of escape from localistic conformity and a form of redemption from purposelessness. The press celebrated the urban world as a kind of apolitical consumer spectacle.[49]

Thus, while crowd psychologists showed that, like a mob, the public was fickle and emotional, the individuals comprising it only sought to imitate that which was modern—fit soil to be tilled by bright and eager young men out to make their mark. Crowds could be persuaded by well-meaning patriots, it was widely believed, whereas mob violence seldom elicited the same fears that it had back in the 1890s. The political language of crowds underlined the exuberant optimism of the prewar period. In 1914 *New Republic* editor Herbert Croly wrote that "Progressive democracy . . . can afford to combine more democracy with more progressiveness than it has done in the past, partly because an attachment to legal matters has become deeply rooted in the national tradition. In no respect does it resemble the omnipotent and arbitrary mob which the constitutional conservatives profess to fear." In fact, he wrote, the American experiment had never become entangled in the cycle of "anarchy and despotism" such as the French had experienced.[50]

As a cultural metaphor of growing importance, the crowd ultimately involved the interaction of imagery and experience that simplified categories of order and disorder. Because it was an easily grasped image, the crowd condensed and ultimately redefined much about the human condition. "Images are not arguments," Henry Adams wrote in 1907, "but the mind craves them, and of late more than ever, the keenest experimenters find twenty images better than one, especially if contradictory; since the human mind has already learned to deal in contradictions." As we shall see, Adams, like Gerald Stanley Lee, believed that the people of the United States needed a new center or "preponderating mass" to simplify their understanding of a complex world. While Adams saw this symbolized in either the medieval cathedral or the dynamo, Lee found this need fulfilled by the personality of the heroic revitalizer of American crowds.[51]

On March 4, 1913, Lee completed what would become the best selling nonfiction book of the year, a book he entitled *Crowds: A Moving Picture of Democracy.* A new president, Woodrow Wilson, was taking office that day and Lee wished him well in language reflecting the impact of the crowd metaphor. "As Winslow Homer takes the sea," Lee wrote, "as Millet takes the peasants in the fields, as Frank Brangwyn lifts up the labour in the mills and makes it colossal and sublime, the President is an artist, in touching the crowd's imagination with itself—in making a nation self-conscious." Lee hoped that Wilson—any modern president—would be the "artist, the composer, the portrait painter of the people—their faith, their cry, their anger, and their love shall be in him. In him shall be seen the panorama of the crowd, focused in a single face."[52]

Lee was the most prominent nonacademic American of his generation to seek a magical personality to lift the imagination of his fellow citizens. The study of his social thought reveals anew that as a people or a public, we do not have crowd minds, that we may actually have a richer history than we have been led to believe, that the fall of public man is not inevitable.

TWO

The Lost Frontier of a Puritan Parson

One Sunday in January 1891, twenty-eight-year-old Gerald Stanley Lee rose before his congregation in the sleepy little northwestern Connecticut town of Sharon. He delivered a talk to help commemorate the sesquicentennial of the founding of the Congregational church. A tall, cadaverous looking man with a long rounded beak of a nose, Lee reminded his parishioners that their town and church "commenced together." In the old days the Congregational parson had been visibly, emotionally, and intellectually at the center of community life; he had "a complete monopoly over the materials of the intellectual and spiritual life of the people. He had no competition." Puritan parsons had been "public libraries, lecture bureaus, magazines and newspapers, all in themselves," retaining their pastorates until death. Those days appeared to have ebbed away, Lee lamented. "Nowadays a minister enters practically into competition with all literature, with the telegraph and newspaper, and people cannot keep him as a pastor but just about so long, for fear of finding out how little he knows."[1]

Lee recognized, as did many of his contemporaries, that by the 1890s the relationship between town and parson had drastically changed. No longer was civic unity buttressed by a common religious spirit; no longer was the parson the pivotal force and guiding intellect of community life. Throughout his ministerial career and his subsequent career as a writer, Lee remained obsessed with the need to discover men who, through their strong, even heroic personalities, could command the attention and the deference of the nation. This quest superseded the need to promote specific social reforms which gripped many of Lee's contemporaries from Jane Addams and Washington Gladden to those involved in the Populist movement. The impact of industrialization, the plight of the poor, women's rights, urban corruption, racial segregation, even the issues of the tariff and civil service reform were all largely ignored by Lee. Placing a high value on romantic idealism and the power of persuasion, Lee struggled to translate what he felt to be the consensus of the early New England village to the context of his tumultuous times.

Raised in middle-class circumstances, Lee attended two colleges located near the homes of his family and followed his father's example by going to Yale Divinity School, in the 1880s. He then tried to fulfill his calling as parson of several churches, first in Princeton, Minnesota, for a year in the late 1880s; subsequently he spent two years presiding over the Congregational church in Sharon, Connecticut, followed by three years at another church, in Springfield, Massachusetts. Finally, in April 1896, he broke with his past and became a professional writer. Yet throughout his writing career Gerald Lee took his religious calling seriously and struggled to reassert the centrality of church and parson as visible and spiritual forces through which all American communities could fully identify.[2]

Educated to assume a dominant role in the social order, many young ministers in the Gilded Age felt that the opportunity structure of American society seemed to be abandoning them. Captains of industry were becoming the central figures of power and responsibility in American society. Numerous young preachers groped for ideas and techniques to increase their influence over congregations who were dispersing into a variety of more worldly pursuits; many were thus left waiting in vain for society's call for leadership. As portrayed in the following two chapters, Lee's interest in three cultural models—the Victorian transcendental hero, the Puritan parson, and the biblical prophet—manifest a pattern in which fantasies of cultural influence would become an obsession.[3]

The contours of Lee's intellectual preoccupations in the period from 1880 to 1896 illustrate several strains in recent historiography addressing the subjects of antimodernism and the adaptation to modernity. An attraction to the religious unanimity associated with medievalism, the protean conception of Puritanism, the obsessive need to find "real life" and authenticity, the nostalgia for youth and frontier vitalism, and the lure of the British writers Ruskin and Morris are all present in Lee. Yet the solution to the problems of culture and personal identity that Lee expressed by the 1890s has largely been overlooked in recent historical accounts. Specifically, the legacy of the romantic hero simplified the cultural complexity of Lee's world. Widely replicated in many other nascent Progressives and conservatives, though admittedly in less rapturous tones, this heroic strain needs resuscitation as a medium through which to view the events and processes in which Victorian America was both challenged and reaffirmed.[4]

Descended from a family whose roots traced back to 1641, when Thomas Lee and his wife Phoebe Brown emigrated with three children from Cheshire, England, to settle in Lyme, Connecticut, Lee was heir apparent to a long line of Congregational ministers. One of his great grandfathers, who had served for sixty-four years as parson of a church he had organized in Hanover, Connecticut, and had been a member of the Yale Corporation as well as a chaplain in the Revolution, was a role model for Gerald, combining the historical aura of Puritan divines with that of the Revolutionary fathers. His paternal grandfather was a Hanover, Connecticut, farmer, William Lee, who lived on a family homestead his entire life and functioned as deacon for forty-one years. William Lee was active in the temperance movement and a zealous antislavery advocate.[5]

Gerald's father, Samuel, born in 1832, left the farm and worked as a teacher while attending schools in the late 1840s and 1850s. He graduated from Yale in 1858. In 1861 Samuel married Emma C. Carter of Pleasant Valley, Connecticut, later a member of the Society of Mayflower Descendants and related to the illustrious Storrs family. Their first son, Gerald, was born in 1862, followed by two daughters and another son. Graduating from Yale Divinity School in 1862, Samuel Lee settled first in a parish in Brockton, Massachusetts, then moved his family to Greenfield, Massachusetts, for five years, after which they presided over a parish in Cleveland, Ohio. (Doctrinal and salary disputes were often at the root of resignations or dismissals of ministers at this time.) After seven years in Cleveland, he accepted a chair in political economy at nearby Oberlin

College, the school founded by the evangelist Charles Grandison Finney and other abolitionists in the 1840s. In the early 1880s Samuel Lee returned to the ministry, taking over a church in Brattleboro, Vermont. Between 1893 and 1908 he concluded his career as a history professor and later president of the American International College, a missionary school, in Springfield, Massachusetts.[6]

As a recent arrival in the Sharon pulpit, Gerald Lee reminded the congregation of their founding father, the Reverend Cotton Mather Smith, and sought to link his own Puritan ancestors to theirs rather than to his father's generation. Smith was a descendant of the venerable Puritan divine Cotton Mather and held the pastorate of the Sharon church from 1752 to 1802, years crucial to the founding of the nation as well as the little church. But, Lee emphasized, it was the power of Smith's personality that made him an "institution of the town." He added his belief that "the history of the town could almost be said for this time to be [Smith's] biography." The behavior of the founding parson, especially during the Revolution, exemplified for Lee the close relationship between the church and society, a time of unified moral authority. While Lee chastised older Puritans for their "baptized morbidness" and the "extravagance of the doctrine of election," he nonetheless sought to restore their spirit and character. Smith had been a legendary figure who was "willing to put his religion into politics, and his politics into bayonets." At the core of Lee's view, however, Smith stood as a "modern David," a shepherd leading his flock, who understood their needs and God's mission for New England.[7]

Although Lee viewed Cotton Mather Smith and the Puritan-Revolutionary fathers as his direct ancestors, the religious world in which he operated was vastly changed from the earlier days. Disestablishment had cost many Congregational churches their public support. A more materialistic culture and competing houses of worship were encroaching upon the serene neighborhoods of the past. In Sharon, the Methodists had built a rival church. By the second half of the nineteenth century, the domination of a community such as Sharon by the personality and imposing intellectual gifts of a Congregational parson had passed, leading ministers to much frustration, nostalgia for more learned congregations, and unstable careers, a phenomenon experienced by Lee himself. In the old days,

Lee noted in 1903, even farmhands had been philosophers in touch with the common community spirit; philosophers "grew like the grass on a thousand hills."[8]

When New England was founded in the seventeenth century, the role of a Puritan preacher had been crucial to community identity. Having been under siege by the agents of England's Archbishop William Laud in the 1620s, preachers had been dramatic figures in crisis, possessing special and ostensibly uncorrupted knowledge honed in a localized context. Although sharing political power with others in New England and limited in their control over social and economic affairs, these men were central authorities over any community's relationship to God. Their power and identity were reinforced by the reality of that which they had escaped—religious tyranny, corruption, and disorder. Moreover, to be a preacher was to know science and business ethics as well as any man. To preach was also to become a spokesman for the community. In fact, the communal sharing of values in colonial days often made opinion formation appear to be an intuitive, almost automatic process embodied in and expressed by the parson.[9]

As magic and superstition had left much emotional and intellectual residue in the mentalities of Puritan preachers, so would more intuitive New Englanders in the nineteenth century continue to feel the nostalgic pull of the older Puritan preacher; and as preachers questioned the nature of their faith, many felt compelled to preach to wider audiences. Ralph Waldo Emerson and Horace Bushnell, for example, questioned the requirements of eloquent, theologically precise sermons that came into conflict with their poetic temperaments, their dissenting theological perspectives, and their desire to influence extended audiences.[10]

With disestablishment, the expansion of the franchise, the Second Great Awakening, the burgeoning power of the press, and the eruption of volatile issues such as abolitionism, the idea of evangelizing public opinion had achieved great urgency to many Protestants in American society. By 1862, when Gerald's father, Samuel Lee, took his first pulpit, this missionary impulse had strongly affected the ministerial calling in small towns and cities alike; the calling was "no longer framed by its role and position in the local community but was shaped by a new kind of translocal structure and professional consciousness." The life of Lee's father reflects these changes in the status of the ministry and the declining power of parson and church to define communal moral life. So while Gerald Lee perceived his heritage from the Revolutionary generation as one of solid authority earned within specific communities, the late nineteenth century example of his father was more problematic and unstable.[11]

Gerald Lee frequently read the writings of one minister who aggressively asserted his role as leader of a national public. Henry Ward Beecher, the pastor of the Plymouth Church in Brooklyn, editor of the influential *Independent,* and famous speaker to audiences throughout the nation, was a man who joined antebellum evangelical fervor with what he considered a new postwar realism. Aware of the deepening threats to the ministry by the early 1870s, Beecher found his calling in "great danger of going under." Beecher's remedy was to call for an expansion of the scope of ministerial concern to include and supply guidance for every aspect of human life.[12]

Although he had lived briefly as a youth among transplanted New Englanders in Ohio, Lee considered himself a son of the beautiful Connecticut Valley region. But a sense of economic decline permeated much of New England. Literary figures like Sarah Orne Jewett, Harriet Beecher Stowe, and Harold Frederic wrote about the loss of innocence and the pervasive pictures of broken dreams reflecting the decline of the northeastern region in which they lived. The empty Maine seaports and the hollow spirits of those who lived in the backwash of the great sea days described by Jewett testified to the lure of the city and the western frontier.[13]

Young Lee's writings provide testimony about the impact of this decline. He wrote to his sister Chris in 1884 that "New England is going to be the old fashioned cemetery of our ancestors, a place of memories and associations, a sort of summer resort for the nation." This sense of residing in a region that had somehow been passed by in the rush of the nation toward cities and the West is reflected in census data of the towns and cities in which Lee lived. Greenfield, Massachusetts, was a small town of about 3,500 souls when Gerald lived there in 1870. It had grown by about 400 people during the prior decade, clearly not on a par with the fast growing towns and cities of the West. Cleveland, for example, where Lee next lived for a few years as an adolescent, practically doubled its population between 1870 and 1880, to 160,446—it was a place with sizable numbers of foreign-born (mostly German) workers. Living amidst the economic dynamism of the city helped breed Lee's impatience and defensive attitude about New England towns. As if to underscore the sense of dissolution, the population of Sharon, Connecticut, actually declined by almost a fifth during the decade before 1890. By the early 1890s the largest city in the western part of Massachusetts was nearby Springfield, the home of Lee's parents, and a bustling industrial city of 44,179 that was to grow by about a third within the next decade. As several historians have recently recounted, social tensions were widespread as the market economy and modernizing forces undermined rural New England traditions.[14]

Lee's fear, confusion, and ambivalence about the forces of urbanization and industrialization were simplified by romanticizing the early New England frontier. In the same month that he gave his nostalgic talk at the Sharon church in 1891 he wrote a letter to the editor of the *Springfield Republican*. He protested development of the "last vacant lot" on K Street in Springfield, where his father was then teaching history at the local missionary college. He saw the vacant lot symbolically connected with natural wildness, providing young boys a link to nature and a definition of "purposeful Christian manhood." The character-developing experience of the frontier, repeated frequently in popular literature, was transposed by Lee to an urban setting. "There's room for everything in a city except a boy," Lee wrote: "But such is the manner of men and the curse of cities, turning playgrounds into parlors and boys into beaus, until all our life [turns] into a deadly, proper, grown-up-ness, and the time is coming when a city boy can't relieve himself with a good lusty yell, without taking out a license for it." Still unmarried at twenty-eight, Lee connected the disappearance of open urban space with the civilizing influence of women. He expressed contempt for the "cult of domesticity": "Behold this effeminate architectural dressmaking in boards!" Open urban spaces formed the breeding ground for boyish vitality, for the "vim" that could only grow "out of doors."[15]

One source for the connection Lee made between the lost frontier, the vacant lot, and his ambivalence toward the urban environment came from his experience in New York City, where he had traveled in the spring of 1890 to take voice lessons. He was shocked by what he saw in walks through the Lower East Side and experienced the stark dichotomy between city and rural life that fills the memoirs of so many people of his generation. "Children, with faces that look as if they had been caressing paving stones and greasy looking children . . . the children! children everywhere, they seem to crawl swarming out of the piles about them like insect inhabitants . . . and they tumble around the sewers until you have the feeling that some of them will tumble in with the other stuff—and certainly not be missed." He was disquieted with lower-class urban immigrant life, showing little compassion for the poor.[16]

Lee was lonely in New York and depressed by his own living conditions, which he felt were probably symptomatic of all that was wrong and artificial in such a large, impersonal city devoid of the focused life of a Congregational community. "By all odds the most extraordinary spectacle in New York is its wickedness," he wrote. He felt bounded by the walls of his room and alienated from the life of the city. He ruminated about symbols of artificial order and spectacles of wickedness were contrasted to the natural order and harmonious community life; church spires were losing the battle over the control of urban space.[17]

The changing social reality of Lee's native region also provided fertile territory for his expanding use of symbolic dichotomies and metaphors. Beyond the loss of geographical status experienced by New Englanders like Lee, issues that involved deepening labor and ethnic conflict threatened the older Puritan social and political values. Massachusetts was the most thoroughly industrialized state by 1880. The 1880 census found that the foreign born and those native born of foreign parents together constituted one-half of the population of Massachusetts; by 1900 they had increased to almost two-thirds. Springfield, besides growing in population by over 40 percent during the 1880s, increased its foreign-born population to one-fourth the total. In Northampton, the small city to which Lee would move in 1896, there were also about one-quarter foreign born in 1885 (about half of these being Irish). The focus of conflict throughout much of western Massachusetts most often involved parochial school support and temperance, which especially roused the older Yankee elements.[18]

Lee rarely commented directly on any threat he felt from immigrants, but his papers do reveal a more generalized anxiety couched in terms of the declining Puritan tradition. In the early fall of 1886, while he was at Yale Divinity School, he described a dream he had had the night before in which he had been drunk in a small town. His dream found him considering that "perhaps the world was coming to an end," and "things were taking a rehearsal so as to know how to act in chaos, when it occurred to me that one thing would be sure to be sober and steady under any circumstance and that was the first Congregational Church." But when he approached it, he found that "there was the good old staid old meeting house keeping time with its steeple and dancing the wickedest sort of a waltz—hugging up to the horse shed for partner!" He expected an Episcopal church to act that way, but to see the church of his forefathers "keeping time with music" was abominable: "I couldn't have been more astonished if I had seen a quotation from the Bible loafing around a bar room and flirting with a bar maid."[19]

The New England of Gerald Lee's young adulthood was dramatically unstable to him, and while the dream reveals his fears of the Congregational church falling in step with the forces of industrializing America, Lee's inability to interpret the dream suggests that social changes troubled him more deeply than he could comprehend. The elusive foe was drunkenness, a distortion of roles and perception—all in all a condition of encroaching ungodliness felt by many Congregationalists. But beyond that, the dream could identify no culprit. Near the end of the dream, he provides evidence of his own adaptation to the new era: "I was getting accustomed to strange sights [and] after seeing the Congregational Church cutting up a caper like that it didn't at all disturb my equanimity to observe that the gutters on main street didn't seem to know that they were to keep off the sidewalks."[20]

One gets a strong sense, therefore, of a split perspective developing in Lee's college-age mind: the frontier and the small town, idyllic and natural, were reminders of the sober, older Puritan communities and were contrasted to the alien, crowded, conformist, and charac-

terless quality of the urban world. Lee's thought reflected the vogu-
ish interest in primitivism, the desire for limitlessness, play, an antip-
athy to rules, as well as a male subculture seeking space from
regulation by Victorian feminine standards. Altogether, his pastoral-
ism evoked a matrix of associations that were under siege.[21]

Yet Lee's memory of the New England town of his youth also
harbored his anger at the constraints of Victorian culture. He wished
he had lived a more exciting childhood. In 1903 he wrote a newspaper article about his childhood years in Greenfield, in northwestern Massachusetts. His main memory of living there was "one
long terrible proper feeling. If ever there was a prig—an unconscion-
able, inordinate, cheerfulminded prig in this wide world, it was . . .
Gerald." He placed some of the blame for this behavior on the fact
that as the minister's son he was forced to be a model child. But he
never publicly criticized his parents for putting him on constant
public display before the town, nor did he identify any other specific
forces of oppression. His anger, constrained by gentility, pointed
toward the amount of time he "wasted" in Greenfield and animated
a set of references: his boyhood, the unity of the town, and the
power of Puritanism. The few surviving letters Lee wrote to his
parents in the late nineteenth century show significant parental
attempts to control any rebellious feelings he might have expressed.
But beyond his evident desire for freedom from social constraints,
there existed a deeper need to be bonded to others. It is in this
context that his formal education becomes relevant.[22]

His picture of the city was also more broadly drawn than his fears
of New York might suggest, especially when one recalls that Lee
spent his tenth to fourteenth years in Cleveland, while his father was
a minister there. Lee looked back on his life in this fast-growing city
as a "glorious straddling-back-fence life, crowded with boys from
morning to night." He remembered Cleveland as not having been
too highly civilized in the 1870s; it still had enough vacant lots
perpetuating a frontier spirit for boys. In sum, he could happily
envision himself as a romantic wanderer in glorious mountain ter-
rain, unfettered by the constraints of civilization; conversely, he
could also conjure up an image of himself in a benign urban environment, but only if he was surrounded by large numbers of boys who
were excited and moved by his personality.[23]

Lee's college education thus reflected the family's geographical mobility and intensified his inner life of reading and dreaming. While his father taught economics at Oberlin, Gerald attended as a student (1880–83); later he transferred to Middlebury College in Vermont (1884–85), after his father became the minister in nearby Brattleboro. From his reading of Victorian literature, Lee gradually developed an increasing anti-institutional point of view, which was buttressed by an ideology, taught at Oberlin, that sponsored the marriage of Darwinian theory of evolution with moral progress. The evangelical spirit, which Oberlin had helped channel against slavery before the Civil War, seemed to be searching through the moral and social landscape of the 1870s and 1880s for a new focus on which to direct conscience.[24]

While he was at Oberlin, Lee wrote pieces that exhibit his affinity for a liberal or mugwump Republicanism, similar to that expounded by the chief newspaper of the Connecticut Valley, the *Springfield Republican,* edited by Samuel Bowles. Lee supported civil service reform, even as he warned against nationalizing the railroads for fear that Democratic party patronage might turn out the Republican brakemen. He wrote glowingly about the "History and Character of John B. Gough," a well-known Victorian temperance spokesman, and he generally looked forward to a society led by men of native stock and high purpose. He held most Europeans to be of a lower order of mind; they were less independent and "in the lowest classes more helpless and unambitious than in America," he wrote in 1878. "Luckily," Lee added, "we are gentlemen, not aristocrats, laborers, not peasants."[25]

These years also exhibit Lee's fears of Catholicism, his envy of its organizational effectiveness, its transnational unity, and the power of papal infallibility. American Protestantism lacked adequate tools, symbols, and personalities with which to combat Catholicism throughout the world, he felt. The Roman Catholic church commanded and received obedience while the Protestants extolled undisciplined freedom and, as a result, were judged to be anarchically fragmented. American Protestantism was in a demographic battle for survival. Statistics proved to him that Catholicism was growing 75 percent faster than Protestantism; that growth was perceived as a vast, adaptable conspiracy of evil against Protestant hegemony, a conspiracy shutting public schools and controlling large cities like New York through the boss control of its cattlelike subjects; a conspiracy possessing vast wealth, often virtually stolen from men and women "who were lured into convents." In an 1881 essay Lee identifies America as a newborn baby, innocent, pure, rural, and Godly, but about to be murdered unless nativist jeremiads were heeded. This dramatic contrast displays an intensity of hatred that would later be masked in more subtle tones; it demonstrates Lee's tendency toward a literary overkill, or perhaps to the rising journalistic styles to be found in big city papers.[26]

While at Middlebury College in 1885, Lee began to focus his reading on the power of great men. He absorbed the mid-century romantic ideal of the hero as fully as anyone of his generation and sought to be its translator to the coming urban industrial culture. Romantic heroism provided Lee with an escape from the boredom and sense of irrelevance he associated with religious theory. It reaffirmed the tradition of voluntarism, which, Thomas Haskell affirms, was under attack in the 1880s by the growing recognition of interdependence mediated by professional social scientists.[27]

Lee's study of heroism and the public image of power was matched by his private view of himself as strange and ugly. His skinniness, large nose, and narrow face obviously greatly bothered him. "I am a queer fellow," he wrote in Brattleboro in 1884, "no doubt about it. But I want something else to distinguish me. I don't think I am a fool exactly—but I've got the materials in me for it, if they should happen to combine." He came from a long line of Puritan parsons with close ties to Yale Divinity School. The legal profession seemed too mercenary and detail oriented, politics too unsavory, and writing and teaching too unremunerative. So Gerald Lee followed the well-worn family path and he entered Yale in 1885.[28]

Thin and ungainly, Lee appears to have cultivated an aura of strangeness about himself at Yale, keeping aloof from his classmates while remaining intensely self-critical and introspective. He was perpetually writing his own thoughts down into small notebooks. "Needed—largeness of movement," he wrote when he was twenty-three years old. "The great utterance of great truths—as distinct [from] the minute treatment of little topics," was his goal.[29]

While he was in New Haven Lee's distaste for the formal logic of theology grew strong. He quit Yale in his final year and later made clear his undisguised contempt for the arid diet of divinity school in comparison to a literary education: "The atmosphere of divinity schools is fatal to the expansive instinct," he wrote, manifesting his desire to experience life whole, rather than through the narrow prism of academia. In judging the journal *Public Opinion* in November of 1890, Lee wrote that the "satisfying part of the periodical is the literary while there was not much food for thought in the theological." Spiritual theology, or what he labeled "religious theology," was fine, "but this dogma-skeleton anatomical theology—is not worth much."[30]

At the center of Lee's growing fascination with power stood the romanticism of Thomas Carlyle and Ralph Waldo Emerson. Lee had read many of Emerson's works in the early and mid-1880s; he read Carlyle's three-volume *History of the French Revolution*, his book on heroes, and *Sartor Resartus* by 1890. From his reading of Carlyle and Emerson, Gerald Lee came to the conviction that he was in tune with the basic harmonies of the world, working God's will out by uncovering the basic metaphorical patterns of human existence.[31]

Lee's belief in metaphor reflected a romantic residue used by many American Victorians who confronted the powerful determinism of the Social Darwinists. Until the early twentieth century, Lee viewed the collector of empirical facts and the scientist as conspirators in a vast crime against creative individual expression. He contrasted the poet to the factmonger or scientist. This formulation aided Lee in disposing of the determinism of Darwinian thought without directly condemning it. Poets should take the simple facts and define their meaning for an anxious world. The poetic hero, Lee felt, would be the savior of American culture before the avalanche of scientific information that was burying traditional authority.[32]

In an unpublished essay probably written in the 1880s, Lee reflects almost word for word the mid-century doctrine of the hero: "The past can be garnered in the influence of a few men. The history of the human race is the biography of a few individuals. Every epoch is the length and character, the multiplying energy of a single man who has risen above his fellows and walked forth from the contented littleness of his times in the heroism of a majestic discord!" Carlyle became a father figure to Lee, both compensating for the lost power of his real father and forming a link to the model of the Puritan parson. Not content to accept the everyday workings of American democracy but interested in gathering mystical companions from the past, Lee exhibited a latent desire to be swept away by a hero who would lead him to the titans of Olympus.[33]

Carlyle answered another of Lee's needs. The Scot's Olympian pronouncements and his writing style sounded radical and daring, while his social prescriptions grew increasingly mystical and ultimately conservative, even feudalistic. "All the best writers have been radicals," Lee wrote, unconsciously defining radicalism in terms of the command of attention rather than the scope or depth of social analysis. Both Carlyle's radicalism as well as Lee's were thus expressions of impatience. Lee continued to be enamored of the figurative quality to Carlyle's language and the fact that it was "full of broad antithesis."[34]

Emerson's writings were easier for most Americans to absorb than Carlyle's. The sage of Concord lived until 1882 and related more directly to Lee's American context than could Carlyle, who moreover was tainted by his support of the Confederacy during the American Civil War. Lee's unstinting admiration for Emerson suffuses his writings of the late 1880s. Similar to other intellectuals of his generation, moreover, Lee relied on Emerson as an "alternative to both orthodoxy and materialism."[35]

The hero that Emerson created possessed few specified ethical principles but was obedient "to a secret impulse of an individual's character." By the end of his life, Emerson, with his heroic theory at the core of his thought, had become the "chief apostle of the emerging cult of self-confidence." Originally seeming to extol nonconformity and antielitism, he was eventually adopted by personal-power theorists and numerous spokesmen for laissez-faire conservatism, such as the corporate chieftains, in their defense of their privileged positions in society.[36]

Lee defined the heroic personality for his own times as a man of genius who could act both as a bulwark against the dispersion of congregational life and as a creator of new and attractive authority in America. In one article published in the *Independent* in 1891, Lee commented on the nature of genius by linking it to a form of dramatic transfer: "The genius carries a kind of relative infinity and eternity in his own consciousness, that ennobles all that it touches with itself, and gilds over his blunders with high meaning. We are lacking this." By 1905 he would explicitly use the phrase "church of the strong men" to describe the extraordinary people—by then defined more narrowly in elitist terms—that he hoped to coalesce on a more national scale. But in the period 1885–1902 he was more concerned with conceiving of an individual of great power in the modern world than in identifying a group of great men or a structure symbolizing or containing the group.[37]

Compulsively self-referential in his exaltation of heroic personalities and contemptuous of the society around him, Lee remained essentially conservative in his social prescriptions. He latched onto the idea of heroic prophecy as a panacea for complex cultural problems, though he was clearly driven toward this solution by his own psychic needs for distinction and power over others. He admonished himself: "Let your life by an inner one. Let books be your friends—thoughts your company. Other men—you live for them— but the more conscientiously you live for yourself—the more you can influence them. Believe in your own destiny as you believe in nothing else except God. Feel it unfolding itself in you day by day. As for fellows, as for women—they are shifting scenes in the drama that you are working out in your own heart—influence them but don't let them more than influence you." Cultivating the self for the greater glory of God and "the people" demanded a relentless form of self-control. "Never cease watching yourself," he wrote while at Yale. "Excesses will be fatal." All of this watching and self-absorption was transformed into Lee's growing worship of power, which was largely devoid of any nuanced understanding or empathy for those in the communities in which he lived and worked. He was what Van Wyck Brooks later labeled a "highbrow," separating himself from the social lives of most people with whom he came into contact.[38]

The ends to which Lee's cultivation of power were to be used became increasingly evident to him; revitalizing the Puritan ideals that tied character to intellect, he sought to promote them as norms for a "natural" aristocracy in American life. His mission was to identify a generation of magnetic personalities who had the power to inspire Americans to build a unified but modern kingdom of God. Avoiding an elitism based on financial holdings or racial theories of character, Lee professed to eschew an aristocracy that "advertise[s] its superiority in the posture of its nose and the affections of an exaggerated refinement." His ideal was based on the older and increasingly elusive republican concept of virtue. He wrote disdainfully in 1885 that the aristocracy of pedigree "is a substituting of blood for virtue. A man of this sort is supposed to carry the distilled excellence of a long line of ancestors in his own blood, each member impersonating, in his turn, the blossom of the race." This notion was, "fortunately," dying in the United States, he wrote, because its representatives' "certificate of membership in society is not the flow of thought in libraries but blood in their veins."[39]

Lee was developing an ideology of modern cultural hegemony based more precisely on a man's success in what he saw to be a democratic marketplace. Technological inventions, poetic ideas, material rewards, and social harmony could all flower if heroic personalities could be identified and nurtured by literary men like himself. But Lee's ideals were narrower than his romantic temperament had led him to project upon himself. He possessed commonplace notions of Victorian respectability, ugly ethnic stereotypes, an intolerance of people who were less literarily inclined than himself, and a malleable conception of acceptable character traits.

In the Sharon address of 1891 and on many subsequent occasions, Lee sought the return of the militant Puritan personality. "Intolerant, unbending, unreasonable, [the Puritan forefathers] were mighty men, farseers down the ways of nations, because . . . they had . . . the sense of human character, the supremacy of manhood, the irrevocable conviction that no knowledge, nor skill of knowledge, nor power that knowledge gives should ever be accorded by the state to one who would not use it to the glory of God." Knowledge, in the final analysis, was "not a man's character, but the multiple of the character he had." The Puritans had an abundance of character. Modern Americans, however, left the "entire problem of American character to the churches they distrust . . . while burying their heads in the Sunday papers."[40]

Lee recognized that the Puritan "had lost ground in the popular mind because those who disliked him have been eloquent and those who have liked him have not." The Puritan was not conquered like the forests, he thundered angrily in a review of Ezra Hoyt Byington's book, *The Puritan in England and New England* (1896), but had remained a "pioneer" and "with the persistence of being in character which always belongs to him [as] his birthright," the Puritan was "fighting still." This sense of being besieged by alien forces and of living in the midst of a national crisis retained all the psychic dangers of the Puritan's frontier. "The fight has only moved on from the musket, the red coat and the Indian to literature and theology and art, but the Puritan has returned. He claims the land . . . He faces his sons, and whether he looks out over a more discouraging wilderness than he had before is a question that can only be decided by our national acceptance of the Puritan spirit as the most essential and sublime element in our American life." Even beyond the specter of class violence experienced by Americans in the late nineteenth century, Lee believed that a cultural state of war existed. Notions about Puritan consensus focused on issues of character, social order, and public opinion were threatened by the ambiguous power of urban industrial culture. By 1900, Lee wondered whether "personality, creative, triumphant, masterful, imperious, personality [was] . . . not at an end." He was to spend most of his adult life attempting to revive the role that a triumphant and heroic personality could play in the maelstrom of America. His jeremiads against modern mass culture were written as he searched for his own voice as a prophet of his times. Needing both to understand the new functions of mass persuasion and to create a workable definition of the public upon which the modern hero could successfully work his will, Gerald Lee remained a self-conscious son of New England romanticism.[41]

THREE

"Parson of the World": Prophecy and Disdain from the Pulpit to the Print Medium

By 1896 Gerald Stanley Lee had become thoroughly dissatisfied with his own role as a Congregational preacher. Parishioners had evidently been divided in their support of Lee from the start, many dissatisfied with his less than full attention and with the time he spent on his writing career. One Sunday in April 1896, the Springfield congregation found Lee absent from his pulpit; his letter of resignation was read aloud. He wrote them that he had "always thought that to be a clergyman was to be the most perfect service that the world affords." In leaving it, he was abandoning a calling that he had originally promised never to give up.[1]

Lee claimed that he sought a higher calling where there were fewer boundaries. "The art of expression . . . has its other pulpits," he wrote, and he visualized an open-air cathedral run by a ministry of print, built on the presumption that the masses always followed an inspired minority.

> Not dependent upon an audience gathered upon a merely geographical basis, alone of all the pulpits, the pulpit of the book admits of that more perfect freedom which is the brother of the truth. By the width of its appeal, rallying about it that inspired minority through the gathering of which the majorities of the world are always led, it is to literature that we must look for the most prophetic as well as expressive of all that we hold to be true.

Few in the congregation could have missed Lee's implicit message: the print medium afforded more freedom of artistic expression to promote the will of God; one who was inspired or prophetic should possess greater avenues of expression.[2]

Lee's resignation letter illustrates several aspects of the Gilded Age in which many ministers called for new techniques of mass persuasion, more effective religious organizations to evangelize a wider public, and more dynamic leaders to revitalize morality and buttress social order. Lee's thought reflected both the impact of recent biblical scholarship that softened the Calvinistic picture of Christ and the accommodation of Protestantism to Darwinian theory. His writings testify to the rising interest in social justice and therapeutic adjustments to industrial culture seen in the Social Gospel and New Thought movements.

All the same, it is necessary to keep in focus the disdain Lee developed toward his congregations in the 1880s and 1890s and his emerging desire to realize a national congregation. "To be a great man is to be greater than a people," Lee wrote in 1896, "and to be a great singer is more than to sum up a nation in a rhapsody or write down its heart in a hymnal. It is to sing more than a nation sings." Lee's dilemma by the 1890s was to uncover the modes of persuasion that would facilitate a consensus of values among widening audiences. His conception of a parson speaking (or "singing") to a church congregation became transformed into that of a writer addressing an unseen audience of readers.[3]

Out of Lee's youthful isolation and a romanticized attachment to books emerged a great admiration for forms of expression that moved large groups of people. As a general principle, Lee later wrote, "a nation's life can be said to be truly a civilized life, in proportion as it is expressive." One writer who was later correctly to recognize this consuming concern in Lee was Randolph Bourne. Reviewing a book of Lee's in 1916, Bourne commented sarcastically that "it is Mr. Lee's function to present to the American people the novel idea that inexpressibleness is the root of all evil." Throughout his career at Yale Divinity School and as parson to three congregations, Lee struggled to express himself dramatically while covertly berating his audiences for their failure to understand him.[4]

Certain words served as master words that painted dramatic pictures, Lee contended, and he was determined to find such words and use them to their maximum effect. He recognized that language evoked emotional responses. "Most of us have words that are sacred to us—locked up with the inner secrets of our being and reserved for only precious uses." While at Yale, Lee began to argue that few modern men were capable of comprehending anything more complex than a simple visual message and that the world was suffused with a dull literalness. "A man's imagination in his picture gallery of ideas," he wrote. "It photographs his thoughts for him." But, "while some of them are mere reflections cast in the mirror of fancy only to vanish with the moment, others print themselves in the warmer colors of conviction and haunt or bless us with their presence ever afterwards."[5]

In order to make words effective, Lee felt, one had to understand how to read and visualize the inner souls of people through their gestures and above all the expressiveness of their faces. This was the key to persuasion: to uncover the mental "screen" upon which human souls, as expressed through their faces, could be accurately reproduced and read—as if they were photographs. "If the minds of two men expressing opinions in the dark could be flashed on a canvas," he mused, "if there could be such a thing as a composite photograph of an opinion—a biography of it—it would prove to be, with nine men out of ten, a dissolving view of faces." The elite tenth of humanity were those whose character and intellect precluded facile visual ascertaining. But the overwhelming majority of faces easily told the whole story of human lives, their aspirations and their sense of despair and helplessness. Nine-tenths of humanity lacked complexity and were barely individuals at all, but living stereotypes to Lee. Thus he reduced the individuals composing most audiences into a simplified mass and showed little appreciation for the texture of their lives; empathy with the diversity of individual problems dissolved under the belief that he could read the lives and concerns of people from their faces. Yet techniques of persuasion obsessed him, overshadowing his observation of the faces peering out at him from his congregations; he accepted the proposition that the central task of the preacher was to shape the congregation, not to represent it.[6]

The first serious test of Lee's opinion-shaping powers came in 1888, when he served as pastor in the small town of Princeton, Minnesota. Far from his native New England, Lee developed an unabashed contempt for the town and its gossiping populace, whose incessant whispering behind his back ignited his anger. Lee was told by one of his parishioners that his style seemed too free-flowing and illustrative, that he seemed too much an impractical visionary to be popular. Altogether, he was discouraged with the ignorance, the small-mindedness, and the pettiness of the town, and he resigned his parish in Princeton on 12 May 1889. In leaving his congregation, he left little doubt about his disillusionment with his midwestern experience, writing in a private note that "Princeton is not a real world but a nightmare . . . and when I leave, it is all over like the shadowy troubles of a dream."[7]

Lee's "real world" was New England, to which he soon returned with a heightened desire to make his preaching abilities equal his power of expression in writing. He took a number of short-term substitute preaching jobs and studied various well-known speakers for their style. After hearing the agnostic orator Robert Ingersoll, Lee commented that the performance was like "lighting a candle and holding it to the star!" Still optimistic about his oratorical powers, Lee proclaimed, in September 1890, "that preaching can be at once popular and very profound. That it may have interest and profit and inspire the most simple minded—and yet have vast sketches of meaning reaching away into the infinity of thought." He felt that if he worked hard enough, he could be both profound and popular, reaching beyond the influence of those preachers who merely aspired to be one or the other. "The man who seeks popularity will not be deep," he wrote, "but he who seeks to express the life of his soul unto the life of other souls—and mingles his love of souls with [one who] seeks popularity—and love of truth which seeks depth—will be both!"[8]

As early as 1890 Lee had considered making writing a career: "With the popular taste as it is, it sometimes seems as if the only way to acquire a reputation, is through the magazines and if a man would write a book in which he can call himself his own, he must first introduce himself quite thoroughly to his public in magazine literature." He characterized this "magazine literature" as "the practice ground before entering the tournament," but the tournament required a national education. The eastern man needs to be westernized and the western man needs to be easternized. Following his

Minnesota experience, Lee believed that he had been westernized and was capable of speaking and writing as a national spokesman, possessing a personality that was able to synthesize and embody the thought and emotion within the country. He would represent the nation in a way done by Sharon's Cotton Mather Smith in the eighteenth century, or by Henry Ward Beecher in his own time.[9]

From 1890 to 1896, while Lee was shifting his efforts into writing, he was also solidifying his perceptions about city dwellers, perceptions that fed his elitist conception of being separated from, superior to, and a spokesman for the masses of humanity. As his writing done during the 1890 sojourn in New York City shows, he had largely depersonalized the condition of the urban poor in the same period that Jacob Riis was evoking sympathy for them through his photographs. Lee's complete lack of missionary zeal to convert or alter the environment of the urban poor of New York seems clear even though his own father was simultaneously involved in sending college-age youth into urban slums; Gerald's interest was focused only on improving his own ability to preach to more familiar congregations in New England. Sadly for him, though, within a month of his return from New York to the country (presumably Springfield, Massachusetts), Lee berated himself for his poor discipline in speaking.[10]

His Sharon, Connecticut, parish, which he joined late in 1890, was taken on a trial basis. From the outset Lee found it too "comfortable," not confronting important issues or problems. To keep him, the elders agreed to increase the salary for the position, but Lee soon became dissatisfied by the yearly review of the minister's salary. It was demeaning, and he left the parish in 1893.[11]

The belief grew in Lee's mind that the market mechanism affected preachers of religion as it did all other professionals. Several years later, in a letter berating the parishioners of his next and final parish in Springfield, Lee declared that salaries for ministers had to be weighed against the salary scales in other allied callings, or ministerial authority would be further diminished. A larger salary meant simply that "demand was greater" for his services while the "supply [was] smaller." "To nine tenths of the public," he wrote, "money is the natural and immediate and legitimate motive of their daily labor and they judge ministers just as they judge artists, from the cash point of view." If a congregation properly respected the widening audience of their preacher, they should reward him and bask in his glory. American values and the laws of the market were the "reality" for up-to-date preachers as well as for business leaders, and to question that was fruitless. Earlier preachers had made this connection. Charles Finney and, in later years, Henry Ward Beecher spoke more and more of the parson's personality instead of his piety, thus manifesting the idea that persuasion and influence were becoming increasingly considered in quantifiable terms.[12]

Moral rectitude had thus become subordinated to the need to attract congregations. Unmixed goodness was deemed "one of the serious evils with which the modern pulpit is confronted." Paul and David were not known for their unalloyed goodness, Lee implied, but for their ability to "sing" to people of all times with an "amazing and suggestive psychology." A great preacher as well as a great writer had to be ahead of his audience, inducing it to imitate his personality. This necessitated the use of "the laws of attention" and the "rules of psychology." The contempt that Lee felt for his audiences, growing out of his inability to dominate them, was being channeled into rationalizing an ethically neutralized use of psychological techniques of persuasion.[13]

"The written word is higher than the spoken word," Lee finally declared to his congregation in his resignation letter, because it compromised less and was able to provide a more capacious forum for artists of the highest gifts. The church and the public could be made one again, he believed, but only through the newer medium of print: books would impart a special wisdom and prophecy to the (unrecognized and elevated) minority in every church who had to suffer through preaching that was directed to everyone—the lowest common denominator. Books were able to select their publics. Lee left little doubt that his own mission was to use his higher literary powers to influence and persuade the leading lights, to be a counselor to an elite. His vision of a two-tiered congregational order—between the educated and the common people—was justified by claiming that it was the "common people" who had not understood Jesus and had "crucified" him.[14]

He defined himself as a "mere camera" that could only reproduce impressions. Not capable of abstract reasoning, only of abstractions, he proposed to break with the categorical method and, as an artist, take information of all kinds as food for his imagination. He meant to adopt the method of Carlyle, who swallowed his material whole, not leaving it in "a half chewed condition in the form of information for the consumption of the public." He would not write reference books: he wanted to write about life, beyond the dictates of institutional constraints. It was strange and wondrous to Lee to observe finallly that "all that art has done for me has been to lead me back to religion. All beauty comes home."[15]

In *The Shadow Christ,* published in 1896, Lee examined ancient Israel in order to launch himself into his increasingly ecumenical definitions of a more all-inclusive church. A meditation on the meaning of the Old Testament to the coming of Christ, the book was the self-acknowledged basis for much of Lee's later published work. Culled from his sermons, *The Shadow Christ* was a hymn to the biblical prophet Isaiah, who stood out in Lee's mind as "an abstract of what a great man will be like when he comes—a shadowing forth of the ideal toward which we strive." Isaiah, Lee felt, was undoubtedly the biblical progenitor of the Carlylean ideal, the figure Carlyle had missed, making his work ultimately incomplete. To Lee, Isaiah was the father of positive thinking. "Isaiah, singing out of his broken life and his broken nation," Lee wrote, "is the most heroic spirit in the annals of man because he sounded the victorious affirmative that has become forever the courage and the destiny of human life." The greatest Old Testament figures, Isaiah and David, were singing salesmen with positive messages as well as poetic spirits who possessed "oceanic" souls as wide as the universe. The grand old days for Lee were therefore not simply the days of his Puritan forefathers but the days of the Hebrews—the days of prophecy, and assertive selling of ideas.[16]

Lee's thought also reflected the impact of contemporary critical scholarship on the Old Testament and such popular novels as *Robert Elsmere* and *John Ward, Preacher.* Both novels raised questions about the authority of the Scriptures and manifested the intense religious doubt of the times. Harold Frederic's *The Damnation of Theron Ware* (1896), for example, was a well-known account of a minister doubting the rigidity of his faith and the dullness of the small-town people. In addition, Frederic gives us the Soulsbys, two characters who are professional religious fund raisers. These are the prototypes of future religious salesmen, people who have adopted modern techniques of attention engineering.[17]

How did Jesus fit into Lee's conceptualization of the great singer-salesman as heroic figure? Lee projected onto Jesus what he understood about himself; he was "intuitive rather than dialectic in his methods, it was the very nature of his commands that they were insights." He pointedly contrasted Jesus to Moses: "The unquestioning obedience that Moses demanded in the Christ became the great sharing ideal—the obedience which questions[;] and then commands itself." Jesus fused mankind into a unity of purpose through love, drama, and his "incredible approachableness." He could, ultimately, get "nearer to men than men could," making fellowship the supreme attribute of God. "With heroic simplicity he risked his mission on the earth, and founded his title to be the ruler of men upon letting them be familiar with him." Jesus was a kind of primal dramatic genius, because he functioned as a common denominator in understanding people.[18]

Lee's interpretation of the role of Isaiah of course fed his own aspirations to act as a prophet of his own times and as a guide and interpreter of public opinion. He felt himself to be part of an elite capable of leading the nation. "With some of us," he wrote in an 1897 book review, "to believe in inspiration for ourselves and one another is about the only religion worth having. . . . To believe in prophecy is prophecy itself and statesmanship and patriotism and common sense." Lee's belief in prophecy ultimately fed a belief in deferential duty toward an elite of his own definition, reflecting as well an increasing tone of compulsion that was beginning to enter into Lee's writing.[19]

From his resignation until June 1905, when he began to publish his own small literary-nature journal, *Mt. Tom,* Lee spent his time writing, preaching, and lecturing in various forums. His ideas were delivered, for a fee, on the platform as well as in print. His published articles and books addressing large and abstract topics—the effects of mass production upon the life of individuals and the attendant loss of religious coherence in a culture basing itself on a quantitative ethic. At first he published only in small journals like *The Critic* and received a number of rejection notices. He remained an obscure aesthete writing criticism in an overblown style. As a struggling writer, he seems to have lived simply.

Most happily for Lee, in June 1896 he married a woman with whom he formed a broad and effective literary and intellectual partnership until his death. His thirty-six-year-old wife was Jennette Barbour Perry of Cleveland, Ohio, whom he had met while traveling in the south of Germany four years before. Two years older than Gerald, she was described by one "of her best friends" as "a little dark woman with very dark hair and very dark eyes and a lot of silence about her." Her silence was seen as "her secret," which gave her an influence over others because "they never know exactly what she is thinking about, and they would like to." She had grown up living with her grandparents and began teaching at age fifteen in a small town near Bristol, Connecticut. The years studying at Smith College were "quiet" ones, and she was "little known by her fellow students." Her aloneness was exhibited in her favorite amusement, which her friend related was "sitting still in the woods." By the time she married Gerald Lee in 1896 she had begun publishing short stories, was a contributor to the scholarly journal *The Critic* (soon to be joined by Gerald), and had taught English and rhetoric at the College for Women in Western Reserve University. She had not joined any church up to 1896 and was doubtless an influence in Gerald's leaving the pulpit. A number of subsequent novels—mostly set in New England—followed until after World War I.[20]

Gerald Lee expressed his admiration for his wife to Upton Sinclair in 1903. "If I had not had a heroic wife, and one who understood and one who was as desperate as I not to compromise I would have lost my soul years ago." After their marriage the Lees had one daughter, Geraldine, born in 1897. The Lees bought a large house on High Street (now named Elm Street) in Northampton in 1896, and five years later Jennette secured a teaching position at Smith College. Their house had an unimpeded view of Mt. Tom in the far distance, and they lived there intermittently, apparently happy together, until Gerald's death in 1944. They collected antiques, then the rage. Jennette had made $2,200 in 1896 and he had made $1,800 before they quit their respective jobs. They found themselves in financial difficulty in the first few years of their marriage, and on

Jennette Barbour Perry,
a writer of fiction and
professor of English
at Smith College. She
married Gerald Lee
in 1896.

several occasions they rented out their Northampton house for the
summer in order to live more cheaply in old southern Berkshire
farmhouses. But they were seldom in such dire financial straits in
these early years to give up vacationing on Monhegan Island, off the
coast of Maine.[21]

Lee's relationship with his parents is difficult to determine, but
letters suggest strong family quarrels. Apparently Samuel Lee was a
rather rigid and doctrinaire Congregationalist. Early family anguish
centered upon the "nervous difficulty" of his sister Chris. In 1893
Gerald wrote a letter lecturing his parents about their responsibility toward the girl, chastising them for their heartlessness. "Our
house—with its constant disagreement, and conflicts—of never give
ups—is the last place for a nervous invalid," he wrote. Gerald's
resignation from the ministry and subsequent marriage to a non-
church woman doubtless produced further strain with his parents.
In later years, however, Gerald makes frequent references in letters
to his parents about the seriousness with which he considered his
religious calling, even though he chose to practice it through the

magazines. On his parents' fortieth wedding anniversary in 1901, he wrote that "you seem very far from one another sometimes and my heart aches and you are far from me. I can only pray that some time we will all know each other." All in all, Gerald Lee displays a rather patronizing attitude toward the old-fashioned quality of his parents' religious views.[22]

Lee lived on the periphery of college life. Many important speakers at Smith stayed at the Lees home, often entranced by the combined erudition of this locally prominent couple. Lee toyed with the idea of teaching at Smith College, and substituted upon occasion, but he wrote of finding little value in the work. The classroom was too confining for him, in the same way as a church congregation.[23]

Northampton was a bustling cosmopolitan city that was in the process of doubling its population to 18,643 (from 1880 to 1900) when the Lees moved there. The silk industry dominated the city, along with the Florence Manufacturing group, which produced such items as sewing machines, hairbrushes, toothbrushes, and stoves. Northampton was serviced by several railroad lines, and by telephones after 1880; it had a hospital and a gothic-style public library, erected in 1894. With all this industrial activity, "Northampton was never dominated by it but remained primarily a residential town ministered to by its industry, and with a high degree of culture." Up until 1900 native labor constituted at least 75 percent of the workers, with labor unions making inroads only in the metal industries. Further, after 1871, the city became dominated by Smith College, the first woman's college to be chartered in New England. Smith's first president, L. Clark Seelye, had been a dynamic and courtly young minister who had earlier taught English and rhetoric himself at Amherst and remained at Smith's helm for thirty-seven years. So the Lees' choice of a home fit their desire for an alternative to a city the size of New York or Boston; Northampton was a city possessing a host of educated people, strong leaders, and close proximity to beautiful rural countryside.[24]

Beginning in the late 1890s, Lee presented a number of addresses and articles explaining the rising phenomenon of the writer as a celebrity with unrivaled power. Writing had become a vocation for a growing number of young men and women by the 1890s; Rudyard Kipling, Harriet Beecher Stowe, and Henry George were models of influence and persuasion for many aspiring writers. Mrs. Stowe's *Uncle Tom's Cabin,* along with the activities of the whole Beecher family, had awakened many, Lee wrote, to the "idea of a public, of creating a market." If Lee sometimes felt "the whole modern reading, book and paper outfit were simply a huge, crunching Mass-Machine—a machine for arranging every man's mind from the outside," then the greatest writers became to him the master arrangers, those who could be modern educators and help "read the world together."[25]

After repeating a lecture on Kipling to a number of local audiences, Lee published in early 1900 an article on the celebrated English author in the *Atlantic Monthly.* There he tried to strike a compromise between condemning the trivia of daily journalism as practiced in the United States and appreciating the power of journalism as a basis for modern literary culture; he sought a balance between managed popular culture and those who possessed "busts of Dante in their houses." Kipling effectively combined the roles of a reporter and a poet and functioned as a pathfinder or prophet and demonstrated how literature could exist not to denigrate newspapers but to raise them to unknown heights of influence.[26]

Another popular author whose work intrigued Lee was Henry George, the single tax advocate. Lee was enthralled with the impact of George's book *Progress and Poverty.* George "has made economics literature, has given to the whole subject a momentum toward its own centre, toward the soul of it, that it has never had in any permanent sense before." Economics was now a subject belonging to everyone, according to Lee, although his own reading on the subject was scanty. Avoiding any serious consideration of George's economic thesis, Lee concentrated on the elements of his writing style that attracted attention.[27]

Clearly, Lee's writing was congenial with the ideology of mainstream northeastern publishers, from Richard Watson Gilder, editor of *The Critic,* to William Dean Howells, the moving force behind the *Atlantic Monthly.* While chafing under the dictates of genteel culture, Lee's work ultimately reflected many of the tensions and ambiguities that kept it alive. One of Lee's articles, for example, condemned the "sex-conscious school of fiction"; obsessive interest in sex was being promoted as a major facet of literature, he felt, while he simultaneously scoffed at the censorious moralists who would banish any consideration of the subject. Another article analyzed the role of parsons in literature, finding that such men had given away their power to the home and the marketplace, to universities and the printing presses, which in turn had become the "parson of the world—with pulpits for assistance." Lee was thus increasingly conscious of the market value of words. In one article, for example, he commented with a sense of resignation on the revelation that Howells had himself finally submitted to the commercialization of the platform by agreeing to have his appearances organized by Major Pond's speaker's bureau.[28]

No matter how abstract they might have seemed, Lee's ideas resonated with the thought of a number of nascent Progressives. Perhaps his closest friend in the decade after his resignation from the pulpit was another former minister, Charles Ferguson. A lawyer and editorial writer for the Hearst newspapers, Ferguson became a loose collaborator with Lee in the early twentieth century. They exchanged ideas and wrote separate books that fed on the work of each other.

Lee admired Ferguson's *The Religion of Democracy,* published in 1900, a book that was neither a critical success nor a best-seller. A vague description of the contemporary condition of American life and an optimistic prescription for the nation's historical mission, Ferguson's book equated the public with democracy itself and found them both sorely deficient. The church he envisioned would "regard itself as constitutionally coterminous with secular society." Written within a year of Spain's defeat by the United States in 1898, the book pictured Spain as representing the passive thinking of the dead spirit of Catholicism.[29]

The movement that Ferguson and Lee envisioned was a cultural and spiritual one. An aristocracy of aesthetic and literary taste, enlightened political leadership, and benevolent public stewards would dominate the nation. In his book *The University Militant* (1904), Ferguson posited that a university was "at bottom religious," having a "gospel that preaches the unity and reasonableness of the ground plan of the world." Toward this end he became president of an organization called the Municipal University, which was conceived to be a church of the industrial republic, "the spiritual organization of the people for adventurous enterprise." In a world where the forces of mass production were undermining so many values, the university would become a "militant order, a self-conscious and self-confident army." Contemporary American universities were characterized as "alms-houses of the arts and sciences"; the "creative intellect" was "pauperized in them and made the parasite of the artless, scienceless drudges of the field and workshop." Ferguson—and Lee—wanted the universities to become territorial aggrandizers as well as employers.[30]

Not content with this, though, Ferguson—with backing by Lee and others such as Ray Stannard Baker, Ida Tarbell, Elbert Hubbard, the poet Edwin Markham, the architect Louis Sullivan, and the novelist Margaret Deland—sought the publication of a national newspaper. The role that the newspaper was to fulfill was the familiar Progressive middle way between plutocracy and socialism, or, as Ferguson put it, as an organizer of "that voiceless middle American public which stands hesitating today between the Machiavellian 'System' and the Deep Sea of Socialism." The newspaper that Ferguson envisioned would be "arrestive," "humanly interesting," and have as its goal the unification of American opinion.[31]

By 1908, with Lee acting as a contributor and George Creel (later to be head of Woodrow Wilson's Committee of Public Information) acting as editor, Ferguson started a newspaper called the *Newsbook*. Embarrassingly unpopular (unlike Hubbard's ventures), the *Newsbook* folded within several months. Creel believed that it was above people's heads and wrote of Ferguson that he "had small use for reform laws and legislative program, branding them as a false approach to democracy's problems." Why, then, did Creel associate himself with such an enterprise? He wrote that "day in and day out, persistently and persuasively, [Ferguson] doped me with the organ music of his voice and dazzled me with word paintings that had a glow of a Titian."[32]

For his part, Lee continued to hope for the containment of the public in a modern church. He did so, however, in more abstract terms than Ferguson, terms that masked his growing adulation of national economic domination by benevolent corporate chieftains. Much of his concern up to 1908 focused upon architecture as a lingering metaphor of contained spiritual consciousness. By 1906 Lee described New York's Trinity Church as a "little toy church" when compared to the "great, splendid, boundless-looking buildings" that seemed to frown down upon it. Hundreds of secretaries (then called typewriter girls) "look down from out of the sky . . . upon the graceful little tower that is still allowed in the great city to stand for God."[33]

In the same year that Henry Adams wrote his now-famous tribute to the sense of unity spawned by the medieval cathedrals, Lee declared that "the church that is going to live in modern life must make itself a kind of city." If the medieval cathedral had remained a great spiritual city, allowing individualistic chapels under its great tent, "we would still belong to it," he asserted. Reflecting the lingering influence of Charles Kingsley, Lee saw the great modern church as the "Church of the Strong Men."[34]

His new attitude was to exalt the limitless possibilities of awakening the tired, listless faces of those around him, transforming them in turn into worshipers in his dreamlike cathedral of unity. "Give me a few blank faces, and I will worship anywhere." A cheap or economical God does not make them worship, he asserted, but keeps them in a kind of trance. His own "mind reading of congregations" told him that a religion of democracy could light up all the individual faces in it as nothing had done before. What was not clearly stated was that this great national cathedral would also possess an elite of far-sighted educated gentlemen who, along with the presiding parson, would possess the real power.[35]

Lee's own personal experience was cited as proof of a universal truth. "I feel the great congregation," he said. "I have seen that the earth would be crowded with worship, I have seen it trooping as in the morning with strange lighted-up men." Yet, Lee retreated here, and reached again into his Emersonian bag. "I do not believe that this mind reading of congregations which I am trying to express is merely personal. I have but dipped into the sea of a universal experience with my own." Nature was the universal truth that confirmed his belief. "I have been with animals or with insects or with trees and

I have not wondered if there was a God." It was only when following the people and the tolling bells beckoning them to what he considered to be an antiseptic God that he sometimes wondered if God really existed. "The dear, hungry people—what has happened to them?"[36]

What had happened to "the dear, hungry people" was that to him they had become a mere faceless mass, a herd to be manipulated in its own best interests. Seeking to feel and express the souls of the American public, the ex-parson was setting himself up to dramatize and retranslate the will of the people back to them, to rule them. The steady disdain that Lee felt toward his church and lecture audiences extended into his conceptualization of the nature of the urbanized reading public. He did not believe that the people should actually rule as a sovereign entity; they had proven unable to rule themselves without heroic figures to imitate. It was a vicious cycle from which the "dear, hungry people" had not been able to escape. By 1906 Lee continued to leave his elite of inspired persons ill-defined, almost waiting in the wings for a modern era to host their appearance for an anxiously waiting world. As Lee waited, however, his dramatization of ideas was becoming an end in itself. Yet, the persistence of his disdain reflected his romantic megalomania and was predicated on his ambiguous personification of the crowd.

FOUR

Psychic Currents: Gerald Lee and the
Progressive-Era Vision of a Beautiful Crowd

By 1900 Gerald Lee believed that finding the key to understanding crowds would prove to be the making of his reputation as a prophet of modern America. His vision joined the literary with the prosaic. If the readers of the *Atlantic Monthly* wanted to become financially successful, Lee hinted in one article, they had to understand that the "crowd principle" was the first principle of production and distribution, and it determined the value of land. Religious life, education, and journalism were all based on catering to large numbers of people. Above all, the crowd principle represented the social consequences of urban spectacle. Americans "live in crowds," he wrote, and "we get our living in crowds."[1]

"Any man who makes the attempt to consider or interpret anything, either in art or life, without a true understanding of the crowd principle as it is working today, without a due sense of its central place in all that goes on around us, is a spectator in the blur and bewilderment of this modern world, as helpless in it, as a Greek god at the World's Fair, gazing out of his still, Olympian eyes at the Midway Plaisance." Americans "are amused in herds . . . Cities are the huge central dynamos of all being," he wrote, and anyone interested in gaining any personal power could measure the task by the "number of miles between him and the city; that is, between him and what the city stands for—the centre of mass." To be an actor in the drama of the world rather than a spectator or passive member of a manipulated audience required crowd consciousness, a knowledge of human psychology, and imitation of inspired modern heroes. For the next twenty years, this was to be Lee's explicit message.[2]

The crowd principle was Lee's way of making sense of the modern world in terms he had appropriated from mid-Victorian times. Although only loosely formulated, Lee's vision of the beautiful crowd became a metaphorical obsession that he would graft onto his theory of the interaction of personality, authority, technology, and the control of human expression. While he evidently feared the power of class-based mobs, strikes, and the encompassing anonymity of mass society—ultimately the loss of personal identity—he also sought to understand and master that fear. To be able to read and interpret the inner thoughts of a variety of audiences and to pass that interpretive power onto other potential leaders was a literary property of great potential power in the transitional period in which he was living.

In a nonacademic, even antiacademic manner, Lee formulated ideas about heroism and mass society that subsumed democratic ideals within a conception of the public as spiritually bonded if only it was properly conceived and led. Lee's nostalgia for the clearly defined authority of the Puritan parson remained to help express an updated—if inchoate—theory of stewardship over a crowdlike public in the Progressive Era. Appropriating the veneer of crowd psychology alongside a mystical identification with machines and electricity, he identified himself with this expectant modernist vision by the first decade of the new century. Like Robert Moses years later, however, Lee had developed, to quote Frances Perkins, as a man who "loves the public, but not as people. The public [was] . . . a great amorphous mass to him."[3]

Owing to his reading of romantic theorists, his personal fears of audiences, and his equally strong desire to dominate them, Lee projected from his personal inadequacy a theory of modern heroic redemption in direct relation to his conceptions of the United States as a crowd culture. Lee joined other writers who wrestled with questions of crowds in relation to lost community values under siege by urbanization, immigration, and the mysterious grip of mass culture. Sadly, neither Lee nor many others sought to link crowd psychology to the horrors of racially inspired lynchings then so widespread.

Nonetheless, even though not always their intention, educated opinion about crowd psychology and public opinion often affirmed widespread anxieties about democratic rule and undermined the belief in a rational public.[4]

In the 1880s and early 1890s, the years before Lee coined his ideas about the "crowd principle," he built up a series of analogies and symbolic references about various forms of collective behavior that remained embedded in his mind through the rest of his life. His primary experiential reference for the "crowd principle," the power of great speakers over their audiences, was rationalized by naturalistic analogies that were commonly used in these years before the advent of crowd psychology. Lee gradually formulated the view that audiences were primarily inhibiters of progressive ideas, and he sought to uncover the techniques needed to attract audiences. He often appropriated naturalistic analogies, as for example, in an extended 1890 monologue he wrote on "Intellectual Life," in which he conceptualized the crowd in terms of the controlled spatial boundaries of a house.

> I have a morbid love for the extraordinary and consequent extraordinary stupidity in appreciating the ordinary. My intellectual tastes, are very exclusive aristocrats, and for an ordinary man, I am extravagant in my ruling that none but genius shall be admitted to the inner home of my intellectual life. Talent may cross the threshold and linger stiffly for a time in the company parlor, common place walks around on the outside and I look out at it from the windows, and notice it just enough to be sure that it is what it seems—the way a man looks through a crowd for a rare face, if perchance there may be one, and watching to invite it in.

The people outside his spatial boundaries were those who could not touch him either physically, intellectually, or emotionally. Lee wanted to control the touch of the crowd upon himself while he cultivated the power to manipulate it as he chose.[5]

The urban crowd functioned as a manifestation of his larger "room" or uncontained congregation. Other nineteenth-century writers—from Baudelaire in Paris to Whitman in New York—had seen the city as a cluttered public forum from which modern heroes

could arise; by immersing themselves in crowds with all their spontaneity, conflict, and color, heroes could emerge as masters of mass
culture and not as its fearful victims. Lee saw that many of the forms
of artistic expression and philosophical formalism were breaking up
under the impact of urbanization and its attendant crowding of
people and experience; and he believed that language, poetic forms,
and the signs and symbols upon which they were built could produce great social changes if the behavior of crowds could be revealed
and channeled. Eschewing interest in parapsychology or occultism
that swept up so many others—notably William James and many
other followers of Whitman—Lee kept trying to justify his role as a
writer in widening arcs of persuasion by returning to the idea of the
crowd.[6]

While Lee eventually appropriated the city crowd as part of his
domain (at least in highly intellectualized terms), back in the early
1890s he reflected the more prevalent provincial fear that saw urban
crowds as symbols of the apocalyptic release from social and religious constraint that had been rationalized by the enlightenment.
As a tourist in 1890, he had been appalled by New York as a
dangerous moral contagion. "New York spread itself like a vast
concrete philosophy over every man's spirit," he later wrote. "It
reeks with cheapness, human cheapness." Paris, to which Lee traveled in 1892, was viewed as a repository of bombs, atheism, radicals, and mass violence. He had spent at least four months wandering with a Baedeker around western Europe and England before
writing of the contrast between the gothic majesty of Notre Dame
and the secular worship of technology symbolized by the recently
completed Eiffel Tower. "Oh city that makes a god of itself—a
worship of worshippers . . . dost thou not feel the wrongs that wait
huddled with their dynamite mouths for time to speak? Hast thou
throned thy Goddess of Reason only to learn that she is the queen of
Dynamite? Christ is the only answer to the cries of the bombs. In thy
fine old cathedral belfries sing the only voices that can drown the
mobs; calling them back to the days of thy faith—and forward to
the Faith that is free." Paris's mobs had been generated through the
misuse of rationalism, which he linked to the alluring quality of
socialism and atheism. The cultural and political life of the city
represented "a Republicanism that makes tyranny democratic; a

literature that makes sin artistic and genius a subtler sort of crime, a philosophy that lays down maxims—and blows up streets, an art of skillful soullessness—and a religion of not being shamed of anything . . . A city whose moods cast their shadows across the seas . . . to tell . . . [us] what not to do." The swirling masses of Paris, and the earlier ones of New York, came to be contrasted in Lee's mind with the church spires "struggling up among its massive structures . . . like flowers that dare to grow among weeds."[7]

Yet while Lee scoffed at the city, he gradually tried to find ways to capture its attention. By 1905 his romanticism provided him with a release clause for his antiurbanism. While feeling ill at ease in New York, which always put him "the first day or so into what seems to be a kind of furor of honesty," he related going "about everywhere in a suspicious, obstinate, country way, buffing against Appearances." Nonetheless, he recognized the city's power and, exhibiting his attraction to Whitman, tried to jettison some of his earlier prejudices. "It is rather inconsistent to come out into the country and hate cities," he wrote. "All nature is a city in a sly way. All one needs is to be bright enough and one feels as miserable and crowded as ever." The city was to be watched from his house with its well-tended garden overlooking Mt. Tom. It was part of a stage that Lee attempted to conjure up everywhere. "I listen to a great city in the grass—millions of insects. Microscopes have threaded it for me. I know this city—all its mighty little highways. I possess it." If you can figuratively possess millions of insects in the grass around you simply by looking at them from above, then why not imagine that you can do the same with a city or a nation? As we shall see, Whitman's vision became tied to the prevalent success ethos in a lesser mind such as Lee's.[8]

Lee's romantic links to the mythical New England past were undoubtedly bolstered by his wife Jennette, as they shared many ideas about nature, the city, and crowds. Her novels and short stories were written in a simplistic style and a preachy tone. Her characters generally represented ideal types, vehicles illustrating values that were typical for the times. Women, for example, played obedient roles to their husbands as good housekeepers and mothers while love and trust always triumphed over greed and materialism. Democracy, especially that practiced in the United States, was the

best system, and readers were never left troubled or confused over
the lesson to be learned at the conclusion of the books.[9]

Jennette Lee exhibited a repugnance toward factory life and retreated to the sanctuary of Christian values in order to preach the
correct attitude toward encroaching modernization. Her writing
exhibits a longing for the disappearing solid, strong male craftsman
whose work ethic, sensitivity, grandfatherliness, and small-town
wisdom solidified community values. In *Kate Wetherill* (1900), the
effects of industrialism are set against an older, more natural, and
deferential order as she contrasted the old street shaded by the elms
and maples with a new one in which elms were sacrificed for asphalt.
In several instances Mrs. Lee also presents a conventional construction of the times—characters who instinctively know the minds
of others. Dr. Burke, the Congregational minister in *The Pillar of
Salt* (1901), for instance, was described as knowing his parishioners
"better than they knew each other, far better than they knew themselves." Jennette Lee left little doubt that rural Yankees who were
true to their heritage could ascertain the character behind the faces
in the urban crowd.[10]

Central to appreciating how Gerald Lee's attitudes toward modernism and crowds were mediated by notions of urban life, church
psychology, and New England values, is the manner in which he appropriated midcentury literary and historical conceptions of crowd
behavior. Lee's personal experience with church congregations was
probably partially formed and undoubtedly reinforced by the dramatic quality of romantic images of revolutionary and violent mobs.
As we saw in Chapter One, ideas about crowds had long been tied to
a definition of respectability and romantic republicanism. Through
numerous writers, ideas about the working class's possessing a collective mind, often controlled by malevolent forces, had become
encased in historical myth. Influenced by the theories and writing
style of Carlyle, Emerson, Dickens, and a number of Victorian
writers, Lee joined many other British liberals and mugwumps in
promoting a perspective that obliquely challenged the benefits of
unchanneled democratic ideals before he was swept away by the
writings of Whitman.

In late 1884, after reading Emerson, Lee wrote an essay entitled "A Plea for the Individual." "We make man a monarch but is there not a good deal of slavery lurking under the horrors of royalty? We stand in awe of majorities. We throw down our sceptre at the feet of Public Sentiment. We love in mathematical times. We measure everything by quantity. But in the name of truth mankind is *force* and not arithmetic!" The average social tendency, Lee believed, was "polite bondage" and "fashionable sameness," with originality being a crime, and ability being imitation of others. Lee's disgust was not with the social and economic forces implementing the conformity— in fact he never mentions them; his romantic temperament conjured up the conformist public as the ultimate victimizers of themselves.[11]

Several years later, after having read Carlyle's *History of the French Revolution,* Lee adopted Carlyle's spectacular characterizations of mobs to describe an auction crowd that he observed in Princeton, Minnesota. He wrote about the "auction carnival—a revel for bargain lovers,—and a studio full of models to an artist in human nature—looking for touching little burlesques on that strange jest and earnest that we call life." The auction was a "house full of starers, and flaw pickers." It was a "selfish crowd, eager to take advantage of misfortune,—to help themselves." The raucous quality of the bidding and the raw competition obviously grated on his genteel sensibilities. But what is more revealing is his desire to render quick artistic judgment on complex human beings.[12]

Another element of Lee's romantic republican conception of crowd behavior, although muted in contrast to later social scientists like Edward Ross and Le Bon, was the subtle reflection of Emerson's racial ideas. Emerson admired the English nobility for their solidity and traced much of it back into the Anglo-Saxon past—to a time when there was a more distinct and cohesive group mind. The Teutonic tribes had possessed a "national singleness of heart," Emerson had written in *English Traits,* "which contrasts with the Latin races." The Germanic people were practical and sincere, proving that "veracity derives from instinct, and makes superiority in organization."[13]

By the late nineteenth century, the implications of Emerson's rather vague ideas about the national mind had become racial dogma in the hands of less sensitive writers. Racial theorists like Le

Bon were categorizing people on the basis of a number of psychological traits, from the shape of their craniums to the extent of their
racial memory. But in Lee's mind, the issues involved went beyond
"scientific" racism. He resonated more closely to the Victorian critics of democracy like the late writings of Carlyle, Ruskin, Bagehot,
Hamerton, and Arnold rather than with the racialist conceptions of
Karl Pearson and Le Bon. The latter, Lee felt, were "factmongers"
and not poets who could express that which could not be seen by
X-rays and microscopes. Ruskin, Carlyle, and Arnold, on the other
hand, hated the imitative quality of modern life produced by machine technology and mass culture. The conceptions of public opinion as merely reproduced and manufactured opinion—effected by
machines (i.e., printing presses and political parties)—thus carried
into political and social thought an aestheticized contempt toward
popular literary and consumer taste. That many of these writers had
not gained commercial success from their own writings only reinforced their attitudes.[14]

Nonetheless, having asserted this restrained racialist perspective,
it is nevertheless undeniable that Lee was also influenced by Le Bon's
The Crowd. Le Bon's hope for a heroic crowd was left largely
undefined. Lee used less racist ideology, less sociological jargon, but,
similar to Le Bon, saw the heroic crowd as passive, a collectivity to
be acted upon. "The solution of the crowd civilization is going to be
the man who shall have it in him to be a crowd-in-spirit," Lee wrote.
Both writers used their ideas about crowds to conceptualize public
opinion and define heroic figures who might embody a coherent
alternative to what they saw as the coming rule by socialistic demagogues. The personalities of emerging national heroes might prove
to be the salvation of both France and the United States, as Le Bon
saw in the Boulangist movement in France and Lee in Theodore
Roosevelt.[15]

In a 1912 letter to book publisher Arthur Page, Lee argued that
his own book *Crowds* was different from Le Bon's. The Frenchman's
book dealt "with the psychology of mobs and is abstract and theoretical and while quite interesting, could not be popular, [and] in the
large sense, does not deal with the concrete and is in direct opposition to my constructive attitude." He distinguished his own work
which addressed a "totally new thing in the world-crowds-groups of

interests-labor unions, and employers associations and how all these crowds in our democracy are about to get together." Le Bon's book, he implied, had assumed a passivity about crowds that Lee believed he was moving beyond.[16]

However murky, the constructive quality that Lee sought to express in contradistinction to Le Bon's determinism was a common American reaction to the book. Theodore Roosevelt, William James, George Mead, and E. L. Godkin all found Le Bon alluring and generally correct in his descriptions of the uniform psychic mechanism of crowd behavior, but they decried his lack of prescriptions for social and political progress. In truth, Le Bon had described the cyclical nature of the rise and fall of civilizations as based on vaguely defined racial or collective souls, but many American reformers and corporate liberals had assured themselves that they had escaped those deterministic jaws of history, that their economic and social order could be made to work for all.[17]

Lee's burgeoning use of the crowd metaphor finally became politicized by the Democratic National Convention of 1896. William Jennings Bryan illustrated to Lee and many other genteel eastern aesthetes how modern political conventions could be seized through use of crowd psychology. Bryan's supporters were seen to be appendages of mobs, irrationally seeking radical reforms that would undermine the natural capitalistic order. Behind the Populist cause, with its volatile "agrarian propaganda," as Rev. Newell Dwight Hillis called it, Bryan was perceived to be unconsciously ushering in socialistic tyranny. After all, Illinois Governor Altgeld, who had pardoned Haymarket anarchists and seemed to have backed the Pullman rioters, was a prominent Bryan supporter. (Some saw Altgeld as the malevolent Svengali behind a more innocent Trilby.) "A class feeling more distinct than ever before has asserted itself in politics," one writer wrote that fall. As the malevolent incarnation of the mob spirit, the Nebraskan had endeavored to embody the will of the people, but when he became perceived as a man raising the ugly monster of sectional conflict and class warfare, Bryan and all the forces he represented had to be repressed.[18]

Back in the 1880s Lee had written that "American eloquence is seemingly averse to politics, where it has degenerated into common places diversified with fine frenzies which are a mere foaming and frothing of words chasing one another in a mad hunt for an idea." In 1902 he still believed that "the public does not expect anything of the politicians." This aversion to politics, converging with his thoughts about his changing conceptions about crowds, was clearly enunciated in an article he published in *The Critic,* shortly after Bryan first won the Democratic nomination in 1896. Entitled "Hullabaloo," it is Lee's earliest and most coherent definition of the crowd principle. A narrow focus upon a political event allowed him to crystallize the social web that made the idea of a "bad" crowd seem so overwhelmingly dangerous and symbolic of cultural degeneration.[19]

The manner in which Bryan had gained his nomination was for Lee as damning as the tenets of any program he espoused. Bryan had brought his "Cross of Gold" speech to a thunderous conclusion by picturing himself as Christ upon a cross. The use of a crown of thorns as the keynote of his speech particularly offended Lee, who saw it as if it were a trick played by a confidence man; he labeled Bryan a "political elocutionist." Yet the Chicago convention was itself a symbol of an artificial and dangerous form of fraternity, symptomatic of the dispersion of modern authority to more secular and commercial agents. "The convention is the most characteristic and ingenious custom of our day," he wrote, "the token of the vast companionship, which is not only the moods, but the very temperament of our time." The convention was more than an instrument of democracy; it was an advertisement of American values, "the billboard of modern thought." Further, he wondered in contemptuous tones "whether, from the caucus of the National House of mis-Representatives to the caucus of the town, our working conception of what constitutes expressing the will of the people will not have to be revised, supervised or demolished."

The problem with a convention was that it "[carries] its points in brute ways . . . [is] swayed by hypnotic and physical forces . . . [is] drunk with itself." Lee's fearful dream of the drunken New England town had been transposed to a national (and partisan) context. He did not mention Populism; he did not concede that the majority of delegates nominated William Jennings Bryan because he might have best represented their opinions on the silver issue or their anger at Wall Street bankers. No, the man who touched the "monster whim[s]" in the convention crowd was scornfully labeled the "voice of the age."

Resist the temptations, the exhortations, and the crowd pressure to join any social group beyond your bond to nature and the universal spirit, Lee urged his readers. "He only is a true believer in the unity of the world, that will make it worth uniting." Stay away from conventions, Lee wrote, because the sense of multitude and applause can act as a narcotic. The convention fool can get used to having "ten thousand men make him think." A convention fool had a "crowd soul, a crowd creed" and was dangerous.[20]

Whether Lee actually attended the Democratic convention is unknown. Nonetheless, the genteel side of Lee's personality revolted at the intellectual simplicity and sensationalism of the Great Commoner. In fact, Bryan was a convincing orator in an era when few politicians commanded the eloquence to attract national political followings. Jealous as well as fearful, Lee had never before written in such outraged tones about a successful speaker; he had usually praised their magnetic style, even when he disagreed with their ideas.[21]

Lee's quick Carlylean sketch of the conventioneer illustrated a wider series of associations about crowds. The convention was "as morbidly gregarious as a recluse is morbidly confined," he wrote, filled with people who were "addicted to conventions . . . with whom anthropomania is a chronic condition of the brain" and "whose jaded spirits ever flag without the fillip of the crowd." He next used Le Bonian language in identifying the full picture of the crowd as an instrument of democracy at which he was aiming: "The recent adventure that the nation has experienced in Chicago is one of those expressive events which the Great Spirit seems to have substituted in modern times for prophecy. It reveals to a popular government the fact that it will have to face—the fact that there is nothing more whimsical, more egotistical, more irresponsible, more thoughtless of everything but itself, than a crowd . . . The inevitable result of superimposing the locomotive upon the printing press in a few frail centuries, when either would have been more than the whirling brain of man could stand, the convention is the reductio ad

Northampton crowds greeting President William McKinley in 1900.

absurdum of Stephenson and Gutenberg, the newspaper run mad—
the massing of men in columns, following fast upon the massing of
ideas—a climax so tremendous that the mightiest men and idiots are
the only ones who can view the field with unbewildered eyes."

Geographical mobility combined with the effects of the mass press were creating a moment-mad culture and a disoriented populace which needed a modern awakening to redefine American identity. Increasingly abstract in outward form, Lee's primary concerns were not with an ethical religion or the promotion of social or political justice, but in excoriating a generalized other—a dimly understood coalition of political and cultural enemies.[22]

It was thus not the Populists by name, or their platform that Lee finally attacked; it was the machine-made organizational culture that became his critical reference. Only by using the ideas of Emerson and Carlyle and with the example of Isaiah before him could Lee have made the following condemnation, singling out, not individuals, but the mechanisms of modern life, excoriating urbanization and the loss of a mythical individualism.

> The convention bestrides the world with vociferousness . . . The smallest hamlet in the land has learned to listen reverent[ly] from afar to its vast, insistent roar, as the voice of the Spirit of the Times. Every idea we have is run into a constitution. We cannot think without a chairman. Our whims have secretaries, our fads by-laws. Literature is a club, philosophy a society. Our reforms are mass meetings. Our culture is a summer school. We mourn our mighty dead with forty vice presidents . . . Charity is an association. Theology is a set of resolutions. Religion is an endeavor to be numerous and communicative. We awe the impenitent with crowds, convert the world with boards and save the lost with delegates; and how Jesus of Nazareth could have done so great a work without being on a committee is beyond our ken.

The organized and unspontaneous quality of American culture was condemned without making any direct references to the forces promulgating it. Neither corporate power nor the processes of industrialization were the culprits; the growth of organizations and crowd-life—the public itself—were all the progenitors of sameness. Aside from exhibiting Lee's antimodernism, the target of his anger in this quotation reflects the growing murkiness with which he understood the causative factors behind the growth of mass culture and hints at the conceptual dead end he was reaching.[23]

Lee's views in "Hullabaloo" were not to change appreciably in the following years, yet he increasingly felt them to be inadequate. Like Le Bon, he could conceive of few specific approaches for individuals who wished to escape the crowd culture in 1896. Containing a myriad of meanings, the crowd metaphor aided him in his search for personal power. The Democratic Convention of 1896, identifying Bryan with crowds and mobs, was a pivotal reference in his mind, as it was to be in the minds of countless other people of the time. It was, of course, also a pivotal political event which helped usher in the dominance of corporate liberalism as the controlling ideology of the nation.

By 1899 Lee published an article entitled "The Printing Press and Personality," which blasted wider targets of a crowd culture: the impact of mass literacy and press sensationalism. His preoccupation with the metaphorical properties of the crowd became so great that his love of nature, his desire to transform cities, his reaction to industrialism, and his need to identify new media of mass communication all became related to crowds and reflected his preaching mentality. He subscribed to the argument that the newspapers mirrored public opinion, and he considered both of these dull and conservative. Papers were not agencies of transformation or change but were "dim, gigantic, stalking shadows of ourselves." Modern man had given the printing press a "soul of its own," making it the "god of machines." To most people God had become the press, with paper functioning as "his prophet . . . That we should dare to base our institutions upon a recklessness like this is one of the many signs we see that the tired end of the Reformation is upon us," he roared.[24]

Increasingly Lee was characterizing the masses as "moment mad," obsessed by the daily news and possessing little coherent direction apart from that derived from organized social life. Individuals in crowds were driven by anxiety to deadening conformity from which they could only escape by a leap of imagination: "Shut in out of all infinity between the high wall called yesterday and the high wall called tomorrow, this nineteenth century of ours is like some vast Roman circus under the wide heaven, the race course of which is drawing strangely now, in hot and eager madness, to its eternal close. Round and round and round we go, droves of us, as fast as we are born, running breathless all our days, trying to catch up, if we

only may, to the News that above our dreams flies onward beyond
our reach in the darkness of the night." Lee recognized that the up-
to-date person had become a popular object of awe, although few
could really keep up with the changing news of the day. In less
sociologically oriented terms than those used by Edward Ross,
Franklin Giddings, Robert Park, or others, Lee saw that the reading
public was being transformed into a cohesive moblike body of
people.[25]

By 1903 Lee's images of both the typical modern man who read
his daily newspaper and the convention-crowd man he described in
1896 were blurred together in his third book, *The Lost Art of
Reading*. Published by G. P. Putnam's, the book sold only 1,800
copies as of 1907. It was aimed at extending Victorian literary
culture to the masses. His prescription followed from his disgust at
what the nineteenth century had wrought: the narrowing of men's
lives into an emulation of the machines with which they worked.
"An Age which narrows the actual lives of men, which so adjusts the
labor of the world that nearly every man in it not only works with a
machine, spiritual or otherwise, but is a machine himself, and a
small part of a machine, must not find fault with its art for being full
of hysterics and excitement, or with its newspapers for being sensational." Such a "crowd of crowds" were becoming literate, he real-
ized, but their reading habits had degenerated. Modern men were
being "mobbed with facts" while generalizations were "trained out
of our typical modern minds." He drew on older organicist notions
of social order (such as those posited by earlier romantic republican
crowd theorists) to express skepticism about the possibilities of
social cohesion in the modern age. "It is getting so that there is
hardly any possible way left in our modern life for knowing people
except by marrying them."[26]

At the center of Lee's diatribe against contemporary society stood
the "modern reader," who was described as a "skimmer, a starer at
pictures, like a child, while he reads, never thinking a whole thought,
a lover of peeks and paragraphs as a matter of course . . . Outside of
his specialty he is not interested in anything more than one paragraph's worth . . . Putting things together tires him. He has no imagination because he has the daily habit of constantly seeing a great
many things which he never puts together." The modern reader

possessed only a "scrap-bag of a soul" and "the faces that pass are phantoms." It was no wonder that he found the typical civilized man to be "exhausted, spiritually hysterical," with "no idea of what it means, or can be made to mean to be a man."[27]

Perhaps the most revealing association Lee made linking the modern reading public with the crowd metaphor was employed to differentiate between those he called the boors and those who "knew a beautiful thing." Apparently boors were defined as didactic and simple modern Americans who conformed to the standard fare of the print media. (Boors may well also have been editors who had rejected many of his manuscripts.) Such people had acquired their culture "largely under mob-influence (the dead level of intelligence) and all they can do with it, not wanting it, is to be teachery with it—force it on other people who do not want it." He continued, "whether in origin, processes, or results of their learning, these people have all the attributes of a mob. Their influence and force in civilization is a mob influence, and it operates in the old classic fashion of mobs upon all who oppose it . . . It constitutes at present the most important and securely entrenched intimidating force that modern society presents against the actual culture of the world . . . There are but few who refuse." To illustrate his point further, he graphically recreated a mob scene using language derived from Carlyle's *History.*

> The fact that this mob power keeps its hold by using books instead of bricks is merely a matter of form. It occupies most of the strategic positions just now in the highways of learning, and it does all the things that mobs do, and does them in the way that mobs do them. It has broken into the gardens, into the arts, the resting place of nations, and with its factories to learn to love in, its treadmills to learn to sing in, it girdles its belt of drudgery around the world and carries bricks and mortar to the clouds. It shouts to every human being across the spaces—the outdoors of life: "Who goes there? Come thou with us. Root or die!"

This mob power was the "intimidator, the aggregation of the Reading Labour Unions of the world." Lee made a crucial cultural link between the psychology of mobs and the modern literate public. He melted all the targets of his wrath together into an indistinct mass.[28]

Literary and theatrical critics as well as historians, politicians, and political theorists used the crowd metaphor as an effective tool in delegitimizing various opponents during the early twentieth century. Critic Henry Dwight Sedgwick published an article in 1908 entitled "The Mob Spirit in Literature." Analogies were drawn from the French Revolution and from Carlyle, as he too concluded that the reading public was essentially a mob, begotten by a system of education that offered no hope for a cure; "art and authority are the only remedies," he wrote. Yale president Arthur Hadley decried the "organized emotion" emanating from the press and whipped to a frenzy through direct primaries, while others were seeing that with the apparent diminution of class-related mob violence, a host of new crowd phenomena, what one writer called "imitation mobs," was springing up around the country. Football mania, the zeal of participants at political gatherings, and the Trilby craze all symbolized a broadening array of social groups acting with psychological properties similar to those seen in mobs. Yet mobs also remained a useful political reference for conservatives as well. D. M. Parry, president of the National Association of Manufacturers and Employers, denied to a 1903 Chautauqua conference addressing "the mob spirit" that organized labor existed for any lawful and beneficent purposes, representing no principle except that of mob rule. Theodore Roosevelt in speeches that outlined his New Nationalism in 1910 effectively staked out his own political ideology by contrasting riotous disorder with greedy plutocrats.[29]

Even though contemporary society was to Lee a conformist "bad" crowd, it could also be a "good" crowd, a kind of incipient divine choral group, orchestra, or crusading army of righteousness. Lee envisioned the "good crowd" led by an unquestioned conductor in terms of analogies drawn from electricity and machine production. He gradually altered his antimodernist perspective into what may best be described as an optimistic modernist. The evolving matrix of associations among the public, machines, and the city nourished his belief that there was a transcendental bonding mechanism or "psychic current" at work in the universe, which an elite of heroic personalities could feel and appreciate and best interpret to the masses. By understanding how Lee's usage of the crowd metaphor was adapted to such "psychic currents," a hidden agenda for his own ascendancy as a cultural prophet becomes obvious.

Being part of a limitless nature had to be reconciled in Lee's mind with the nostalgia in the 1890s for a more regimented and nationalistic society. One medium that proved useful to Lee in this reconciliation was music. He occasionally used the musical analogy to reinforce his idea about the value of the good crowd in the restructuring of the social order. In "A Plea for the Individual," written in the mid 1880s, Lee wrote that not only did great musical thoughts exist in nature, but the "whole human race is like a vast orchestra with an infinite precision and an endless range of notes." History itself was the "echo of the terrible vibrations that have been sounding through the past. Nations are its noblest, grandest chords." He was bothered by the fact that the orchestra "has no leader. A thousand million parts—the music of life is only gained when the triumphant strains of the majority drown the discords of the few." Nonetheless, he was worried that "the prevailing public sentiment tries to run the business of living like a huge foundry, turning humanity into molds and casting them into shapes most in vogue."[30]

This early association of conformity with machines would be reformulated—even though Lee continued to hope for a more organized public sentiment. In the 1890s Lee was one of many Americans following the lead of Ruskin and Morris in extolling handicrafts as ennobling individual accomplishment. By the early years of the new century, Lee's attraction to the arts and crafts movement— like so many others—shifted as he lauded the social and poetic benefits of the machine. How did he make that leap? How did his love affair with technology fit with his ambiguous usage of the crowd metaphor?

The roots of Lee's "rhapsodic exposition of machine aesthetics" can be traced with some precision. As a young boy of twelve he had visited the Philadelphia Exposition of 1876 and was ecstatic—converted, he claimed, to the new power of electricity. The Corliss engine overwhelmed him as it had done to many other observers. This great machine, he wrote in one early essay, "and its well performed duty remind us not only of the power of steam, but of the power [of] human genius, human enterprise and their results."[31]

The electrical current functioned as a model for Lee's ideas about modes of imitation and attraction among people. He used the analogy of an electromagnetic field of attraction as a controller of "crowds" because it was capable of transferring dramatic impulses and practical information over further distances and to immeasurably larger audiences than a local minister could ever hope to do from his pulpit. He was, in a fundamental manner, anticipating television. To capture the essence of dramatic transfer in oneself and to translate that through the printed pages to the public was a rare gift that Lee set out either to embody in himself or to identify for others. To somehow be able to do that through electronic means was becoming more and more a possibility. Late Victorian era writers were fascinated by the metaphor of the machine and by mesmeric theories, in which the human brain was claimed to be controlled by electromagnetic currents. In Lee's diary of 1886 he wrote that "thought is electricity—of the spiritual world. There are two poles and the affinities of thought have corresponding affinities in men. Certain thoughts are magnets." Words and poetic expression could evoke currents of sympathy that could galvanize America as a homogeneous unit.[32]

More than any other modern writer, Walt Whitman had described the dramatic properties that Lee was seeking to define more precisely for his own age. More clearly than Emerson or Carlyle, Whitman proclaimed the idea that a heroic, democratic man was not necessarily a contradiction in terms. As William James and Robert Park and so many others noted, such dramatic personalities could mingle with the crowd and by so doing achieve an understanding of it sufficient to claim the right to be a spokesman of its collective soul. H. L. Mencken's version of this—less identified with democratic man—was derived more clearly from a Nietzschean definition of reality. After talking long into the night about Whitman with Lee, naturalist John Burroughs wrote a correspondent in July 1902 that Lee was "deeply moved by Whitman . . . but I feel that he forces the note a little—he is almost violently individual. He asked me if I knew how long it took Whitman before he could say "I" in that magnificent way. He wants to do it himself, but I fear he never can." But Lee kept trying.[33]

In an article in *Putnam's* entitled "An Order for the Next Poet," Lee used Whitman as a model for the poet the modern world needed. Whitman was "the only man that can be named who is the alembic of us all in this modern age . . . He flocks the age together in a book. He groups it under one name. He is its spirit. He is the singing down in its vast, struggling, self-lifting, speechless heart." He was a "greater master of the modern poet's spirit than any other poet," partly because he was a "greater master of the modern poet's technique— symbolism—the one possible poetic device for making the finite infinite, for bringing out the spirituality of matter." Lee believed that one had to bow before a more modern conception of technique. The "poet of the modern man takes his cue from the silent machines the man has made. He sits at the feet of Electricity." The habits of the modern man "have become more galvanic, less panoramic and pic- turesque," for he has become "addicted to the dynamo habit."[34]

This bowing toward electricity as a god, similar to that of Henry Adams and Brooks Adams, became for Lee a way to explain and encapsulate the mind of modern man. Modern man "sees with a current," Lee wrote; "the current makes him feel things more as he wants to feel them—all over, with all his senses at once, and with his body and with his soul. He does not read descriptions of faces. The author who tries to give him a map of a soul—the old, elaborate, empty feature list—for a human face, is yawned over. Unless an author can flash the face of a hero into one's being, in some way that one does not know, and that the author himself does not know, he is not quite modern enough." The modern poet could "induce . . . the current in others" when, like Whitman (in his poem "I Sing the Body Electric"), he saw himself as a worker like everyone else. In pushing the electromagnetic imagery as far as he did, Lee curiously avoided sexual connotations. Whitman's display of sexuality in his poems, which had hurt his reputation in genteel circles, was not a topic to be broached by Lee, whose own masculine sensibility—much as he might deplore it in theory—was bounded by late Victorian social constraints. Lee's tolerance had become aestheticized and was twist- ing into an affirmation of modern mass culture as long as it was properly guided.[35]

It is small wonder that Lee was fascinated with the power of the photograph and, later, the motion picture to transmit common images to the public. His language of social cohesion had long sought to conceptualize visualizable signs bonding modern people together, signs that were reproducible through the print medium and expressed through new heroic personalities. Lee's romantic vision of mastering time, space, and extended publics had been rationalized through an identification of the American tradition largely in terms of its literary giants like Emerson and Whitman. Further, his understanding of crowds and crowd psychology was created and sustained through an historically inaccurate analogy to the modern democratic mass public. French Revolution mobs thus became the ultimate foil used in rationalizing a new industrial-era elite to interpret the aspirations of all Americans. That mastery could not be the province of the public itself but only of intermediary artists, religious figures, or intellectuals who could interpret and express the public will. The distinction is crucial and is at the heart of Lee's preaching mentality.

Yet the new century saw Lee cutting off the notion of constraining the power of machines. There was an inevitability to their dominance and their ceaseless exploitation by market forces. Modern man, in order to be fulfilled and happy in the world, must bow before the power of the machine-made crowd. As one of its chief flatterers (and secret enemy), Lee looked at what he saw to be the new power sources—technology, business leadership, and democracy—and readily found himself able to adapt his religiosity to it. If a man "lives in an age of democracy, an age of crowds, he will make the crowd beautiful, or he will be crowded out of it," he wrote in 1900. "If he lives in an age of machines, the machine shall be beautiful or he will be crushed by it." His age of machines and crowds, like that of so many other nascent modernists, was backward looking, eschewing any consideration but brief references to the corporate control over the economy. Others in England and the United States, from Gustave Stickney, to H. G. Wells, Van Wyck Brooks, Walter Lippmann, and Arnold Bennett, were struggling to define these new relationships. Only Lee was so narrowly fixated on seeing crowds, machines, and heroes in such stark relief. To Lee, it was the end of Luther's Reformation era and the beginning of a period when religion needed to appeal to a national public, a "religion of the crowd" made beautiful by truly modern poets.[36]

By the middle of the first decade of the new century, with the publication of Lee's *The Voice of the Machine*, adulation of the machine had become a cultural imperative for him; people could become fused to each other only by accepting machines and the leadership of great poets who saw beyond contemporary social and political constraints. Like so many of his contemporaries, Lee saw the engineer as a creator of webs of interdependence or organic tentacles in which the attention of all urban residents could become organized. Exuding a phony empathy for machine workers, Lee saw technology's superimposition on the landscape as a rationale for imperialism over the environment. His language betrays how nature lovers acted to defer abjectly to a "capture thesis" simultaneously created over both technology and the masses.

> I only know that so long as there is no poet among us, who can put himself into a word, as this man, my brother engineer, is putting himself into his engine, the engine shall remove mountains, and the word of the poet shall not; it shall be buried beneath the mountains . . . [S]o long as we have more preachers who can be hired to stop preaching or to go into life insurance than we have engineers who can be hired to leave their engines, inspiration shall be looked for more in engine cabs than in pulpits . . . The telephone, the wireless telegraph, the X rays, and all the other great believers are singing up around [the church].

Lee sought to define success in modern life through his own iden-tification with technological achievements, a classless social de-meanor, and deference toward a solid work ethic. "What is true of the men who make the machines is equally true of the men who live with them. The brakeman and the locomotive engineer and the mechanical engineer and the sailor all have the same spirit. Their days are invested with the same dignity and aspiration, the same unwonted enthusiasm, and self-forgetfulness in the work itself." Clearly revealing his ignorance of the routine of factory work, Lee ended up idealizing machine labor, neglecting to distinguish be-tween the owners (and inventors) of machine technology and those who worked with them on a daily basis—and increasingly under the dictates of scientific management. Lee could not understand how anyone could justifiably be alienated from the whole industrial pro-cess. Switchmen, Lee wrote, "love a railroad as Shakespeare loved a sonnet."[37]

Lee sent copies of *The Voice of the Machine* to influential people in hopes of gaining a favorable response. George Hodges, the dean of the Episcopal Theological School in Cambridge, Massachusetts, wrote of being thoroughly convinced by the book. "Ruskin's retreat into the Middle Ages, cursing the machines as he went, was a temporary mood and not a worthy one," he wrote. "This glad welcome to the machines in the name of poetry and of religion is the true end of sane and helpful thinking."[38]

Not everyone was so positive. The British author W. H. Mallock commented that "your claim for machinery, as such, is somewhat too wide," while Havelock Ellis found the book to be "genuinely American," then added:

> Although I am quite able to see poetry in machines, I do not myself go quite as far as you do. I consider that for machines to be genuinely beautiful and poetic they must fulfill two among other conditions: 1. Have reached a high degree of efficiency in their specific functions and 2. have become entwined with the emotional life of humanity. A sailing ship, for instance, has developed slowly through long years to a high degree of perfection and has been familiar to a large part of mankind. But most modern machines are still far from perfection and are constantly changing their shape; they are, moreover, unfamiliar and incomprehensible to most people.

Ellis hinted what seems true from a later vantage point: that Lee had attempted to define man's relationship to machine technology prematurely, without waiting to see how man's emotional life would develop.[39]

As first enunciated in the *Atlantic Monthly* magazine article of 1900, Lee's ideas on the poetry of a machine age had been highly praised by none other than William James. From Switzerland, the noted philosopher and psychologist wrote to the publisher and asked, "Who on earth is G. S. Lee? Write me about him. His is a god like article, and he will be a new force in literature if only he doesn't degenerate into subjectivism and mannerism." The publisher sent the card to Lee, who was greatly heartened by it. It was not surprising, then, that Lee sent James a copy of the machine book in 1907, writing in a covering letter that he wanted to write a practical book, a book that people "could get the good of afterwards every day, so that as they went about, the sights and sounds of streets and cities would be full of cheer to them." He added that "the feeling I have been groping toward in "The Voice of the Machines" is something akin to the love of nature except that it is for town use. James responded that he liked parts of the book and that Lee possessed "extraordinary verbal felicities, and the deeper road of interpretation." "I am sure the book will last," he added, then commented critically that "for me, there strayed into the latter chapters too much of the *Mt. Tom* voluntary whimsicality and straggle. But my taste is peculiar." James, the scientist, clearly couldn't identify with Lee's strained attempt to transfer Whitman's vocabulary of romance and nature into an urban industrial context.[40]

"I tried to keep Walt Whitman out of my book on machinery," Lee had earlier written one correspondent, "but he edged in finally and in sheer despair I found myself writing on him as if he were all the book was about." But lee also sought to identify with other midcentury romantics, writing Frank Sanborn, a friend of Henry David Thoreau's and president of the American Social Science Association, that "somehow I feel [that] if Thoreau had had to live in New York instead of Concord, he would have fussed around and believed what I have believed in the machine book." Thoreau, however, was never so arrogant as to pretend that he could speak for a city as Lee did. Clearly, Lee was transforming his ideological coloring to fit the prevailing winds of power and influence. His fantasies, fed by Whitmanesque linguistic excess, by obsessive use of metaphors, and by shifting social targets, had changed from an antimodernist stance toward affirmation of modern culture. He did not know he had become possessed by a metaphor. By 1916, however, he admitted that he had gotten "into a kind of rut in my mind—ever since I began writing 'crowds'—of connecting up everything that interests me with crowds."[41]

Seldom using the specific term "crowd mind" in discussing his ideas, the former parson developed the more literary image of flocking as a human instinct in which people might gleefully melt into something greater than themselves, a collective soul. A person as the sum of his numerous ancestors would thus be someone who acted as more than himself; he became magical or charismatic and by the power of his magnetic personality attracted the bad crowd to himself and transformed it. "The world follows the creative spirit," Lee wrote. "Where the spirit is creating, the strong and the beautiful flock."[42]

Yet as we have seen, Lee perceived the American public as a

debased crowd that could be uplifted only when it saw itself in the manner in which he saw it. If human beings didn't follow his prescriptions, he had little use for them. "If we deliberately prefer to live in crowds for the larger part of our lives, we must expect our lives to be cut and fitted accordingly," he had written. Images of childlike simplicity, employing a variety of code words with their own distinct historical development, were woven together in a critique of American pretensions as a democratic society. Those who were not gifted poets must accept the consequences of being crowd-oriented beings who fit the machine-made patterns of modernity; they were logically less deserving of real power than those with greater gifts of interpreting nature. "People who prefer to be educated in masses must conform to the law of the mass, which is inertia." One didn't have to "believe . . . in the mass of men—as men," he wrote. "One needs to believe in them very much as—possible men." The heroic performer, the passive audiences to be manipulated, and the conceptualization of the stage on which America would achieve its destiny were all intertwined, Lee believed, with his own fate. If he could but formulate more precisely the face of the hero he was looking for, then the magnetic quality of his own personality might well be revealed to an ungrateful public, and he too could begin to hear "crowds . . . cheering in the dark."[43]

At the heart of Lee's thinking, however, was his reverence for the dominance that older Puritan personalities exerted over crowds. In his article entitled "The Dominance of the Crowd," published in 1901 and later inserted as part of *Crowds,* Lee wrote that

> The church of our forefathers, founded on personality, is exchanged for the church of democracy, founded on crowds; and the church of the moment is the institutional church, in which the standing of the clergyman is exchanged for the standing of the congregation. The inevitable result, the crowd clergyman, is seen on every hand amongst us—the agent of an audience, who, instead of telling an audience what they ought to do, runs errands for them morning and noon and night. He does his people as much good as they will let him . . . until he dies at last, and goes to take his place with the Puritan parsons who mastered majorities.

Nowhere else in Lee's writings can one better appreciate the motivation behind this man so imbued with metaphor. Protestant divisions and loss of centrality in a market-driven culture could be circumvented by appealing to this higher plane of spiritual life.[44]

Only in the late twentieth century, as we witness the full flowering of the crowd metaphor, can we see that Lee's words are something more than ridiculous: the ambiguity that attended the crowd metaphor became a subliminal but invaluable ideological weapon to Lee and others in rationalizing corporate capitalism and the power of the modern state, while it tempered the reach of alternative social forces (like labor unions) and delegitimized alternative economic systems as fit vehicles for civilized people. The Parisian mobs breaking into the mansions of the French nobility had become the prototype for altogether dissimilar forms of collective behavior.

Although Lee never recognized that his thought involved a selective usage of such a vague formulation, others before and after him would understand the power of ambiguity in the use of collective nouns. Sociologist Walter Shepard, writing in 1909, was plainly worried about the increasing use of "serviceable terms . . . which assume a theory of society." Involved, he hinted, was a battle for national direction and human rights under the guise of shifting code words such as "national sentiment" and "social will." Those rights were becoming tenuous as men like Lee grew more interested in managing the nation's attention than in listening to the voices in the crowd, or appreciating the diverse forms of collective behavior. Lee fit the description given in 1899 by the French sociologist Gabriel Tarde, who commented sadly that "not only does a crowd attract and exert an irresistible pull on the spectator, but its very name has attraction for the contemporary reader, encouraging certain writers to use this ambiguous word to designate all sorts of human groupings."[45]

Ambiguous yet real, engendering hope and fear, adaptable to a variety of collective forms, and evoking fears of class conflict among "respectable" Americans, the crowd metaphor ultimately sanctified the power and deference accorded the values of the business leadership of America. With Gerald Lee, a dangerous perception of personality in relation to crowds comes sharply into focus.

FIVE

"Redeemer of Wealth": Business Evangelism and the Search for Heroic Leaders, 1900–1916

After receiving rejection notices from numerous publishers, Lee published a book entitled *Inspired Millionaires* at his own expense in 1908. The book initially received little attention, but within several years Lee's ideas were widely discussed; the book was soon republished in several languages. *Inspired Millionaires* found Lee using the most conspicuously rich man in the United States, Andrew Carnegie, to explain the dramatic role that millionaires could play in promoting social progress. "By sheer prominence and representativeness," Lee wrote, "no possible device the modern world would have, for thinking out money, could excel Carnegie." Lee was attracted to the artistic ways Carnegie used money, his role as a model philanthropist. Being rich wasn't like it had been in the old days, Lee felt, for the press and the public demanded greater social responsibility.[1]

Carnegie's private secretary soon responded that Carnegie had looked over proofs of the book and "believes that the 'Inspired Millionaire' will be developed as you say and that the large employer of labor can improve industrial conditions to such an extent as to win rank among the true benefactors of his race." Yet Carnegie recognized "that will be more difficult to do in corporations owned by thousands of stockholders, whose consent would be necessary. The experiment would cost much but would be worth it. Meanwhile the condition of labor improves and the day is coming when almost every workman will be a shareholder in the corporation. The United States Steel Corporation has made a fine start in this direction and has already, Mr. Carnegie is told, sixty thousand of its workmen joint proprietors." Lee's and Carnegie's ideological matrices converged as they recognized that the era of the old-style robber barons and the attitudes of "the public be damned" were ebbing; a new age was dawning in which "people's capitalism" and broad concerns for the public welfare were being promoted by modern business statesmen.[2]

Sadly for Lee, his proposal to Carnegie was never joined; he never became Carnegie's éminence grise. Nonetheless, Lee's use of the crowd metaphor in defining and rationalizing the behavior of heroic personalities illustrates how the image of corporate power was reformulated, personified, and projected as a benign reflection of the public will, an inevitable historical development. *Inspired Millionaires* can best be understood as part of a widespread offensive against muckraking critics of corporate corruption taking place in the decade following the Panic of 1907. If corporations could only create coherent personalities (or souls) for themselves, the increasingly popular argument went, if they could be led by business statesmen who had the trust of consumers, employees, and shareholders, then a peaceful social order could be inaugurated that would further God's will. This was often the message of Social Gospel ministers, writers of self-help manuals, liberal businessmen, and reformers themselves.[3]

Indeed, personifying corporations and picturing corporate capitalists as heroic public servants has been a recurring phenomenon throughout much of modern American history. In the 1980s entrepreneurialism was touted as a spiritually endowed calling, the essence of American life. From George Gilder to Lee Iaccoca and Victor Kiam, from the Reverend Pat Robertson to Ronald Reagan, the recent versions of the ideal of capitalist heroism limits success to the notion of being rich, embodying the essence of public service. Often cynical about human nature, with boundless trust in the market mechanism, entrepreneurialism has become the reigning ideal of our times, infused with divine favor. "It is the entrepreneurs who know the rules of the world and the laws of God," George Gilder has written in his recent book *The Spirit of Enterprise.* "They overthrow establishments rather than establish equilibria. They are the heroes of economic life."[4]

The journalist Mark Sullivan looked back on the years of the early twentieth century and wrote that the "talent for exhortation which in former eras taught men to prepare for the next world now has taught him to use more goods in this." The best-known business evangelists in the early twentieth century were northern Protestant ministers or former ministers, academics, journalists, and self-help authors out to make money or gain influence or they were business-men dispensing advice to young men by defining their own social utility. Like Gerald Lee, these latter-day evangelicals often promoted a "social religion" and waxed nostalgic about replicating the simple life and elusive forms of small town cohesion not found in the more anonymous large cities. Increasingly, personality or personal force became accentuated in the self-help literature, the offspring of both romanticism and New Thought philosophy. The extravagance of the rich was periodically condemned, of course, but the more perva-sive message was that the sole concern for profits was not in the long-term self-interest of businessmen, nor did it fit with an in-creasingly benevolent God who loved all his children.[5]

As government investigations and muckraking attacks under-mined the authority of politicians and businessmen after 1902, the need to channel the conduct of the "modern" big businessman was widely discussed in mainstream journals. The burgeoning market for muckraking articles, rising political insurgency, and the public's anger at the mine owners during the 1902 coal strike had all alarmed businessmen and business evangelists, fueling the hope that pub-licity would cleanse the pervasive corruption.[6]

Then in the aftermath of the Panic of 1907, the intensity of the muckraking criticism of big business began to lessen as the press and fictional treatments showed an increase in what Otis Graham has called a "reigning fantasy" that "all problems yielded to inspired leadership under true principles." By 1910 one could read comments in any number of forums about the value of what William Jewett Tucker called an "authoritative mind," be it a politician, millionaire, scientist, or efficiency expert. Carl Hovey published a laudatory biography of financier J. P. Morgan (which Lee read), lionizing him for bringing businesses together under effective leadership. Herbert Croly's biography of Marc Hanna showed that a businessman with brains had been the key force in the making of a president. The author of *The Promise of American Life* and future editor of the *New Republic* felt that Hanna embodied "the most vital social and economic tradition in American history—the tradition . . . of the pioneer . . . who overflowed with good-will and good fellowship. He and his neighbors were all striving for the same port." Thus, like Lee and so many of his contemporaries, Croly linked the role of wealthy businessmen to the frontier spirit, democratic idealism, and national greatness. The continuing attraction toward former president Theodore Roosevelt's political leadership that grew alongside the plodding style and political discord evident under his successor William Howard Taft fit neatly with this yearning for strong leadership.[7]

A number of historians have observed that social commentators in the Progressive Era expressed a need for new types of public leaders to combat plutocratic greed and mob rule, the twin evils identified as threatening the nation. The contemporary novels of Theodore Dreiser, Jack London, Colonel E. M. House, William Allen White, Upton Sinclair, Bourke White, Ernest Poole, Winston Churchill, and many others also provide testimony to this attribute. Simply put, anticipation was rampant for heroic public men who could provide social cohesion for a disoriented populace.[8]

But doubts and tensions persisted about the cultural utility and moral rectitude of great industrialists or political saviors during the Taft and early Wilson administrations. The Pujo Committee and the ideological stance of Wilson's New Freedom undermined the credibility of the trusts, while the status of men of wealth became a topic of great interest. A living legacy of midcentury values, the venerable and wealthy Bostonian Henry L. Higginson wrote in 1911, "The strong man has won his pile, but has he succeeded?" "The day has come for him to show to other men that his life and his work are henceforth [for] them, and not for his own gratification. He must prove that he has labored for the common good, and that he knows the rightful, wise use of his profits." Altruism and idealism were in the air, Higginson reminded his readers, and "surely our forefathers did not come to this country to win material success alone." True success was going to be made in the field of education and mass persuasion where all would be bound together for the commonweal.[9]

A change in the philosophy of business was widely noted by 1912, almost as if a generational conversion on behalf of service to the public interest had taken place. Americans were being reminded that railroad mogul Cornelius Vanderbilt's comment "the public be damned" reflected an antiquated attitude. William Gibbs McAdoo, president of New York's Hudson and Manhattan Railroad Company, reflected this new sensitivity back in 1908 when he announced that his company's intention was that "the public be pleased." Courteous service to customers became highly prized as a business strategy. Profit sharing and other corporate welfare policies were said by Morgan's partner George Perkins to be giving souls to corporations, making them "quasi-public" enterprises. Lawyer Louis Brandeis told a 1912 graduating class at Brown that business had finally become a profession fit for men with imagination. Progressives yearned for heroic personalities who understood science, the contours of city life, consumer psychology, and what was then loosely conceptualized as the public will. *World's Work* magazine, published by the Page brothers (who also published Carnegie's *The Empire of Business* and Lee's *Crowds*), sponsored countless articles noting changes in the philosophy of modern businessmen. One of its writers, C. M. Keys, showed that of seventy-six men who had led American industry seven years before, almost half had either retired or died. Readers were told that the new leaders were not interested in exploiting labor or consumers; these men were intent on providing more "real service to the country," he reported (ironically after describing the power of Samuel Insull who later fled the country).[10]

Business groups were also busy organizing new conventions and service organizations for themselves in the early twentieth century. The quest for fellowship and the marriage between business and civic consciousness can be seen in the creation of service organizations like the Rotary Club, founded in 1905 by four lonely Chicago bachelors, nostalgic for small-town community life. Also significant in this regard, business groups held bigger and more frequent national and regional conventions by the early twentieth century; at these the rewards of salesmanship, product identification, and the glories of service to the public became a recurrent litany.[11]

Walter Lippmann, one of the most influential intellectuals of the prewar era, took note of the popularity of ideas about business "statesmenship" in *Drift and Mastery,* published in 1914. After decrying the "sense of conspiracy and secret scheming" about muckraking accounts of corruption, he commented that the "real news about business is that it is being administered by men who are not profiteers." Big business (and more particularly the recently invented trusts) had "created a demand for a new type of business man—for a man whose motives resemble those of the applied scientists and whose responsibility is that of a public servant." Lippmann, however, was apprehensive about business evangelists like Lee who, although they had good reason to be joyful about the improvement in business motives, "might in decency refrain from erecting upon it a mystic and rhetorical commercialism."[12]

By acting as honest brokers between public opinion and the possessors of great wealth, ministers, former ministers, or even the sons of ministers like Lee (he fit each category) had been attempting to appropriate an enlarged sphere of influence for themselves within America for decades. In prior years, many aided in the creation of new institutions of social cohesion: Lyceums, the Chautauqua, the Chicago Civil Federation, and social service organizations. Most were dependent on funding by wealthy contributors. Gerald Lee's father, for example, a Congregational minister, was involved with one such urban outreach group in 1890. Perhaps this broker role was most cogently symbolized by the former minister Frederick Gates, who rationalized the distribution of millions of Rockefeller family dollars through charitable foundations; forthrightly attacking fraud in the disbursement of funds, he also worked to make the public appreciate the utility of wealth in alleviating human distress. This mediating role between spiritual values, business statesmanship, and what he saw as the economic realities of the day was what Gerald Lee attempted to play for all it was worth.[13]

In making the leap in the early twentieth century from being a romantic critic of the United States as a mass culture to a cheerleader for inspired millionaires, Lee mixed the more institutionally based economic assumptions propounded by his father with facets of British social thought. But the channels of his economic thought retained a vital core of belief in an entrepreneurial basis of corporate capitalism combined with his recurrent fears of social disorder.[14]

The elder Lee's own mugwumpish thought is revealed in an

article he published in June 1888 in the *New Englander and Yale Review*. Entitled "Men of Wealth and Institutions of Learning," the piece sought to coax newly wealthy Americans to continue donating large sums of their money to colleges and universities. Simultaneous with Carnegie's publication of his essay on "Wealth" and John D. Rockefeller's formation of the University of Chicago, the argument used by Samuel Lee exhibits a conservative defense of philanthropy combined with a warning that education should be appreciated as a form of social control by men of wealth. "Architects of their own fortunes, and efficient promoters of the general wealth," men of wealth were "entitled to generous appreciation and admiration," Samuel Lee wrote. Their record in the United States was labeled "brilliant, beyond comparison with that of their class in any other land or time." Lee believed that entrepreneurial activity had made the wilderness "blossom . . . as the rose," while the ongoing consolidation efforts by railroad magnates were deemed beneficial in reducing rates for the public. From such evidence, Samuel Lee added, "the current relative exaltation of the laboring class in discussion and in politics is unjust and injurious."[15]

The elder Lee used two underlying arguments to frighten men of wealth, who were his real audience. The first was to castigate the spirit of Mammon, which he found to be "terribly dominant in American life." This materialistic preoccupation could "seriously impair and imperil the stability of the economic order"; it could "break down the confidence which is the basis for commercial prosperity." The other warning was the threat of labor upheavals. To avoid mobs of strikers, he wrote, follow the example of industrialists such as Peter Cooper and Charles Pratt and set up institutions for the improvement of workers' minds. One can almost hear one of Gerald Lee's role models, preacher Henry Ward Beecher, whispering in the background that "the way to make a man safe is to educate him." The generous funding of colleges, the elder Lee wrote, "reaches men in their highest needs, and so meets all needs." The object of giving should be more than alleviating social problems; it should be to prevent their development. He completed his article by asserting that "when men shall use wealth more largely for the benefit of their fellows, its acquisition will no longer be looked upon as sordid, but an exercise of noble self-sacrifice for high ends." He sought to create the institutional base for socialized millionaires.[16]

Beyond his own father, however, young Lee was also influenced by a number of English social critics who had for years been writing about the need for greater cooperation between industrial leaders and workers. Carlyle had originally coined the term "captain of industry," writing that "to be a noble Master among noble Workers would again be the first ambition with some few; to be a rich Master only second." His captain would thus lure the working classes away from riotous disorder and into a more regimented atmosphere. Workers would identify their interests with righteous captains who in turn would benignly fuse their own interests back into the lives of their workers. By toiling alongside the men they employed, captains would achieve loyal, efficient labor and create enduring social cohesion outside the context of war.[17]

The work of John Ruskin and William Morris had a profound impact on both Lee and many of his contemporaries. The arts and crafts movement attracted many Americans in the 1890s, reflecting widespread disgust with mass-produced decorative arts and a belief in society as a social organism which demanded greater sensitivity toward the working class. In his 1862 collection of essays, *Unto This Last,* the great English art critic John Ruskin had stressed the duties of employers to assist the welfare of their employees. Lee avidly read about Ruskin's advocacy of profit sharing and other reforms. The essence of wealth, Ruskin asserted, lay in recognizing that "the persons themselves are the wealth." From Ruskin, Lee also learned about the value of patronage. Great individuals should be sponsored in preference to dubiously effective institutions, he felt. As we shall see, however, through Lee and other American disciples the ideology of Ruskin and Morris became twisted into celebrating contemporary mass culture by the early twentieth century.[18]

Aside from Ruskin, several other writers at the turn of the century had an impact on Lee's ideas about wealth and great men. Rudyard Kipling, for one, wrote popular stories extolling wealthy persons who had the wisdom to appreciate the lives of ordinary folk. H. G. Wells was also concentrating more attention on the agency of elites in changing the social order. More importantly, however, Lee's book lists and notebooks reveal that he was very familiar with the writings of W. H. Mallock, whose *Aristocracy and Evolution: The Origins and Social Functions of the Wealthier Classes* was published in 1898. Raymond Williams has called the Englishman the "most able conservative thinker in the last eighty years." Mallock transferred earlier Carlylean concepts about an "aristocracy of talent" to such early twentieth century writers as George Bernard Shaw and H. G. Wells.[19]

Lee accepted most of Mallock's argument and restated it in *Inspired Millionaires*. According to one scholar, Mallock wanted to "reintroduce the great man into the evolutionary system from which Spencer had eliminated him." While Herbert Spencer had berated Carlyle's Great Man Theory of history as impeding social science, Mallock saw evolutionary theory as ignoring the natural inequalities. "The movement of progress is double," Mallock wrote, "one movement being very slow, the other rapid. The survival of the fittest causes the slow movement. The rapid movement is caused by the great man." Evolution, Mallock argued in a restatement of the earlier argument William James had had with Spencer, was the unintended result of the intentions of great men. Through full appreciation of this double movement, heroism could easily coexist with Darwinian theory.[20]

Facilitating Lee's later attraction to the work of Frederick Winslow Taylor, Mallock was able to graft the value of efficiency onto the heroic ideal. But where did this leave the average man? Mallock's answer was that "the average man should be taught to aim at embellishing his position not at escaping from it." There was thus little fluidity in Mallock's class system outside the stray hero. Not surprisingly, socialists were condemned as having forgotten any sense of exceptional motives behind individuals, producing only agitators who stirred up workers. In the final analysis, Mallock defined the unrestrained freedom of wealth as a proper response to socialism and existing social problems.[21]

By 1907 Lee's admiration for Mallock's thought came into clearer focus as he saw the political initiative within the United States passing to insurgents. The previous year the American Federation of Labor began to endorse political candidates; the socialist newspaper *The Appeal to Reason* had over 500,000 subscribers. A growing band of legislators were pressing for legislative reforms to curb corporate excesses and extend the basis of democracy. The Socialist party, the newly formed International Workers of the World, and the radical press all seemed to be ascendant.[22]

Counterposed against images of mobs, the strong man solution became an attractive antidote to this growing critical coterie. Charles Ferguson invoked the dual extremist ogres of anarchic class warfare and plutocratic exploitation of workers when, in 1906, he wrote a series of articles for the *National Magazine*. "America is threatened with a deadly class struggle between the money power and the mob," he warned. The respectable classes would seek something that was clearly opposed to both extremes. Theodore Roosevelt found this dichotomy to be effective as well, telling an audience in 1910 that "in the interest of the workingman himself we need to set our faces like flint against mob violence just as against corporate greed; against violence and injustice and lawlessness by wage workers just as much as against lawless cunning and greed and selfish arrogance of employers." Writer Frederick T. Martin commented in 1911 that "the moment has arrived when the people demand a Marius." What, he asked, was the alternative for the society that did not find its Marius? The specter that presented itself to him was of "the days of the Terror, the bloody hands, the brutish mob, the wild eyes, frantic leaders of the hosts that stormed the Bastile, set up the guillotine."[23]

Lee was forming ideas about business heroes into a conception that left out much of the concern for social change and democratic rights that one could find in the writings of such Progressives as Herbert Croly, Walter Weyl, Jane Addams, and Robert La Follette. Lee seldom stopped to answer the key question that Randolph Bourne later demanded of business idealists: "Should not the workers' welfare be the concern of the community at large rather than of the individual corporation, to which it means only a more powerful instrument for control of the habits, ideals, attitudes of the worker, and for his ultimate feudalization?"[24]

Part of the reason behind Lee's failure to adequately address Bourne's question derives from the translocal context from which he was taking his cues about wealth and social control. He was also becoming more responsive to the daily headlines and the vast changes in politics, science, and social life. As reflected in both his small monthly magazine *Mt. Tom* and his book *Inspired Millionaires,* Lee felt that a new business ethic was surfacing throughout the country due to the growing interdependence—what he cryptically called the "modern ideas about dust and germs," which were "at work day and night, millions of them to a cubic inch, socializing us."[25]

In political terms, Lee joined others in seeing the 1902 coal strike as an important turning point. Coal company executives were widely chastised for appearing callous and selfish; the strike, lasting way into the fall, had underscored the self-righteous intransigence of business leaders, producing scores of "semi-inspired millionaires" according to Lee. While Theodore Roosevelt acted as the "public's representative" ending the strike and averting possible social disorder, coal company president George Baer had sanctimoniously invoked God as an ally of business leaders in a manner that undermined both business and religious authority. Lee wrote that Baer had been "proceeding upon the old common business ethics of always getting all one can. It was not that he was different from what he ought to be, but that he brought the difference out when we were cold and thoughtful . . . We began to quite generally conceive [of] . . . the type of business man that would not have to be apologized for by saying what a fine personality he had in private life." The public personality of business leaders conveyed through the popular press was thus seen to be of seismic importance in perpetuating their power. Lee's concern was primarily focused on the appearance of business ethics to the public mind; Baer was not condemned for his actions, merely for his failure to understand how the public perceived them. Baer had needed better advice.[26]

The man who most clearly personified the assertive man of wealth and education able to galvanize public opinion by acting openly and forcefully was Theodore Roosevelt. Lee gushed in admiration of Roosevelt, extolling his "moral genius," his political successes, and his temperament. Roosevelt had made the presidency "seem almost like a new position," acting toward the American people as if he were talking to them on a one-to-one basis. "There is a certain dead earnest way that Roosevelt has of taking a nation as if a nation were the best confidante a President could have—which has something almost religious about it," Lee wrote. Roosevelt exuded sincerity; his leadership was based on his effectiveness in communicating his personality, not his role as an ethicist, moralist, or champion of the people. Roosevelt's "personality is a Program," Lee wrote, "a program for all parties, whatever they believe"; he was a man who could personify the national will. The implicit message was that as a bulwark against socialism, the power of sincere and assertive public men, be they politicians or businessmen, was invaluable to cultural order and personal success.[27]

In Lee's own state of Massachusetts, moreover, a new kind of public-spirited business leadership was symbolized by the election of William L. Douglas to the governorship in 1904. A prominent shoe manufacturer, the wealthy Douglas had become successful through the intense use of personalized newspaper and magazine advertisements that featured his face. A conservative Democrat who had voted for Illinois Senator Palmer in opposition to William Jennings Bryan in 1896, Douglas nonetheless "stood well with labor interests," according to historian Richard Abrams. On election day 1904, Massachusetts elected a conservative millionaire who had the widespread backing of labor as their new governor, a man who had run without identification with the state or national Democratic party, a man who seemed to be above the party system.[28]

Lee used Douglas to illustrate the unique role millionaires could play amidst the institutionalized lethargy and petty bickering that made politics such an unsavory calling for men of character. Men like Douglas could revitalize voter loyalty beyond party labels, focusing it on dynamic leaders who had already passed the test of being successful in an economic marketplace before they had entered the political arena. That Douglas had used his own money and the familiarity of his face as electoral tools was no crime; the reverse was closer to the truth: his election implied the consent of the voters for this new technique of personalization.[29]

While to Lee Douglas seemed to be the right public man who could weld a statewide consensus, the Panic of 1907 proved the country's need for strong nationally oriented personalities who could preserve order and act as models of behavior. This important but historically underappreciated panic began in October 1907 and was soon settled, in the eyes of the press, not by political leadership, but by the talents of J. P. Morgan, the titan of finance, who came to the rescue of several ailing banks. But while the crisis soon abated and was superseded by an increasing concern over inflation, it left a warning cloud in the minds of many. Robert Wiebe writes that the Panic of 1907 "roused memories of the dark days of the Nineties" and acted "catalytically upon the trend from local, disorganized reform to optimistic national programming." The influential editor and columnist William Allen White, observing the seat of the panic, New York, reported that he had never seen the city "gloomier and shabbier, nor did I see the nation droop and wilt as we saw it wither under the Panic of 1907" with "crowds of idle workers" milling in the streets almost like cattle before a storm.[30]

As he penned *Inspired Millionaires,* Lee congealed a view of heroes, crowds, and dramatic expression that illustrates the widespread critique of strict Social Darwinian thought. Advocating an "organic" factory system comprising contented factory workers, adroit and sensitive superintendents, as well as magnetic and inspired millionaire owners, the book extended many ideas Lee had earlier published in the *Atlantic Monthly.* His next two books, *Crowds: A Moving Picture of Democracy* (1913) and *We* (1916), were further explorations into the cultural utility of inspired millionaires.

In all these books millionaires were criticized for their lack of awareness regarding the new business ethics which the public demanded, but it was labor which received the most withering attack from Lee's pen. Few labor advocates would have agreed with a writer who commented that "nine men out of ten in the factories are not interested in working. They are working as little as possible for their money . . . They are merely interested in getting all the values they can that other people have created." Workers were referred to as "tired herds" who were so dulled as to be unable to formulate any coherent positions on social issues. He somberly wrote that the real oppression of the poor came from a distortion of evolutionary laws—namely the "mob of weak men intimidating the strong." Sounding like the popular violently antidemocratic social psychology of the French theorist Gustave Le Bon, Lee wrote that workers were part of the masses and "masses not only cannot do things, but they do not want to." The chief problem was that so many of the workers could find no inspiration in their work. Curiously, Lee did not consider himself antilabor, but sought to appeal to the hidden higher selves of working people. Meaningless hyperbole and vaguely wrought arguments about reform took the place of a coherent argument.[31]

One of the many contradictions in *Inspired Millionaires* is that Lee never fully reconciled his idealized factory reforms with the means which would effect them. For example, he believed that every factory worker, if he wanted it, should be given the chance to learn all the functions of the factory and should be fully able to switch from one job to another, while gaining a view of the big picture in the workshop, a kind of exchange system of employment. He believed that too much specialization undermined creativity, which was spawned by a cross-fertilization process of men working with different machines, and that unless this kind of "rotary employment" took place, work becomes mechanical and workers become dull and tired. But this idea was thrown out without any further discussion about its viability. He often tried to bridge the gap between conservatives and radicals by projecting glimpses of far-reaching reforms that should take place in factories but then left the ultimate decisions consistently in the hands of superintendents and owners.[32]

There was no problem with the market mechanism of capitalism, Lee felt, only with those inclined toward socialism or with governments that tried to equalize the conditions of labor and throttle the genius of inspired employers. Socialism was a "scared machine," he later called it, which "scared people have invented for not letting people choose to do right because they may choose to do wrong." However, Lee never showed a deep hatred for individual socialists and sought to enlist a number of them in his crusade for benevolent or "socialized" millionaires. To Eugene Debs, Lee wrote of the "groping towards [the] Socialists that pervades all my thought." Yet he candidly continued that "unless the Socialism is of the sort that lends itself to the ideas and gifts of great individualists, I am afraid of it. I am afraid of what it will do with us. I believe in experts and men of genius who represent the people."[33]

One reader of *Inspired Millionaires* threw Lee's gaping ignorance of socialism into relief. Robert Hunter, the author of *Socialists at Work,* wrote to Lee: "You really do not understand the subject at all . . . Your whole conception of our aims seems drawn from a lot of trashy sentimentalism such as some utopists have written . . . The trouble is the system. It destroys us all . . . The millionaires can help themselves no more than can the most miserable of us." If Lee found socialists to be suffused with conformist tendencies, he also feared Leo Tolstoy's Christian anarchism. Tolstoy was labeled a "nobly blind old hero . . . who does not believe in men at all unless they are poor, and who does not see any hope for any of us, either in our religion or our art, or our lives, but to level us down into Russian peasants, and begin over."[34]

The Christianity that Lee espoused saw Jesus in a vastly different light from the simplicity and love promoted by the great Russian novelist. While admitting that in ancient times Jesus had given up entirely on "a few crude, provincial-minded millionaires . . . before a single church had been founded," it did not follow that he would despair of finding inspired millionaires in the modern world. Christ was great because he exuded an infectious positive attitude. "The one thing of all others that Christ did with people," Lee added, "was to make them believe in themselves and in one another more than they wanted to." Above all, Lee felt that Christ would not "believe that the world was going to be saved (like the socialists) by dropping off over the edge of the planet one entire class of men in one indistinguishable mass. If a world is going to be saved at all, it is going to be saved by the men who see things first." Here was Lee defending millionaires as a class by excoriating radicals who viewed them as a monolithic force, exactly the image that he himself had of labor.[35]

What were the specific qualities that inspired millionaires should possess in order to lead the nation? Their sense of mutualism with workers and consumers, their professionalism, and dramatic insight were all elements that Lee sought to highlight. Above all, millionaires should use their money artistically, galvanizing labor and the public away from any possible affinity with class warfare and toward cooperation with business leaders. The best way to do this was by the construction of Lee's "organic factories" which would act as a new kind of church. Using such a conception, clearly derived from the ideas of Ruskin, Morris, and Elbert Hubbard, Lee idealized future factories in terms that he used in recalling the New England church of his forefathers.[36]

The organic factory, as Lee saw it, was a place that could be "as spiritual as a church and as educational as a school," where "the employees and owners and the public become as members of one body moving and growing in conscious health, and in strength and joy together." The reason that factories had not previously become organic, Lee felt, was because most people no longer had faith in anyone: "It is getting to be a literal business truth that what the typical modern factory needs most to go with its plant today is a creed—or possibly a church on the premises, where all the people could go—master and workmen—and kneel together until they amount to something—that is, amount to enough, have religion and insight enough, to work their souls together." Here is a clear prescription for a civil religion which would be identified with the deepest traditions of American civilization, harkening back to a time when church influence on social behavior was largely unquestioned. Similar sentiment was later expressed by Lee's fellow resident of Northampton, Calvin Coolidge.[37]

Beyond the inspired millionaire, though, the superintendent of the organic factory was the crucial person in Lee's "system." Chosen by the inspired millionaire to manage the factory, the superintendent would begin his tenure by having it explicitly understood among all concerned that

> he is . . . the personal representative and champion of every man who works in it, and of every man who owns it, and of the great public outside that is buying its goods. He will proceed on the principle that every act of every day of his life is to be governed by the interests of these three groups of men, that in proportion as he can braid these interests together, make them inextricably mutual and keep them so, he is establishing a permanent and prosperous career for both the business and himself.

The superintendent was thus the man in the middle, reconciling class conflicts with his "dramatic insight," determining wage scales, work rules, pricing, and levels of profits to the owners. It was the quality of his character that would make or break the organic factory experiment. This left the inspired millionaire free from the daily concerns of the factory with which he was supposed to be so intimately related. Lee was placing an impossible burden of reconciliation among three conflicting forces onto the back of superintendents.

Consumers, workers, and the owners of capital would all gain, Lee believed, if the right superintendents were chosen for their jobs. Yet consumers wanted low prices, owners wanted high profits, while workers wanted higher wages, improved working conditions, and a series of other benefits which would obviously eat into profits or raise prices. Lee was hypothesizing that a progressive equilibrium could be effected among these three mutually antagonistic groups when, and only when, they could be induced to work within a great spiritual consensus.[38]

All in all, the factory was rationalized as a work of art with those acting under the inspired millionaire serving as his dabs of paint. The inspired millionaire functioned as an amalgamation of Whitman's poet and Barnum's showman—men who could "invent" other people and create new publics and an expanding marketplace. Selfishness was legitimized through faith in the good intentions of the wealthy. There was to be no strong government arbiter in Lee's scheme, no countervailing power other than the market. Stop worrying about "mixed motives" if you are inspired, Lee admonished businessmen. "If the employers are voluntarily and habitually generous, if they make common cause with their best men, the best men will make common cause with the men below and the whole factory will be keyed to a new spirit." To imitate the men who accomplished this feat most successfully was to imitate success, to improve oneself, and become a dynamic personality. Social transformation was thus totally contingent upon the quality of leadership from above.[39]

Lee's attitude toward the problem of trusts followed from such a simple faith. Although critical of their past performance, he defended them as being so big that they served a quasi-public function. The trusts seemed to be made for "getting the truth big enough—taking just any ordinary truth from out of the New Testament and making it so big almost anybody could see it." A corporation had become the central institutional stage for proving Lee's vision for a revitalized Christianity. The essence of Lee's conception was that inspired millionaires of the new era, in order to preserve or increase their wealth, needed the power to create monopolies if they produced what the buying public wanted in the way of price and product. Inspired millionaires became the best barometers of public opinion. Lee saw no contradiction in defining such men as both molders and reflecters of public desires. The power of personality to dramatically control social relations remained paramount. "The aristocrat in America," he concluded, "is the man who is more of a democrat than other people have the brains to be, the man who can identify himself with the interests and with the points of view of the most kinds of people."[40]

By 1910 Lee felt that the mission he had begun when he resigned from his church parish in 1896 was finally coming to fruition. He was regularly corresponding with important Progressives, including businessmen E. A. Filene and Joseph Fels, journalist Lincoln Steffens, and others who were clearly intrigued by what seemed to be the network of inspired millionaires Lee was identifying. He distributed hundreds of free copies of his book to leaders, through the financial assistance of Fels. Louis Brandeis, whose writings reflect some of Lee's ideas, hoped that *Inspired Millionaires* could be used in the Harvard School of Business. Alfred Stieglitz and Louis Sullivan were clearly intrigued with Lee's book. Lee visited factories and lunched with business executives while promoting his book as a cultural panacea of great importance.[41]

Then, between 1910 and 1912, the Lees made several prolonged visits to England. There they met many important authors who confirmed to Gerald that he was finally gaining the stature he had long sought, proving as well to his parents that his switch to a writing career was furthering God's work on earth. His father, however, remained rankled that Gerald identified Jesus with ordinary "reformers or exceptional men of any kind." As Gerald was departing for England, he tried to soothe his parents' discomfort over the unstable character of his career. He justified the trip in evangelical terms: "It is my business and my religion to be in England now—and the most important crisis in my life work. It is my parish and my next parish and I have to be there and I belong there, whether I like it in all respects or not." An English edition of *Inspired Millionaires* was published by Grant Richards and Lee's reception in England lifted his spirits. Distance only confirmed his feelings of superiority. From England he wrote to his parents that "we are too hurried in America to have the deeper slower understanding, and

The Lee house on High Street, Northampton, Massachusetts.

our big men—while they decline to be as hurried as the others, are still a little superficial as compared with the big men I have met here."[42]

Business, politics, and religion had become inextricably intertwined in his mind, with business becoming the dominant partner. Lee wrote to former secretary of the treasury Lyman Gage that "in spite of the humor in my book [I] have come to consider my ideas . . . as a cause—as a national movement and it looks as if, as a national campaign document for better conditions, a great deal might be expected." Any expression of support from his correspondents was cited by Lee as testimony of a groundswell of opinion for himself as a prophet. To John Graham Brooks, another social critic and frequent correspondent, Lee wrote in 1910 that he detected a significant recent change in the intellectual climate toward business. In a manner that exhibited his recurrent tendency, through metaphor, to contain the consciousness of the American people, he commented: "Now we have all moved into one great living room," he wrote, "and there is a great fireplace and hearth on the world and we are getting together and beginning to live."[43]

Not surprisingly, many businessmen responded enthusiastically to Lee's book, with some seeing it as an effective ideological tool against socialism. Ralph Easley, the chairman of the executive council of the National Civil Federation, the group James Weinstein has styled the penultimate expression of emerging corporate liberalism, wrote Lee in late June 1908, soon after the book was published. Striving to create alternatives to attract workers away from socialism, Easley wrote that an optimistic book was needed in the times of crisis in which they were all living and "certainly is quite in demand at this time when so much revolutionary socialism is being propagated by people who ought to know better."[44]

The response of business writer John Moody illustrates the skepticism that many more sophisticated analysts must have felt toward Lee's book. Moody ran an influential data-gathering business service and wrote an exposé, *The Truth about Trusts*, in 1904. The book detailed for the first time the extent of industrial concentration that had overtaken the United States since 1898 and how interlocking directorships aided the Carnegie, Rockefeller, and Morgan interests. An admirer of the single tax scheme propounded by Tom Johnson and Joseph Fels, because they were "not striving to be model millionaires and to perpetuate modern millionairedom, but to end it," Moody denied that millionaires could be anything other than that which their class defined for them. "The modern millionaire, the man whom you would inspire, is not possible of inspiration . . . Even though he spends his own money profits as fast as they come in 'bettering the conditions of the masses,' he must continue to stand for a political and social economy which filches wealth from

its creators to hand it back to them in part as gifts and donations."
Moody expressed moral outrage at the exploitation of nature and
human labor by monopolistic corporations. The conflict, from
Moody's vantage point, was between monopoly (which he defined
as the "private appropriation of socially created values") as against
capital and labor working together.[45]

Another response to Lee's book exhibits the manner in which it
sparked debate even from doubters. The prominent Cambridge University author and literary critic G. Lowes Dickinson wrote Lee in
December 1908, praising him for his efforts, though criticizing him
for his neglect in addressing the "inspired public servant": "It strikes
me as almost the only American book I have read—outside Walt
Whitman—that is really American; has a vision . . . that seems to
belong to a new country and civilization . . . I agree that the artist (as
you conceive him) is the man one wants . . . But the rank and file—
are they not going to continue to turn a crank or whatever it may be,
so many hours a day? And how is that going to be anything but sheer
necessary drudgery?" Dickinson believed that the object of reform
should be to increase people's leisure time, and get them to use their
leisure more artistically. He, as well as Lee, seemed oblivious to the
possibility that leisure itself was being commodified in a manner that
could reflect and reinforce the mechanization of the factory system.[46]

Dickinson continued his critique by noting Lee's propensity to
downgrade public service, a comment that speaks to the rhetoric of
Ronald Reagan in the 1980s as well as to Lee in 1910. He wrote that
Lee's

> "Inspired Millionaire" is more chimerical than an inspired public ser-
> vant. My kind of man, at any rate, has existed; whereas yours is some-
> thing you want to evoke . . . In practice, I believe your ideal would end in
> a hereditary aristocracy, which, according to all precedent, would degen-
> erate into a hereditary oligarchy. Or are you going to rule out the
> inheritance of wealth? In that case you go a long way with Socialists. You
> in America don't seem to me to know what we in Europe are after with
> Socialism. We are after equal opportunity and individuality.

Dickinson had penned a critique that points out not only the naiveté
of Lee's ideas about socialism but underscores the lack of attention

placed on public service in modern times. Even in the early twentieth century, success had become habitually equated to wealth derived from dominating an economic market with scant regard paid to one's contribution to any local community.[47]

Lee had Dickinson's critique printed in the back of a later edition of *Inspired Millionaires* and added an afterword of his own to defend his ideas—or rather to exhibit their plasticity. The book had been put forward, he wrote "not so much as a repudiation of socialism as a substitute for it." He was quite willing "to admit that a few semi-socialistic-looking government regulations about land or about inheritance might well be introduced by the inspired millionaire, if the uninspired ones drive them to it."[48]

Lee frequently used such rhetorical excess to mask the authoritarian strain that emanated from his early frustrations in dominating his church congregations. Yet there was always the tart remark that leaves the impression that he was dancing through the ideas of his times as an ideological gadfly. To Lowes Dickinson, for example, Lee wrote in the summer of 1909 that "whether your kind of socialism swallows my kind of feudalism in the end, or my feudalism swallows your socialism we will both stand by cheerfully and watch 'em swallow, won't we?"[49]

By 1915 Lee had gained a wide audience among influential writers and businessmen. Tall, thin, and sporting the clothes of his former calling, Lee spoke to numerous audiences. He wrote a column for a number of months for the *New York World* in 1915, and possessed contacts with important literary figures and businessmen, claiming to be uncovering a group of inspired millionaires. Such a stance allowed him to appeal to businessmen with intellectual aspirations as well as to intellectuals who wished to appear practical. As if following Lee's admonition, 1914 had seen automaker Henry Ford announce that he would distribute over $10 million to his employees and pay a $5 base salary to each worker. Public opinion, led by the press, exploded in admiration. In an article published in *Harper's Weekly* that March, Lee announced that Ford was filling out his prescription of an inspired millionaire. "Everybody is a partner in the Ford Motor Company . . . sharing . . . if he likes, in the profits of the Ford business." The drivers of Ford cars were not the only ones who enjoyed them. "They fly through the streets addressed to all of us—happy valentines about the world and about the way things are going in it."[50]

Yet the line between Lee's fantasies and his "practical" idealism, barely evident in *Inspired Millionaires,* eroded quickly as he gained influence and a national audience. Unable to successfully adapt the residue of his own preaching mentality to the modern world of marketing, science, and business, Lee had naively tried to extend the Christian mission to effect the amalgamation between labor and capital, making it a movement which would be all-inclusive under the leadership of his strong men. He provides a vivid example of the latent desire on the part of many Americans—then and now—to emulate personalities whose material success and organizational abilities have become bathed in a quasi-religious unanimity of purpose. Clyde Griffen has written of the Progressive Era that "the very vagueness of the vision and rhetoric of a Christian democracy created a semblance of national unity of purpose, encouraging the progressive generation to minimize divisions between various kinds of reformers and conservatives within and without the churches. In the Twenties that vision and rhetoric no longer attracted many native middle class Americans and the divisions had become all too obvious."[51]

The vagueness of Lee's scheme for inspired millionaires and organic factories, combined with the responses of intrigued readers, manifests a naive side of the Progressive Era, a hopeful voice from a more innocent past in a world being swept by the aggressive doctrines of modern consumerism. What became abundantly clear in the 1980s, however, is that the romance of what is now labeled entrepreneurialism has had its price as well as its benefits. Heroism has become a fully marketable commodity like soap, relentlessly promoted throughout popular culture, politics, and religion. Neither Lee nor his contemporaries could appreciate how that commodification process could become an end in itself, nor how the scope of public cynicism would grow.

SIX

Righteous Crowds and Moving-Picture Minds: Managing Public Opinion during the Progressive Era

The Progressive Era was a pivotal period in both the conceptualization and management of public opinion. Politicians made more effective use of publicity to influence voters than had their predecessors. Ad men increasingly spoke about the "science" of marketing, often viewing the public as an irrational, controllable mass. As human experience fell further under the influence of commercially sponsored, mass-produced definitions of modern reality, both advertising and an ideology of consumerism presented themselves to most Americans as inevitable, progressive achievements; they were linked to the revival of spiritual values, democratic idealism, and expanding economic markets.[1]

By 1910 Gerald Lee had completed a conversion, incorporating into his developing ideology the goal of inspired millionaires working closely with wordsmiths to express and mold public consciousness. Twelve years before Edward Bernays defined the term "public relations," Lee had conceptualized a profession that he variously labeled "news" or "attention engineering," which in effect involved the management of public opinion. Consulting prominent advertisers, publicity agents, journalists, businessmen, and politicians, Lee formulated the utility of the "lord of attention" to redeem America's lost unity. He called this notion a contribution to democratic idealism, but never far from the surface of Lee's mind lay fantasies of a bounded public opinion that had captivated him since the 1890s.[2]

In 1913 Lee finally achieved national recognition after a 561-page pastiche of his ideas on such subjects as crowds, heroes, machines, inspired millionaires, consumerism, and news was published by Doubleday and Page under the title *Crowds: A Moving Picture of Democracy*. To Theodore Roosevelt, Lee wrote of his fervent hope that he had written "the textbook of the Progressive Movement—in a sense, even the classic—the Uncle Tom's Cabin of American business." It became the best selling nonfiction book of the year and Lee, for a brief time, became a national celebrity.[3]

Along with other advocates and business evangelists in the prewar era, Lee attempted to explain the potential of advertising and publicity management for achieving social harmony. He bestowed the nascent "profession" with a cloudy exuberance over its service to the public. However, the heritage of his nineteenth-century Protestant past remained imbedded in his thought. Lee's was an appeal that failed to span two eras yet leaves traces of crucial metaphorical relationships from that transitional period in our history.[4] More specifically, Lee's thought helps explain an important paradox in the early twentieth century: how could so many Americans promote the increased democratization of the electorate while simultaneously viewing the public as a dull herd, easily manipulated by new techniques and media of mass persuasion? Many conservatives such as Yale president Arthur Hadley argued that if America extended the franchise to a wider public, "organized emotion" would be controlled by lower-class demagogues and irresponsible editors, possibly renewing the political disorder of the 1890s. On the other hand, such notable reformers as William Allen White and William Jennings Bryan expressed optimism that through publicity and advertising, corruption could be revealed to the public and corporate power channeled toward socially beneficial ends. Corporate power would thus be contained by a truth-seeking press and by public understanding. Lee spoke indirectly to Hadley's concerns and his writings help explain the paradox, in that the language of reform is suffused with his romantic notions of collective behavior.[5]

Lee's writing illustrates how the language of social cohesion functioned to rationalize social engineering and the corporate dominance of advertising and public relations. Historians have shown how "efficiency," "group process," and "laws of psychology" became buzzwords in the Progressive Era. As we shall see, Lee's ability to transform his use of the crowd metaphor from a formal religious context into advertising and public relations illustrates one facet of how these fields became legitimized and how they enlarged their power in American society.[6]

Lee is but one example of a growing prewar group of people who sought, as he himself put it, to "steer . . . people from inside their heads" toward a modern consumer state through techniques of mass persuasion. Through his writings we can see how advertising, "crowd" control, and direct democracy became compatible; how a preaching mentality, formed in the late nineteenth century, finally became adapted to the world of efficiency movements and consumer culture.[7]

All power was "rapidly coming to be based on news—news about human nature," Lee declared in *Crowds*. News was to be dispensed to markets that he labeled crowds. These crowds could best find their voices through businessmen and wordsmiths. Ultimately, as he understood it, the control of news would provide an invaluable tool for "good" men with fertile imaginations who were trying to mold public opinion. But how did Lee conceive of news and how did it fit into prevalent conceptions? The definition of news was changing dramatically by the 1890s as the partisan press had been superseded by a mass press that sought to appeal to the broadest possible market. As we saw in Chapter One, concern over the guidance of public opinion was widespread in the genteel and scholarly publications.[8]

Lee's imagination stretched most conventional definitions of the news. By the early years of the new century Lee believed that office buildings, display windows, mass-circulation print advertisements, moving pictures, and even the newsworthiness of celebrated personalities could all function as emblems of a national consensus. He conceived of news in broadly inclusive terms, involving information, physical structures, or values imparted by a variety of visual sources. Large buildings, for example, should be appreciated for gaining the attention of the public as symbols of power. All in all, the definition of the news became opaque in Lee's consciousness, confused with older Puritan assumptions about deference due the ordained cultural authority.

If the dynamo was the symbol of modernity to Adams, Lee saw the cathedral of commerce as his own totem. Technological achievements in building the skyscraper were divinely inspired, fueling both the Progressive movement and democratic idealism. Lee noted that New York's recently completed Metropolitan Tower, "with its big clock dial, with its three stories of telling what time it is, and its great bell singing hymns above the dizzy flocks of the skyscrapers, is the soul of New York." It was a "steeple of democracy" and functioned, undoubtedly quite unconsciously, as a symbol of male power to Lee. Peering down from high up in the tower, the clock tolled a new gospel, the "religion of business" into the minds and souls of people. Trinity Church, which had earlier alarmed Lee by appearing as a little toy church dwarfed by the new imposing buildings, was now pictured as gracefully and deferentially bowing to these new power centers of the consumer society. Lee was linking economic dominance with democratic choice. More importantly, moral rectitude was preserved and promoted by deferring to corporate leaders as the reigning cultural force within the United States and England.[9]

Corporate dominance also became tied to news through the functions of a department store. Lee saw such grand emporia both as reflections of the public's desires and as institutions to channel consumer behavior. Of necessity, department stores ought to be imbued with a religious spirit based on fully embracing the democratic market society through their spectacular architectural designs and their organizational expertise. After all, Lee wrote, "the shopping of a country is . . . from a psychologist's point of view, the most spiritual energy, the most irrevocable, most implacable meter there can ever be of the religion a country really has." No clergyman could make as great an impression on the American crowd man as someone like A. T. Stewart, the creator of America's first department store. Stewart's innovative standardized pricing policy had "touched the imagination of the crowd because he had let the crowd touch him and had seen what crowds, in spite of appearances, were really like."[10]

Although privately contemptuous of the masses, Lee told readers of *Crowds* that when people were presented with clearly identifiable choices between good and evil, between the modern way of life and outdated customs, or between efficiency and lethargy, they invariably chose the correct path. Betraying little appreciation for ethnic diversity, the subtlety of social relations, or the complexity of ethical choice, Lee set up a simplistic moral analogy:

> If two great shops could stand side by side on the Main Street of the World and all the vices could be put in the show window of one of them and all the virtues in the show window of the other, and all the people could go by all day, all night, and see the windowful of virtues as they were, and the windowful of vices as they were, all the world would be good in the morning. It would stay good as long as people remembered how the windows looked . . . [A]ll they would need to do, most people, when a vice tempted them would be to step out, look at it in its window a minute—possibly take a look too at the other window—and they would be good.

This statement reflects the prevalent Progressive belief that if people merely saw "truth" revealed, then right would prevail. Such was the faith of many of the nation's most illustrious journalists, sociologists, and reformers. Nowhere in Lee's statement does he define his criteria of "the good"; he ignored the ethical implications of using psychological techniques to attract people to the good window. He simply assumed an instinctive or primordial attraction to the window of virtue, in the same way he could assume a nineteenth-century gentleman would know the difference between right and wrong. In this way, Lee extends the idea of absorbing moral distinctions in a visual glance as Carlyle had externalized character in his historical sketches and as Whitman had extracted from the photographed face. The public was implicitly admonished by Lee not to be concerned with anything beyond the display window, to avoid the chaos and spontaneity of the street. Although more a fantasy than a serious proposal, Lee's notion about the flash of moral recognition in viewing a store window revealed his compulsive desire for a shorthand device to control the public's attention.[11]

The recently created medium of motion pictures brought together all the properties Lee had envisioned for galvanizing public attention. Movies were standardized, machine-made dispensers of news, literature, and dreams. Beginning in 1896 and spreading quickly to the working classes through nickelodeons in the early 1900s, movies were beginning to attract the middle classes by the time that Lee published *Crowds*. As Lary May has noted, more and more Progressive Era observers were seeing that film, as a "centrally controlled medium might arouse the various groups and classes in the city to transcend their selfish interests in favor of a higher moral law." A few critics were increasingly optimistic about the possibilities of dominating the public mind through the use of film while some filmmakers, D. W. Griffith among them, saw the new medium as a wider pulpit for themselves to promote a moral social order.[12]

Lee wrote an article in the *Atlantic Monthly* in 1913 that found the new medium possessing the mysterious powers of collective expression. Then in *Crowds* his hopes for film were phrased in the following exuberant manner: "What we want is a vast white canvas, spread, as it were, over the end of the world, before which we all sit together, the audience of the nations, of the poor, of the rich, as in some still, thoughtful place—all of us together; and then we will throw up before us in the vast white screen in the dark the vivid pictures of our vast desires, flame up upon it the hopes, the passions of human lives, and the grim, silent wills of men." Both a window in a store and a canvas in a movie hall became devices to draw out people's hidden desires; both elicited dreams and provided a collective record of what Lee, as a preacher, had found largely unobtainable from his earlier congregations.[13]

As advertisers and publicity agents grasped for professional status, Lee lent his pen to their cause in arguing that their cultural value complemented the reformist aims of the Progressive Movement. Many self-styled Progressives came to believe in advertising "as a kind of democratic education which could be applied to any arena of life." Further, many ad men had close connections with religious organizations and were creating ideological associations between progress, modernity, and advertising. George Coleman of Boston, for example, addressed Boston's Ford Hall Forum in 1909 on the subject of "the religion of the crowd." A prominent leader in both Baptist and advertising circles, Coleman believed the "democratic spirit" was moving through American history, a "common platform or moral and spiritual truth that all broad-minded and right-hearted people can get together upon."[14]

Like the pamphlets and speeches disseminated by leading ad agencies, Coleman eschewed explicit religious content in his remarks, preferring to connect democratic idealism and modernism with advertising. Important code words such as *charity, altruism,* or *fashion* were featured in the work of many advertising proponents. Some language evoked religious authority in a manner bordering on humor. For example, Seymour Eaton of the J. Walter Thompson advertising agency entitled his 1907 pamphlet promoting advertising "Sermons on Advertising"; it addressed readers as if they were a congregation listening to its local parson. Chicago's leading firm, Lord and Thomas, published a pamphlet, "Altruism in Advertising," in 1911 that proclaimed the virtues of "higher advertising" which "compels action," either in making people spend money for things they did not previously want or "cause people to go to Church—make them more Charitable, more Kind, Sober, Honest, or Industrious."[15]

By that year Lee's attitude toward advertising had undergone seismic changes. In 1890 he had written of being outraged at seeing an ad stating that a soap manufacturer would give away a copy of a popular English novel with every cake sold. While rapturous over the literary power of the romantic writers, he was then aghast at how far literature seemed to have fallen. It appeared there was "no dignity in writing a book nowadays," when writers were placed on "a level with the quack adventurers in patent medicine." Nonetheless, Lee grasped something about the wide scope of advertising's influence on religion: "The newspaper has taken the place of the church bell as a means of keeping people in mind of sacred affairs. The public mind has the idea of advertised merit so thoroughly worked into it that unless the public knows all about a thing it stays away and assumes that a good thing will make itself known. Businessmen find themselves forced to advertise. Unless they keep themselves in the front of public attention in the usual way and places they are crowded out. The same rule applies in a modified way to churches." He believed that churches "must take up their share in the public prints," while also warning against allowing religious journals to dominate church affairs. His solution, reflecting his own career change, was that churches should "appear in the papers at large, and the religious sentiment of the public should be reflected in them." Drawing little distinction between advertising and publicity in 1890, Lee thought that "the church should use this great modern weapon or it will use her," assuming an attitude of awe toward a new power that he saw triumphing over live preaching by intellectually competent clerics.[16]

By the 1890s American attitudes toward advertising were in the process of being altered by the changing visual style and tone of ads, as well as by their increasing ubiquity. Until the 1870s, advertisements had presented little more than the name of a product. Then by the 1880s ads became increasingly extravagant. At the time of the Chicago General Strike in May 1886, for instance, one merchant advertising in the *Chicago Tribune* used the fear of labor violence to capture the attention of readers by exclaiming in bold letters, "Tremendous slaughter in immense large lots of hosiery, embroideries." Such an ad was clearly written to fool people into reading it as a news item connected to labor violence. Yet genteel scorn at such ads was becoming more and more resignation to their continued existence.[17]

Further, the picture of advertising was not uniformly negative; it received a positive reception from many mugwump publications and from political operatives, as well as from some leading ministers. Whereas Washington Gladden resigned from the *Independent* in 1873 because of the paper's acceptance of questionable advertising, few objected when Henry Ward Beecher received $1,000 to endorse a truss or a brand of soap for an advertisement. Advertising was increasingly perceived to represent the commercial energy that gripped American life. The *Nation* magazine commended advertising in 1875 as "a token of healthy energy, and the ingenuity in it may even command admiration, though it can never be the index of any intellectual effort above the level of shrewdness." Politicians were increasingly shifting to more sophisticated advertising campaigns.[18]

By the 1890s advertisement revenues in newspapers were outstripping those made from the sale of the papers to its readers. In addition, as Neil Borden has pointed out, manufacturers of consumer goods who advertised were increasingly dominating the merchants who bought and sold their products, creating a dependence on themselves as the recruiters of large groups of potential consumers. This affected not only the scale but also the content of advertising. The literary quality of ads was upgraded as their production was centralized among ad men who resented being considered practioners of a black art. The upshot was that slogan writing was becoming both more remunerative and more intriguing to ambitious men and women.[19]

The early years of the new century saw advertisers describing their work as a new and vital force in American business, one that provided a crucial link between the public and manufacturers and that applied new concepts of social psychology. A new assertiveness arose about advertising's contributions to American national identity. The ad writer for Wanamaker's department store, John Powers, declared in 1903 that advertising "benefits society by bringing the extremes of the country together, making all more cosmopolitan, and permitting all to enjoy the same luxuries and comforts."[20]

Yet Lee's ambivalence toward advertising persisted, reflecting in part his growing awareness of the power of personality in ads. In 1897 he chided the noted author Charles Dudley Warner for allowing his picture to be used in magazines to sell encyclopedias. He felt that this endorsement was like "receiving a blow at literature from literature itself." Gazing at Warner's reproduced face clearly unsettled Lee's assumptions about the separation between huckstering and his image of the Victorian literary artist as a contemplative aesthete. To him the ad illustrated the tendency in American letters to "appeal to the irrelevant and the little and the personal."[21]

Who, wondered Lee, was this "phantom thing we call the public"? Was it as irrational as sensationalist editors supposed? Lee acted as spokesman for what he saw to be a passive public when he penned the following invective against the dominance of society by commercial forces, a view he was later to reverse when he tried to interpret the public to businessmen.

> To do our reading everywhere, to do our very thinking from day to day under the oligarchy of advertising that rules the world, to have the books we read determined for us by the subtle or furtive quality of flagrant advertising in the very news that is placed before our eyes—to know that whichever way we turn, for pleasure or profit, or inspiration or knowledge or wisdom under the sun, there is some business interest at stake,—this is to strike at the very soul of literature, at every latent possibility for creative or beautiful thought.

In a handwritten addition that Lee later included in an unsuccessful book proposal, he elaborated that "the ascendency of the advertisement confronts us on every hand. Fences are reading matter . . . The palisades proclaim soap . . . Concerts advertise pianolas and churches advertise themselves."[22]

Yet, given such attitudes, how did Lee's subsequent accommodation to advertising come about? How did he become converted to the notion of advertising as religion's handmaiden? In 1910 Lee recounted how he initially became fascinated with advertising. Although he does not say when this change occurred, it was probably during the opening years of the century. His first response was that "reading the advertising department of a great magazine is a little like strolling up and down the Midway Plaisance at the Chicago Fair. You go on and on . . . all these Firms waving their arms, flourishing a little, and attracting attention to their gates." But as time passed, his attitude changed. He "began going into the advertising department of a great magazine and sitting down all alone like an audience and watching it, profoundly and strangely absorbed—this vast immeasurable pantomime of business—this silent tussle of the Trusts to feed the people, to build their homes for them, to put out chairs for them to sit in, mattresses for them to sleep on, telling them what to read and what to play and how to work and how to be good and happy."[23]

By chance he then looked through a pile of old newspapers from Boston dating back some seventy years, and it slowly dawned on him that one could tell more about Bostonians from reading and studying the advertisements than from the hard news and editorials; one could, in short, perceive in the advertising columns the "inner history, the dramatic truth—the truth as they were acting it out—the naked life" of people. Authors had a limited impact on readers in the new mass-circulation magazines because, unlike advertisements, they did not address the whole nation. "In the advertising section all crowded up together a Nation speaks. What we really are is there—all of us are there; calling to one another . . . To me it is an ocean or sky, or continent of Desire, and the smoking factories and the vast surf of the voices of cities and the echoes of all the little hills and valleys go rolling through it."[24]

Lee's romanticism saw the entire public in the advertising pages, every facet of the recent history and consciousness of a people. The literal embodiment of the collective will of the people was to be found in their buying habits. He felt that equipped with this truth he was then in a position to define the "face" of the public. "There are days when . . . I think I see a face . . . a mighty amorphous boundless face. But oftener it is more like a play, a vast pageant—a colossal silent spectacle of Us, of our people, of our ideas, of our Things—the things we pour our living into, the vast landscape or valley of Desire in the United States." Just as he had believed he could embody the people in himself, so ads could be visualized as a singularly identifiable Whitmanesque reflection of collective desires in magazines like *McClure's* or *Everybody's*.[25]

By 1905, several years after his series of articles on America as a crowd culture had appeared, and after entering into close association with Charles Ferguson, who had penned articles on "the genius of business," Lee set about writing ads for his own journal, *Mt. Tom*. Partly motivated by the financial rewards of advertising, he also became fascinated with the idea of imparting a new tone of personal familiarity to the readers of ads. Uninterested in becoming associated with an advertising agency, Lee preferred to remain a free agent—not a hired pen but a literary man composing advertisements that would read as well as, if not better than, the text of the magazines. In the November 1905 issue of *Mt. Tom,* he presented a few of his advertising principles designed to uplift the copy writer's stature. "An artist is a man who has the power of taking anything on earth he is interested in, stuffing it into a hundred words, and making other people feel about it the way he does." A great ad writer would never be a servant, but should reflect in his work his superior character, good taste, and his love of human nature. Clearly Lee was attempting to set a place for the inspired ad man at the tables of American financial power, using Whitman's democratic ideal as appetizer.[26]

Lee's view of the irrationality of the public, however, remained central to his thought. He appears to have bought the arguments put forth by Walter Dill Scott, a Northwestern University psychology professor who was gaining renown by promoting the principle of "ideodynamism," whereby techniques of imitation-suggestion psychology were used to induce people to buy certain products. Scott had in turn appropriated many of his ideas about social psychology from Le Bon's *The Crowd*. Scott, Le Bon, and Lee all believed it was a primary instinct of mankind to imitate those one considered to be social superiors. Scott and Lee felt application of this basic law of psychology could make advertising techniques more effective.[27]

Some of Lee's early ads treated readers merely as beings who would imitate those with higher status. Fear of social disapproval and jealousy of those with elevated tastes were psychological states of mind his copy projected to sell his clients' products. One must be respectable, fashionable, and hyper-conscious of other's opinions— this was the implicit message in most of his ads, a complete reversal of his earlier emphasis on Emersonian individualism. One of his ads, for instance, entitled "Social Philosophy," avowed,

> Everybody wants the same things that the people in the tier above them have. The people in the tier above them do not want everybody to have the same things that they have. They buy new ones. This is why we have new fashions. Being in fashion (in writing papers, for instance) requires: 1. Being at the top so that one can determine by merely looking around on what people at the top will do. 2. Being a prophet, so that one can foresee or guess what people at the top will do. 3. Buying one's fine writing papers from the Eaton-Hurlbut Company.

In an ad for the nearby Florence Manufacturing Company, which made toothbrushes, Lee wrote, "Wherever one is, look anywhere, among any class of people, for the best teeth. They are PROPHYLAC-TIC TEETH." Clever and conversational, Lee's ads drew upon the fear that people were always watching each other with a critical eye. The commodities one purchased were an extension of one's status. Although certainly not an inventor of this style of advertising, Lee showed a complete lack of concern over any ethical boundaries implied in such psychological manipulation.

That Lee was obsessed with advertising as a redemptive tool became clear in a letter he wrote to ad man John Powers on 5 October 1909.

> I would rather be an ad writer, and with the ad writer's stand, than to have a crown upon my forehead and a book within my hand . . . [T]he fate of the world is lying to-day in the hands of the men who can reveal and interpret their fellows, sketch them in big vivid words, and uncover

men to themselves, and to the world . . . And so far as business is concerned it is the ad writer—in the larger sense—who has his finger on the pulse of the time . . . I believe once more in words . . . The man who can build sky scrapers with a sentence and rolling mills with an adjective is the coming man . . . To make men believe things without even seeing them, to make them believe them . . . all with little quirks of ink on smooth paper which can be endlessly reproduced until they cover the earth—the man who can do this is priceless.

Powers was a modern Kipling, Lee felt, a man who used words to their greatest current effect. Trading on techniques similar to those he used with other businessmen—notably Edward Filene and Joseph Fels—Lee posed as their confidant, a man who possessed an inside track to the public mind and the future.[28]

One advertising man who shared Lee's belief in his prophetic powers over the public was Lord and Thomas ad man James Howard Kehler. Lee and Kehler complemented each other—one a belletrist, another a professional publicity agent—both seeking greater respectability for their parallel concerns. After the publication of *Inspired Millionaires,* Lee dangled the carrot of fame and power before Kehler when he wrote that "there are things that you and I in a common spirit could work out together which would be the making of both of us." The relationship was to be that of a prophet to a more practical worldly man.[29]

By November 1909, after Lee sought advice about publicizing his book, Kehler responded that "a work of art" could not be marketed in the same way as merchandise.

> The problem is simply to get free publicity and in order to get the most of this one must not only be a good writer, but an exceptionally good press agent for one's self and must be willing to devote a great deal of time to the cultivation of personal relationships which will insure wide-spread attention for whatever is done in the line of art. It is a problem which you must solve for yourself, so far as I can see and if I know you as well as I think I do, it is not one the solution of which appeals to you.

Kehler impressed upon Lee the idea that success as a writer required manipulating one's own image; it was a practical lesson to Lee in the art of the publicity agent, which went beyond the narrower traditional outlines of advertising. Lee's interest in press agentry, while not particularly novel, nonetheless harbored an intense yet changing evangelical vision.[30]

Lee's first statement about the new profession he called attention engineering was composed in 1910 and left unpublished under the title of "The Lords of Attention: A Study of Publicity in America." In 1916 it was partially incorporated into Lee's book *We*. In the existing fragment of this earlier piece Lee related that a major crystallization took place in his mind in early April 1910, while he was on the Twentieth Century Limited train between Chicago and New York, presumably after visiting Kehler. Lee was ecstatic about a new kind of publicity agent that he associated with Kehler. "I was going to write your life before you have lived it," he wrote to Kehler. "I shall gather it around you and haunt you with it and bathe your days and nights and it shall be a vow and a sacrament between us." Lee proposed that Kehler collaborate with him in producing a book that would have an important mission in the world. His romantic fantasies, however, were reaching an unstable and absurd level when he wrote: "Before all the world, between your heart and mine, you and I together will build our vision in stone and in mortar and in iron and in real men's daily lives and we shall write our love for each other and our hope for each other upon a Nation and upon the face of the earth."[31]

"The Lords of Attention" presents Lee's view of Kehler as an advanced agent of "goodness" in a newly elevated profession. Lee had been attracted to ad men because they took words seriously and "seemed to have discovered what words were for." He then observed that advertisements with style had been created by "good men" and those without any style were the products of financially motivated "bad men." If people rejected his product it was only because he had failed to express the thing that is good "as it is." An inspired advertiser had become the trustworthy intermediary between the producer and consumer, the person who decided the moral worth of material and spiritual things, acting as endowed priest and persuader.[32]

The persuader must above all believe in himself. "The man who wants greater power of persuasion than other men gets it by believing in persuasion," Lee declared. Persuasion was eminently practical and could be translated into dollars if one understood that "the literal hard business-like-market value of an advertisement on a printed page depends upon the amount of sincerity per square inch that can be gotten into it. An advertisement of an automobile that brings twenty thousand dollars worth of business might bring a hundred thousand, if the goodness in the man who writes it should happen to be twice as much and twice as lively and penetrating." Lee was formulating a creed of material success for those adept at exploiting the appearance of sincerity. It was a naively optimistic and tautological view: inspired millionaires hired wordsmiths to express the essence of a product to the consuming public. The market mechanism, when properly appreciated by all, would bring out the hidden "goodness" of mankind through consumerism; gratification without coercion.[33]

Lee's vague affinity to the Social Gospel movement led him to redefine Jesus' primary contribution to world history as a grand persuader. In *Crowds*, Jesus became the consensual hero, compelling attention to himself, a man possessing enormous egotism as well as a "simplicity and frankness" that projected a "sustained nobleness" through his dramatic persona. In one early sermon Lee wrote that Christ had seen that "his disciples loved him—and more than they did the Lord—and so used their love of him deliberately—as a language—and interpretation of God. He used himself as an illustration—he was a picture—of his conception." In *Crowds*, Jesus was cast as the ultimate public personality, a newsmaker, actor, organizer, and inspirational figure who would oppose modern egalitarians like Tolstoy, Marx, or Upton Sinclair. This rendition placed Jesus in tune with nature—a man of will power, yet sensitive to the masses. Jesus combined the qualities of cooperation and individualism. A nationalist and a creator of great publics, Jesus possessed an "instinct for psychology," as well as a "power of divining people's minds . . . which made possible to him those extraordinary feats in the way of telling short stories that would arrest and hold the attention of crowds so that they would think and live with them for weeks to come."[34]

In his early writings, Lee had pictured Jesus in terms of his intuitive fellowship with mankind and his ability to define men to themselves. He used this conception again and again as he identified Jesus as an attention engineer. By 1901, however, he wrote, in increasingly authoritarian tones, that "the crowd can only be made beautiful by a man who lives so great a life in it that he can make a crowd beautiful whether it allows him to or not." Jesus rationalized this notion by being the ultimate expression of the crowd's personality. "The one ability Christ had, that included all the others, was his ability to be all men in one,—the comprehensiveness of his temperament . . . The degree of a man's Christianity in any age may be exactly measured and counted off by the number of the kinds of men he can put himself in the place of. The Golden Rule was offered to the world as an ability . . . the one ability that can . . . ever make the crowd beautiful."[35]

Christ, as both representative and expression of the crowd's will, was thus able to support Lee's image of service to the crowd. The truly open personality, virtuous, charismatic, almost transparent as well as mesmerizing, could thus bring together the little, mean, and selfish crowds into one beautiful and righteous Crowd. "The Crowd is dumb, massive and silent," he wrote. "There seems to be no one in the world to express it, to express its indomitable desire, its prayer, to lay at last its huge, terrible, beautiful will upon the earth. It is the classes or little crowds—the little pulling and pushing, helpless, lonely, mean, separated crowds—blind, hateful, and afraid, who are running about trying to lay their little wills upon the earth." In other words, to Lee the good Crowd waited for its modern heroic redeemer, but the little separated crowds (more accurately he probably meant interest groups) were selfish and fearful obstructionists, subconsciously desirous of being part of the beautiful Crowd.[36]

Transposing his concept to a modern context, Lee added that Christ would have appreciated the work of the father of scientific management, Frederick Winslow Taylor. If Christ wanted to get businessmen to love one another "he would begin by trying to work out some technical, practical way in which certain particular men in a certain particular place could afford to love one another." Christ, to Lee, was thus a pragmatic as well as an approachable man. For example, "he would find a practical way for employers and pig-iron handlers in the Midvale Steel Works [Taylor's firm], to come to some sort of common understanding and to work cheerfully and with a free spirit together. I think he would proceed very much in the way that Frederick Taylor did." In these remarks Lee is implicitly criticizing a number of Social Gospellers and the muckrakers. He wrote that Christ would "not say much about the Golden Rule" but would "give each man a vision of his work and leave the Golden Rule a chance to take care of its self. This is all the Golden Rule, as a truth or as a remark, needs just now."[37]

The image of Jesus was becoming protean, imbued with Lee's conception of the updated Carlylean hero. Through Lee, one can also appreciate how traces of the Spencerian obsession with a ruthless competitiveness was becoming socialized. As Lee put it in a letter to journalist Lincoln Steffens in 1910: "The hero who takes you by the throat has been displaced by the hero who takes you by the arm and who so conducts himself that you will let him do it. Combination or cooperation is the tremendous heroism of our present life and this heroism is based upon human understanding, upon psychology, upon a vision or divination, a sublime guess upon what men really want and what they will be bound to have, in order to be happy." Cooperation and competition could develop alongside each other only through the agency of the thoroughly advertised modern hero. Lee had "come to believe," he added, "that hero worship in some form is one of the great elemental energies in human nature [and] must be served, that it must be regulated and used, that it has an incalculable power that we were meant to turn on to run the world with." The "hero habit" was a mechanism that should be extended into innumerable fields of endeavor.

> I believe in crowds and I believe that the more they have the hero habit, the more heroes they have to compare and select from, the finer, longer, and truer heroes they will select, the more deeply, truly, and concretely the crowds will think, and the more nobly they will express themselves . . . Appealing to the crowd's ideal of the beautiful in conduct, its sense of the heroic or semi-heroic, is the only practical, hard headed understanding way of getting out of the crowd, for the crowd, what the crowd wants.

In this era when movie stars were first becoming known and dramatic political and labor conflicts resounded through the daily newspapers, it is small wonder that Lee insisted that the public thought only in terms of great men or in "simple, big, broadly drawn events, or words of one syllable, like coal strikes."[38]

The cult of the hero remained an important ingredient to many advertising and publicity practitioners in the Progressive Era as they sought to demonstrate their skills of persuasion. Advertising men Ernest Calkins and Ralph Holden, for example, had found Napoleon the "fairest prototype" of their profession for his understanding of human nature, and of the power of the press, and for his organizing genius and tireless capacity for leadership. "Such men have gone into business," they related in 1905, and those who had found business commonplace in many instances had gone into the master field of business—advertising. Lee's parallel argument in *Crowds* and later in *We* (1916) was that the twentieth-century Napoleons were those who led armies of well-chosen words rather than soldiers; engineers of news, or attention, rather than ineffective local preachers. "We conquer now by getting inside of people and by getting inside first and then dealing with outside things together." The new heroes knew their battle lines, involved the public mind, and had no qualms about it.[39]

The 1913 prototype of Lee's heroic politician was, as it had been since 1905, Theodore Roosevelt. He had provided a glimpse of what a president could be, which was the "Comptroller of the people's vision" or the "Chancellor of the People's Attention." The president gave "at last the Face of the United States an expression!" Earlier, in "Lords of Attention" Lee had written that Roosevelt was a "highly concentrated extract" of the people at large—a Crowd Man. The example that best described Roosevelt was a picture in *Collier's* magazine in 1908 in which countless faces were massed together as dots in his face. It was, Lee wrote in 1910, impossible to overestimate the "moral market value of Mr. Roosevelt's skill in advertising anything he likes," for he was a "kind of P. T. Barnum for the United States," exuding his genius and energy to "vast circuses of people." In *Crowds* Lee expressed further hopes for presidents who would become "the organic function, the organizer of the news about our people to ourselves." He would be the "public made visible . . . a moving picture of us."[40]

"The business of being a President," he wrote, "is the business of focusing the vision, of flooding the whole desire or will of a people around a man and letting him have the light of it, to see what he is doing by, and be seen by, while he is doing it." The real power of the president came from his ability to advertise the national ideals instead of legislating them: he was "Head Advertising Manager" of the United States. Parodying Lincoln's Gettysburg Address, Lee went so far as to state that "the precise measure of the governing power a man can get out of the position of being President of the United States to-day is the amount of advertising for the people, of the people, and by the people he can crowd every morning, every week, into the papers of the country." The updated parson for the national community, the president would become "the great central, official editor of what the people are trying to find out—of a nation's news about itself. By his being president of what the people think, by his dictating the subjects the people shall take up, by his sorting out the men whom the people shall notice, this great ceaseless Meeting of ninety million men we call the United States—comes to order." If the trusts were a serious problem in the United States, a president only had to make an example or two of them, as Roosevelt had done. There was no need for extensive enforcement of the law, or checking on compliance through elaborate bureaucratic guidelines, or even lengthy discussion in the halls of Congress. The president just needed to say "Look." "The people who stop being theoretical and logical about each other," Lee wrote, "and who will look hard into each other's eyes will be the people whose ideas will come to pass."[41]

Labor disagreements, for instance, could be easily overcome by seeing them as news problems, circumvented by governmental manipulation of both public opinion and union members. "If a President were to appoint a Secretary of Labour," Lee wrote, "and were to give him as one of his conveniences, a news engineer—an expert at attracting and holding the attention of labor unions and driving through news to them about themselves that they do not know yet, who would be practically at the head of the department in two years? The Secretary or the Secretary's news engineer? News is all there is to such a department, finding out what it is and distributing it." Still contemptuous of Congresses that appeared to produce nothing but compromise, Lee maintained that a government without his sense of a positive vision was not really a government but a group of selfish politicians and lawyers. He had only scorn for such people: "Let the lawyers—the little swarms of dark-minded lawyers, wandering to and fro, creeping in offices, who have tried to run our world, blurred our governments, and buzzed, who have filled the world with piles of old paper, Congressional Records, with technicalities, words, droning, weariness, despair, and fear . . . let them come out and look! Let them catch up." They were, of course, being admonished to catch up specifically to corporations and the market mentality. Corporations had "expressed or focused the employers of labor" and labor unions had "focused or expressed the will of laborers," Lee claimed (contradicting his earlier assertion that union leaders did not speak for the true spirit of the individual workers). The government's role was to "focus and express the will of consumers, the will of the people as a whole, rich or poor, so that Capital and Labor [would] both listen to it, understand it and act on it."[42]

Crowds advised socially mobile men to recognize the primacy of a new field. It was both a self-help book for young men and a philosophical primer for business magnates seeking to rationalize their status. "In every business it is the man who can recognize, focus, organize and apply news, and who can get news through to people, who soon becomes the head of the business," Lee observed. The "salesman of news to people about what they want to buy and about how they are to spend their money—soon rises to be Head of the Factory." With all its verbosity, contradictions, and whimsical posturing, *Crowds* should be fundamentally understood as an elaborate rationale for a business aristocracy, supported by a sliding scale of civil liberties and allowed a preponderant influence in shaping public opinion.

> The first trait of a great government is going to be that it will recognize that the basis of a true government in a democracy is privilege and not treating all people alike . . . We will have rules or laws for people who need them, and men in the same business who amount to enough and are American enough to be safe as laws to themselves will continue to have their initiative and to make their business a profession, a mould, an art form into which they pour their lives. The pouring of the lives of men like this into their business is the one thing that the business and the government want.

Discrimination and inequality became the hallmarks of a government that dispensed a two-tiered system regulating only the working classes; those proving their worth by the wealth they had made were left to pursue their initiatives.[43]

Lee pleaded for the admirers of Hamilton, Emerson, Jefferson, and Marx to outgrow them. He hoped that the new president in the White House, Woodrow Wilson, might measure up to his ideal. "If we have a poet in the White House, this is the main fact he is going to reckon with: he will not be seen taking sides with the Alexander Hamilton model or with the Thomas Jefferson model or with Karl Marx or Emerson." He will melt them all down, "glowing them and fusing them together into one man—the Crowd Man—who shall be more aristocratic than Hamilton ever dreamed, and be filled with a genius for democracy that Jefferson never guessed."[44]

The harmony Lee advocated in extirpating all democratic discord and disagreement was thus achieved by cooperation among strong individuals who retained the power—through attention engineering—to command agreement from all citizens. He called for "search parties" to work within a nation that was "wired throughout" to "establish the current between the people and the books, to discover the people one by one and follow them to their homes, and follow them in their lives, and take out the latent geniuses." Carnegie's method of donating libraries had become insufficient. It was only by "employing forces that can be made extremely small, invisible, personal, penetrating, and spiritual," he alleged, "that this sort of work can be done." Above all, the rewards flowing from Lee's vision of compulsion and persuasion would create a spiritual unity for the nation and provide material success for those who had the right vision.[45]

The engineers of news or attention would steer a nationalistic congregation from inside their heads. Years before Lippmann gave a more sophisticated and critical treatment of this idea in *Public Opinion*, Lee wrote that "the art of steering heads inside, which has come to be the secret art of all the other arts, the secret religion of all the religions, is also the secret of building and maintaining a civilization and a successful permanent business." Any feelings of class antagonism would be negated by controlling the images people absorbed. Fundamentally, however, he was appealing to the business elite in terms that played on their fear of labor violence and strikes that might threaten the capitalist system. "It is hard to believe," he wrote, "how largely, for the last twenty years it has been overlooked by employers as the real key to the labor problem—this art of steering people's heads inside."[46]

Crowds provided a summation of the ideal of the inspired millionaire, and an extension of Lee's preaching mentality into the burgeoning fields of public relations and advertising. The book has largely been overlooked by historians charting the rise of the "profession" because Lee is considered to be a literary man and not an ad man. His is a unique and quirky expression of the high Progressive Era. Yet Lee always remained tentative. To Louis Brandeis, for example, Lee admitted that "of course 'Crowds' is not a literal book but I do not want to swerve from the spirit of the facts." Yet, he had very high hopes for its reception. To Theodore Roosevelt, on the day *Crowds* was published, Lee wrote that he had wanted "to express the universal human background—this time—and sketch a nation and then let people line up into parties themselves"; he had wanted to put "into a book the spirit of the new [Progressive] movement."[47]

In June 1913 *Crowds* was published in both the United States and England; it went through numerous editions and was condensed into a thin volume entitled *Crowds Jr.* a year later. It would up as the best-selling nonfiction book of 1913. The reaction to the book exhibits the convergence of reform thought and business evangelism in the late Progressive Era. Writers like Walter Lippmann, Lincoln Steffens, Van Wyck Brooks, Vachel Lindsay, and Randolph Bourne, publicity men such as Ivy Lee and Carl Byoir, numerous businessmen, novelists, and politicians saw Gerald Lee as the spokesman for a business culture led by news engineers, inventors, inspired millionaires, and charismatic political personalities. Progressive businessman E. A. Filene thought that the book was prophetic of a new type of public man. Although Lee was occasionally chastised for his turgid writing style, the opacity of his ideals, his egoism, and the implausibility of his solutions for industry, even those opposed to his ideas noted his mystical appeal.[48]

Ten years before *Crowds* was published, Lee had written that "a true book does not go about advertising itself, huckstering for souls, arranging its greatness . . . It waits." Lee had waited a long time for the greatness that he felt was due him. To have the reading public buy *Crowds* and make it a fulcrum for national discussion was his fervent wish. Toward that end, he turned to Kehler's advertising talents to make the book a bible for the Progressive movement. Through ads in prominent newspapers, testimonials, and publicity stunts, the book became widely discussed in the summer and fall of 1913. *Inspired Millionaires* had reached a wide audience in England in the previous year or so—the result, in part, of Lee's promotion of it during his extended visit in 1912. So he now had himself promoted as a man with an international reputation. It is curious that it took an effort at mass manipulation to sell a book on mass manipulation.[49]

The impact of Lee's book on religious leaders was divided between those who could or could not indulge his embrace of business and efficiency as the central concerns of Jesus. Many ministers, including his own father, saw Lee's characterization of Jesus as a news engineer as blasphemous. Serious proponents of the Social Gospel (whose correspondence with Lee seems to fall off by about 1913) were beginning to see his antilabor bias more clearly. Yet many Protestant ministers, including public relations man Ivy Lee's father, quoted long passages from Lee's book in their sermons.[50]

The influence of Whitman in *Crowds* struck many readers. Frank Lloyd Wright and Louis Sullivan had read Lee and commented favorably about his Whitmanesque democratic vision. From England, the *New Statesman* claimed that Lee was "the modern incarnation of the spirit of Whitman," although the reviewer also affirmed that throughout the United States he had "encountered commonplace embodiments of that audacious spirit, men who talked in large, vague terms about fellowship, individualism, national self-consciousness, and the genial love of your neighbor—men who dwelt at length on the subject of teeming cities, tilled fields, and pioneers of progress." "Braggadocio" was considered to be a peculiarly American quality that was "demanded from preachers and orators." The *Brooklyn Eagle,* the paper where Whitman had worked, noted that "Whitman wrote before the modern world of machines had been organized and exploited for the benefit of the exploiters," adding that there was a "large field in which his primal warwhoop for a man's soul and democracy [could] be amplified and applied to concrete conditions. That is the field which Lee fills, if not entirely, yet more conspicuously and hopefully than anybody else." Perhaps it was the reviewer for the *Springfield Republican* that caught the essential discrepancy between Whitman and Lee when he commented that "in truth they are very different in their attitude towards the average man. To Walt, the crowd and the people in it were good enough and [he] was of them; Mr. Lee on the other hand says: The average man in a crowd does not want to be an average man, and the last thing he wants is to have an average man represent him. He wants a man to represent him as he would like to be."[51]

American magazine and newspaper reviews were mixed. The *Independent* said that even though Lee wrote "panegyrics" about both crowds and machines "in a staccato style that enraptures some readers and exasperates others," he was a man who could, nonetheless "see more than most people." Wallace Rice of *The Dial* exalted what he saw as its democratic optimism. Charles Shinn, the reviewer for the *San Francisco Star,* saw Lee's resemblance to Carlyle. *Crowds* was a "brilliant restatement of Carlyle's masterful doctrine—that machines and crowds must be run by great men." It was no wonder that "lots of business leaders are said to be giving copies to their employees, and that dozens of reviewers have shouted, for it is the unanswerable word against Socialism and the howling have-nots." Shinn concluded, however, that "some of us think the Carlylean philosophy of [the] last century is belated," and wished that "this brilliant writer knew more about inspired co-operators." Floyd Dell, writing in the *Chicago Evening Post,* claimed that Lee's accomplishment was "something comparable to what Kipling did in the nineties, when he made us see the romance of steam, and the loyalties and codes of soldiers and department officials." Lee's specialty was in seeing "the romance of business, and the codes and loyalties which bind together the great industrial fabric." When not eloquent, however, Lee was deemed "a little absurd" and "uncritical to the last degree"; in sum the "apotheosis of the advertising man."[52]

The book had a verbal charm for writers like Hamlin Garland and Jack London. Garland wrote Lee that "from the standpoint of the optimistic democrat [*Crowds*] is an inspiration to gay and fearless thinking." In a letter to James Kehler which was forwarded to Lee, Jack London, in a style reminiscent of Lee's, revealed from his Glen Ellen ranch in Sonoma, California: "I swore by Gerald Stanley Lee before I ever entered the writing game. I have sworn by him through all my years of the writing game, and to-day, reading his book, "Crowds," I swear by him more than ever. His style is tingling and electric. Also, and more to the point, he KNOWS. What I like about him is that he sees the present, past, and the future all in a radiant vision." London may well have appropriated some of the ideas about crowds that Lee expressed in his early *Atlantic Monthly* articles; his novels fairly bristle with descriptions of packs and mob instincts.[53]

After he had read *Crowds,* Edward A. Filene wrote to Lee, "Your book, or if it is too early yet, some day a trumpet note like it, will martial the big men of the world to make it a big man's world." Yet while Lee extolled Filene for his inspired leadership in *Crowds* and undoubtedly appreciated Filene's compliments, he refused to lend his own name to support an arbitration board that Filene & Sons had set up in 1913. To one letter of inquiry from a Filene subordinate, Lee responded that if workers in the store could only look through clear moral looking glasses they "would be their own arbitration boards" most of the time and "discipline themselves."[54]

Aside from Kehler's publicity and the book reviews, *Crowds* gained attention in a number of other ways. The New York Telephone Company sent out a notice to its subscribers bearing a quotation from it. A self-help book, *The Art of Public Speaking* by Dale Carnegie and J. Berg Esenwein, opened one chapter on "influencing the crowd" with a quotation from Lee's book, asserting that "success in business, in the last analysis, turns upon touching the imagination of crowds." The book further advised its readers to "get the most and the best out of the crowd-spirit" or to transform an "audience into a crowd" by "unifying the minds and needs of the audience and arousing their emotions. Their feelings, not their reason, must be played upon." Logical arguments had their place on the speaker's platform, "but even its potencies must subserve the speaker's plan of attack to win possession of his audience." Carnegie and Esenwein's book shows the influence of Walter Dill Scott and Gustave Le Bon, as well as the religious sanction which Lee provided in rationalizing the control of crowd behavior.[55]

Not surprisingly, ad men were often ecstatic about the book that had elevated their "profession" to a higher plane than that occupied by either the law or the ministry. It was publicity expert Ivy Lee, however, who showed the scope and subtlety of *Crowds* in reconciling crowd theory and democratic idealism to a business-dominated culture. Generally considered to have invented public relations as a concept, Ivy Lee was highly impressed with the ideas of his second cousin for several years. Gerald's professed idealism sanctioned the publicity agent's work as public service.[56]

Gerald's influence was most evident in an important speech Ivy made in the spring of 1914 to the American Railroad Guild, later reprinted in book form as *Human Nature and Railroads*. The speech leaves little doubt about several sources behind Ivy's conceptions of crowds. Lincoln was quoted as saying that the "crowd" had become "enthroned" as the new sovereign with "courtiers who flatter and caress precisely as did those who surrounded medieval emperors." These courtiers, Ivy added, "are sedulously cultivating the doctrine that to be weak is to be good, and that to be strong is to be bad." Railroad men had to understand the psychology of the multitude if they were to "assume the place to which they are entitled as leaders of the public." Above all, Ivy maintained, a public must be emotionally aroused through the use of convincing and dramatic facts, however trivial they might seem. "The public is disposed to take little incidents and to talk about them, and from these small incidents judge the whole." Use this form of personalism to counter the appeal of muckrakers, he was admonishing them.[57]

Gerald Lee's ideas were also attractive to several people connected with the theater and film industries. His expectant modernism and democratic idealism, his dramatic pictures of crowds, and his fervent search for heroic personalities to channel the mentality of the masses all spoke to several contemporary cultural currents. Those pushing civic pageants and the civic theater movement, then in their heyday, had also sought to create grand forums to persuade and guide the masses toward proper American ideals. Percy Mackaye, for example, a leading proponent, used religious language similar to Lee's when describing the groundswell of idealism and artistry that could combine to create new "cathedrals of expression."[58]

Similar themes of civic redemption through righteous crowds were also projected in a number of D. W. Griffith's films, especially "Intolerance," a film that Griffith hoped would help Woodrow Wilson's reelection bid in 1916. While I have found no evidence that Griffith ever read Lee's work, the final scenes in both "The Birth of a Nation" and "Intolerance" find dramatic tension resolved in celestial-like scenes with massive groups of people mingling in harmonic bliss around Christian totems. One can begin to appreciate the cinematic quality of Lee's work more precisely, however, through the poet and film critic Nicholas Vachel Lindsay. Readers of Lindsay's book, *The Art of the Moving Picture,* were warned that Lee was "far from infallible in his remedies for factory and industrial relations." What dazzled Lindsay was Lee's "sensitiveness to the flowing street of humanity." Reflecting his own Whitmanesque predilections, Lindsay declared that nations and races were the "total gestures of crowds." Like Lee, Lindsay was an optimist and believed that "as we peer into the Mirror Screen, some of us dare to look forward to the time when the pouring streets of men will become sacred in each other's eyes, in pictures and in fact."[59]

Both Lee and Lindsay yearned for a civic unity modeled on an older, spiritually based community. Both used various versions of the crowd metaphor to explain the meaning of collective life in modern times. What the nation needed, both felt, were films that could re-create the festivals and dramatic rituals that had sustained the spiritual life of ancient Athens. That, of course, was precisely what Mackaye and the civic pageant movement was all about as well.

Aside from Lindsay, there were other visual modernists with whom Lee resonated rather closely. Lee was attracted to the lively, irreverent Italian Futurists with their acquiescent attitude toward modernism and political heroics. While introducing a copy of the Manifesto of the Futurists in *Mt. Tom* in 1914, Lee declared that he found the manifesto too strident for his own taste. It nonetheless reflected his own attraction to visual shock, his accommodation with the frenetic energy of industrialism, and the use of spectacle to galvanize attention. Extolling "aggressive movement" and the "beauty of speed," the manifesto finds true glory in the "man at the steering wheel, whose ideal . . . transfixes the Earth, rushing over the circuit of her orbit." It continues: "We shall sing of the great crowds in the excitement of labour, pleasure or rebellion, of the multi-coloured and polyphonic surf of revolutions in modern capital cities. . . ; of the greedy stations swallowing smoking snakes; of factories suspended from the clouds by their strings of smoke . . . and the gliding flight of aeroplanes, the sound of whose screws is like the flapping of flags and the applause of an enthusiastic crowd." Like the Futurists, Lee attempted to accomplish an impossible task, placing the spectator in the center of the picture instead of merely arranging figures and objects in a line of vision. Lee had neither the wit nor the critical frame of mind to see the regimentation implicit in these ideas, how crowds could also be outlets for deep-seated alienation, a condition that an artist such as James Ensor and later the writer Nathanael West were to see with greater clarity.[60]

Few critics were able to explain what was precisely so wrong about Lee's notions. The most effective analysts were three writers who would have a strong influence on educated opinion in years to come. H. L. Mencken savaged *Crowds* because Lee's style seemed pretentious and masked a lot of outdated ideas. *Crowds*, said Mencken, was

filled to the brim with vague, windy mush. [Lee] . . . clothes common-place—and often downright silly—thoughts in ornate and stuffy garments, and so gives them a false air of importance. He is always announcing the obvious in terms of the revolutionary, and with all the trappings of a blood-tub dime novel. The astounding discovery that every man has a Theory of the World—why does he overlook weltan-schaung, that juicy term?—is set off in a separate paragraph . . . The author describes for us, with great particularity, just where and when this or that Great Thought was hatched in him.

Mencken chided Lee for maintaining that America was a tune, and warned his readers that the odds were that *Crowds* would have a "large sale in our fair republic" and that the "virgin" reviewers would hail the author of "a profound and penetrating thinker." But not Mencken. He was angry at the popularity of New Thought authors like Lee, adding:

The way to get a reputation for sagacity is to translate platitudes into mystical rumblebumble. That exhorter whose meaning is plain at first hearing, that propagandist who thinks his thoughts out clearly and puts them into sound and simple English, has a hard time catching the crowd. The taste for the moment is for more subtle and puzzling stuff—for nonsensical gabble about Avatars, Oversouls and Zeitgeists, for copy-book maxims with their eyebrows penciled and feathers stuck in their hats, for long rows of meaningless italics and capitals, for mellow Mae-terlinckain cadenzas on penny whistles.

Mencken was outraged that the work of writers like Lee and Orison Swett Marden outsold T. H. Huxley's essays, adding that "Americans show a childish weakness for sonorous and empty words, for the shallow trick of typography."[61]

Perhaps it was Van Wyck Brooks's essay "The Precipitant," published in 1915, that came closest to uncovering the tenuous position that Lee had attempted to occupy with his ideals of the "inspired millionaire" and "the attention engineer." Brooks's essay was a paean to the influence of Whitman, the man who, he wrote, "precipitated the American character" by combining so many incoordinate pieces into "a fresh democratic ideal, based upon the whole personality." Whitman created an ideal which aimed to foster an "emotional attitude" of a "perfectly free personality" but had avoided social constraints. A series of "spurious social ideals" had emerged from the Whitmanians, Brooks continued:

> The more dangerous the more plausible, and even the more "American" they are. One of these, and perhaps the most typical, is that of the "inspired millionaires," which has had such a vogue during these later years, and which, for all its tincture of "privilege", has many of the traits of Whitmanism. Just as Carlyle's Hero may be taken as a projection of what the typical Englishman seems to aspire to be, a sort of Lord Cromer with a halo, just as Nietzsche's Superman is a projection of what the typical modern German long struggled to be, a sort of Bismarck with a halo, so the "inspired millionaire" is a projection of what the typical American apparently struggles to be, a sort of Henry Ford with a halo. It is the type towards which the personal forces of the generality of Americans appear to be directed, heightened and justified as an ideal.

Nonetheless, Brooks found Lee's ideal to have a certain validity, for business was the "most engaging activity in American life."[62]

Brooks's main objection to the ideal of the "inspired millionaire" was that it was not disinterested, nor was it based upon a coherent moral program for the individual. To be an "inspired millionaire" was an ideal that "plainly contradicts itself. For although a man may be disinterested after he has become a millionaire, it is a quite impossible, except through inheritance . . . to be disinterested during the process of becoming. . . . [A] millionaire is itself not a moral entity like heroism or superhumanity: it is a situation, and a situation moreover that is not the inevitable result of any kind of activity, even the activity of a genius for acquisition." Nevertheless, Brooks found Lee's ideal to be a "landmark and a touchstone," for it was in the "direct line of the American tradition[;] it is the climax of our old Transcendental individualism. It springs, like the flower of the century plant, right out of the apparent heart, right out of the apparent centre, of American society." Lee's concepts fed the paradoxical, peculiarly American condition in which the "mind of a nation is given over, in a potentially disinterested mood, to an essentially self-interested activity!"[63]

Later, Brooks apologized to Lee for his comments. Nonetheless, Lee had provided an example for Brooks's explanation of the low state of critical thought in modern American culture. According to his biographer, Brooks understood that "Lee had enough intelligence to see that something was wrong with the social system and enough courage to attempt to offer a new ideal. But in the absence of a school of rigorous critical thought to force him to think straight and see that socialism was the logical conclusion of his premises, he was at the mercy of his sentimental Yankee individualism." By affirming everything, Lee, like Whitman, had failed to distinguish between the ideal of the liberated personality and the real social and economic structures within which all Americans existed. Brooks found this typical of Americans' dangerous intellectual confusion.[64]

Walter Lippmann, writing in *Drift and Mastery* (1914), found Lee's ideas to be out of touch with the modern economic reality that separated ownership from management. Lee's paternalistic capitalism was deemed a simplistic solution for America, in that "workers, politicians, consumers and the rest are to have no real part in the glorious revolution which is to be consummated for their benefit . . . Those who have seen the change in business motives have, I believe, good ground for rejoicing, but they might in decency refrain from erecting upon it a mystic and rhetorical commercialism." Lippmann took a tack different from Brooks's, however, when he indirectly attacked Lee's rationalization of advertising as a tool of business. Advertising was the "weed that has grown up because the art of consumption is uncultivated" and involved the "effort of business men to take charge of consumption as well as production." Business-men were not "content to supply a demand, as the textbooks say; they educate the demand as well. In the end, advertising rests upon the fact that consumers are a fickle and superstitious mob, incapable of any real judgement as to what it wants or how it is to get what it thinks it would like. A bewildered child in a toy shop is nothing compared to the ultimate consumer in the world market of today." To posit that advertising was "merely a way of calling attention to useful goods," which many theorists, like Lee, had been doing, struck Lippmann as a "gorgeous piece of idealization." Lippmann welcomed the future role of consumers as an interest group, capable of pressuring government and becoming a force to reckon with in society, though he increasingly believed that scientifically trained experts ought to rule modern America.[65]

Mencken, Brooks, and Lippmann all testify to the popularity of Lee's ideals among business and religious circles. Their sharp criticism of his book signaled the rise of a more critical intellectual generation that was carrying less transcendental baggage from the nineteenth century, a generation that would lead the widespread attack on so-called Puritanism by the 1920s. However mistakenly *Crowds* might have been grasped, it was nonetheless an important reference for many Progressive intellectuals and business leaders. Lincoln Steffens, perhaps using utmost tact, wrote to Lee that reading *Crowds* had been a "pleasure," while Louis Brandeis labeled it "brilliant." But the accolades from friends and others whom Lee pestered in promoting his work over the years would not last. Over time, his work increasingly became the object of ridicule. J. Ward Moorehouse, the public relations counsel in John Dos Passos's novel *The 42nd Parallel,* mouthed the platitudes he had read from *Crowds Jr.;* Upton Sinclair, in *The Brass Check,* wrote that he had "made a fortune and a reputation for Doubleday Page & Co. which imme-diately became one of the most conservative publishing houses in

America—using 'The Jungle' money to promote . . . the sociological bunkum of Gerald Stanley Lee."[66]

If one reads the political rhetoric of many Progressives in the 1910s or the advocates of crowd psychology, the civic pageant movement, or business evangelists, one can detect a widespread view that characterized the American public as crowdlike by those who so often acted as their champions. The writings of Gerald Stanley Lee present us with a perspective with which to view the fragile Progressive ethos in the year or two before the shots fired in Sarajevo. "If our preachers are not saving us, our business men will," Lee had written hopefully in *Crowds*. He had found compensation from his own failure in the pulpit by creating a business ideology of wide scope, great momentary impact, and little logical consistency. After a number of twists and turns, his use of the crowd metaphor helped legitimize the emerging professions of advertising and public relations; his modern hero finally found a face. "The imagination of crowds is convinced only by men who have real genius for expression," he declared, "for making word pictures of real things [and] . . . moving picture minds." Businessmen of the 1920s responded favorably to similar blandishments from Bruce Barton and Elmo Calkins, in part because prewar writers like Lee had paved the way, acting as transitional figures for an evangelism that made the management of public opinion seem so essential to capitalist expansion and American identity.[67]

SEVEN

"The Soul of Advertising Is the Soul of America": The Final Years of Gerald Stanley Lee (1914–1942)

By 1916, twenty years after he resigned from the pulpit, Gerald Lee had become more hopeful about advertising men than about preachers, because, he wrote, "as a class they are more spiritually robust about their profession. Most advertising men act as if they believed in persuasion more than most preachers do." Advertising men lived by the rule of the market: when they failed to attract attention they accepted their fate of dismissal by their clients. Ironically, as a New England preacher turned prophet of what he labeled attention engineering, Lee was in the process of becoming anachronistic to his own age, eclipsed by a younger, more specialized generation.[1]

After *Crowds* was published, Lee's stature had risen across the country. He was asked to address a number of prestigious businessmen's groups and was inducted into the Players Club for writers in New York. His notions seemed to be fulfilled by the new policies of Henry Ford and other evidence of welfare capitalism sponsored by large corporations and groups such as the National Civic Federation. By 1914 he became a popular weekly columnist for the *New York World*. After twenty years of obscurity, the former parson was beginning to reach the dual audiences he had always sought: the elite men of wealth and power as well as the diverse public. Meeting and corresponding with powerful people, Lee was seeking to translate his self-professed knowledge of human nature and the techniques of crowd persuasion into an attractive commodity to be bartered for national influence. Into this hopeful period of Lee's life, however, a

more complex and violent reality intruded that mocked any lingering romantic idealism.

Events from 1914 to 1917 reinforced the perception of the public
as irrational and herdlike, possessing crowd minds, ostensibly proving the popular theories of Le Bon, Tarde, Ross, and many others. In
1915 a writer for the *Springfield Republican,* while discussing war
preparations, saw little around him but "the insanity of the crowd."
One could read articles and books about "herd instincts" and the
public-as-crowd in journals of all political persuasions, as an older,
more genteel view of American individualism confronted machine
guns, barbed wire, and tanks. An important book published in 1915
by British writer Wilfred Trotter was entitled *Instincts of the Herd in
Peace and War,* positing biological analogies and simplistic social
typing of national characteristics. By the 1920s notions about a
crowdlike public had become widely disseminated, although more
and more analysts began using Freudian or behaviorist conceptions.[2]

The Great War provided an expanded stage for many Americans
to act out their fantasies of social cohesion and national regeneration through organized collective behavior. For his part, while at the
pinnacle of his power, Lee expressed growing desperation to solidify
his prophesies by conjuring up grandiose schemes of national regeneration. Rival suitors—from social scientists and business journalists to experts in advertising and religious salesmanship—promoted seemingly more sophisticated ideas about crowds and public
opinion. But Lee's writings still reveal the outlines of a preaching
mentality that wouldn't stop.

From the outset of the war Lee remained a sidelines critic, urging
powerful men to find better ways to confront the chaotic world than
with guns. America's best defense, Lee argued, was an advertising
offense; the nation should sell itself through relentless advertising of
its goods in foreign countries. As he wrote in the *New York Evening
Post,* both the government and private business should spend "hundreds of millions of dollars to tell what we are like," which he was
convinced would prove more profitable for the country than "a
massive overbuilding of armies and navies." Writer G. K. Chesterton

criticized Lee's ideas for being influenced by the semipacifistic school of thought which "admits that he cannot really blame any of the combatants and therefore proceeds to blame all of them."[3]

Lee gathered the material he published in various magazines along with his newspaper columns into a 740-page volume he entitled *We: A Confession of Faith for the American People during and after War. A Study of the Art of Making Things Happen.* The book was published in the spring of 1916, after his cousin Ivy Lee made special arrangements, despite a strike, to have the Pennsylvania Railroad move enough paper to print it. In this repetitious and topical discussion, Lee addressed such subjects as Carnegie's peace campaign (which he opposed), Ford's automobile factories (which he found to be examples of his own industrial prescriptions), and Roosevelt's bellicosity (Lee's judgment was that the bellicose former president was no longer a good attention engineer). He praised Woodrow Wilson for his idealism and John D. Rockefeller, Jr., for being seen dressed in overalls with his workers in Colorado after the Ludlow disaster.

Lee claimed that the origins of the war had arisen from the Europeans' failure to adequately communicate with each other, leading to the use of violence as a language. The war's ultimate cause was based on the "failure of our machines for expressing our real selves." Machines had gotten ahead of words and the war was "a stupendous breakdown of the European languages." Peace was defined as an "energy of mutual attention, a genius for pursuing and overtaking mutual interest," while militarism kept people "in holds where they cannot see [so] that they shall be ready to die when the order is shouted down to them." Peace could be maintained by organizations like that headquartered at the Hague Peace Palace or by the creative appreciation of the market mechanism as practiced in the United States. "Getting people to want ideas they do not want is like any other kind of salesmanship," involving the ability to interrupt people who might not think they want to be interrupted. But, as Lee had demonstrated in *Crowds,* certain "good" people had the right to "interrupt" the public.[4]

Advertising continued to serve as the secular arm of Lee's religious sensibility, supplanting face-to-face persuasion by less direct means of communication while preserving the broad rhetoric of his idealism. Picking out the words for ads had become the "greatest . . . most . . . terrific power in modern life and the most noble and colossal of all the professions." Great advertising had developed a religion of its own, the spiritual secret of civilization, he felt, while it remained based on the example of Christ. Publicity, which Lee now defined as "the art of persuading crowds, of fertilizing and organizing what people see, and creating the visions as to what they shall be and what they shall have," was destined to be great art as well. "The art of attention, of organizing, of massing, of composing the picture of every man's thoughts, is the . . . most determining art form of modern times." Men involved in it had their fingers on the "motor nerve" of mass attention. Bruce Barton would repeat much of what Lee said—albeit in fewer words—ten years later.[5]

Extending the analysis first published in *The Shadow Christ*, Lee asserted that if Isaiah had only possessed the capital to promote his ideas, Israel would have been saved from destruction. The modern Israel, America, had to save itself by appreciating the fact that the "soul of advertising [is] the soul of America." The spirit animating America's great inventions such as the telegraph and the Atlantic cable manifested a special national mission to facilitate worldwide communication by using the most modern forms. World peace would inevitably follow as the full benefits of the consumer society became fully appreciated; the United States would then fulfill its historical role as a beacon to the world by illustrating the beauties of the democratic market mechanism.[6]

The best material symbol of Lee's nationalistic advertising ideal was the automobile. With the automatic appeal of the earlier moral show window, the modern automobile factory of Henry Ford was the prototype for all future industry. Henry Ford's assembly line dispensed mass-produced dreams of consumer fulfillment and cultural melioration. Millions of Ford cars "go rolling, whispering, almost softly shouting through the streets how he treats his public and how he treats his men." Ford's Sociological Department was applauded for creating workers into more efficient machines. Ford possessed the "We-vision" and "We-Spirit" and "We-Will" to educate the nation in mutuality and interdependence. Yet Lee never showed concern for the workers' dignity, then being steadily undermined by the paternalistic intrusion into their private lives by agents of the Sociological Department. Although he didn't state it, he would have been ecstatic about Ford's "Melting Pot" drama in which workers became Americanized through a theatrical rendition that saw them shedding their native clothes and emerging from a huge pot with American flags.[7]

Aside from the automobile, the most useful human purveyor of dreams remained Lee's updated hero. By 1916 movie stars and sports heroes were becoming marketed as national phenomena; the faces of Charlie Chaplin, Mary Pickford, and Douglas Fairbanks were familiar throughout the nation. Experiencing such phenomena in the movie theaters of Northampton, Lee began to demythologize his heroic ideal; fame became an end in itself, a prosaic commodity that crowds themselves insisted on having as "advertisements for themselves," he felt. "Crowds seem to be seized by some kind of unfathomable, elemental passion for compact self-revelation, self-consciousness, self-expression," he added. Famous men ultimately reflected the irrationality and narcissism of crowd men. Famous men functioned as a nation's "luxuries, or orgies," serving in a representative capacity as a peg to hang the wandering minds of a crowd and pull its attention together. "Making a man famous is like smoking for a crowd's nerves," Lee wrote. Extending ideas he had first written in *Crowds,* Lee wrote that national salvation was predicated on appreciating how crowds and famous men interacted. The public was a primitive emotional beast which needed to be controlled by the managed use of famous men. Fire, as energy and a symbolic form of common attention, was what the commodified hero needed to appropriate. People looking at a fire together "converge in the flames and enjoy it. A great man is a kind of crowd fireplace," he wrote. Of course the members of a crowd so envisioned could all be expected to observe the fire in a room which Lee dominated. He was the hidden hero seeking to galvanize public attention.[8]

To a variety of correspondents, Lee demonstrated an increasingly self-referential and imperious attitude that was only dimly muted by self-deprecating humor. The publishing success of *Crowds* and the prominence of his newspaper columns fed his hopes for the publishing success of *We.* By 1915, however, Lee exhibited increasing des-

peration for power and influence, cogently expressed in his correspondence with "cousin" Ivy Lee, who from 1914 to 1916 was a
publicity adviser to the Rockefeller family. Ivy sought to dampen
criticism of the Rockefellers following the Ludlow Massacre. Many
liberals and socialists now saw him as a horrible ogre, but not
Gerald. Writing to Ivy in late March 1916 Gerald illuminates a
growing strain between the two, and provides a glimpse of his
growing megalomania. The humorous use of overstatement, which
may have charmed many, was discarded as Gerald revealed the true
intentions of his life's work. "I have invented the next five hundred
years of my country," he declared, "and I want my invention advertised and organized, promoted and put on the market." His invention consisted of his divinely inspired vision of the proper relationship between business, the public, and technology in modern life.

> If I am able by the personal daily persistent use of my invention to make
> my own career and what I believe and what I do with it a determining
> and dominating factor in American national life, everybody as a matter
> of course will soon be daily using as a driving force in business the
> spirit . . . I have wagered all I have or could be on . . . [O]nly the man
> who is better than himself . . . only the man who is a superman toward
> himself and a free servant toward others, can hope to win a permanent
> happy or inevitable success under the conditions of modern life.

This statement was but the appetizer before the main course as the
former parson extended an invitation to another parson's son. Gerald continued: "We plan the founding of a new profession and the
introduction of a new art, the art of making things happen, the
control of business and affairs and the government of the world
through advertising, through the power of attracting, holding and
organizing the attention and the vision of men."[9]

He was, of course, identifying the concept of public relations—as
Edward Bernays would later define it—and as Ivy Lee, in 1916, was
already practicing it. Gerald attempted to attach himself through Ivy
to the Rockefeller family and their fortune. *We* was going to make
Rockefeller "ten times the man he thinks he is" if only Ivy would
help Gerald to formulate Rockefeller's "greater career in the public
understanding and in the public will." Ivy had done the "initial
work"; what was needed was to have "some disinterested person

with the ear of the public and in the foreground of the public mind standing by ready to interpret it." Hand the control of Rockefeller's reputation over to me and we will both make a mountain of money became Gerald's message in no uncertain terms. "I am soon going to be in a position to turn over, and am going to be practically obliged to turn over to the men I believe in, opportunities which are beyond computation. It is necessary for me to do what I do and say what I say without reference to money in order to make it most effective, and yet I cannot see finished what I wish to do without creating and handing over opportunities for others to make money on every hand, and I shall have to be searching for the men to do it." Ivy was admonished to consider the time he devoted to Gerald Lee as an "investment," and he warned him to "deal with me and with my religion and with my art on a par with the Pennsylvania Railway and the Rockefeller fortune." While striving to elevate his own status as prophet, Gerald was gambling that Ivy needed the spiritual rationale for his work badly enough to cement this alliance. He was wrong.[10]

By 1916 the management of public communications had achieved legitimacy in all its essentials and didn't need the religious gloss provided by a frustrated former parson. The voice of Gerald Lee was fading from the ears of the powerful. His final words to Ivy were bold, yet greedy, and have a pathetic ring to them. "There has never been such a partnership as yours and mine in the world before," Gerald avowed, "one in which either of us would need to bargain with the other because our careers are helplessly, implacably wrought in with one another and we are as necessary to each other to express our full selves as vowels and consonants."[11]

About the time that Gerald was transmitting his proposition to Ivy (whose response is not recorded) he privately expressed a sinking feeling about the popular reception to *We.* (The book turned out to be a flop, with sales totaling only 5,194 as of February 1917.) In his diary Gerald wrote that "for the moment, being in the midst as I am of the difficult feat of waiting for the country to do something to me instead of doing things to the country, I hardly know who I am." His career was in serious jeopardy. If he, a man who had glorified advertising and the ability to command attention, a man who had pulled off a publishing coup with *Crowds,* was not able to make a splash with his new book, then the unique role he had created for himself might be repudiated as well. He would lose the wager of his life.[12]

After musing that perhaps he took himself too seriously, Lee characteristically proceeded to thrust blame for the book's lack of popular appeal on the prevalence of "machine-like" institutional minds. The book's fate was due to the "newspaper book-reviewing machine" and the "bookstore's machine" which "crowd between me and the public everywhere. The only people who are deeply interested in 'We' are the people and the author." Oddly similar to the personality of Hitler's Great Man as described in *Mein Kampf,* Gerald found his ultimate defense in the unimpeded relationship between the heroic individual and the public. He had convinced himself for years that only he could serve as the intermediary between the public and the institutions of industrial America. In sum, he intended to dominate the public by using the "reviewing machines" when they responded positively toward him and condemn them as mass-produced, myopic, and anti-individualistic when his work was ignored or scorned.[13]

Lee had long recognized that he was competing with newer, more precise practitioners and theorists on the diverse subjects he dealt with: the redemption of wealth and the management of public opinion. By praising inventors like Edison and Marconi, by acclaiming the genius of Frederick Winslow Taylor as akin to Christ, and by scorning the efficacy of romanticism in favor of the "fact spirit," Lee had sought to develop the aura of being a practical "spiritual engineer." But by late March 1916 he commented to G. K. Chesterton that "the trouble with my ideas seems to be that there are certain assumptions which I need to develop and establish as my premises before my point of view has a fair chance in the reader's mind." But instead of developing these premises, he plowed ahead with new schemes for a national audience, casting aspersions on others along the way.[14]

By July, Lee's publisher blamed the poor reviews and sales of *We* on its critical stance toward military preparedness. Arthur Page claimed that when Lee had called for the running of the War Department by Sears and Roebuck, the military leadership had not been pleased, nor was public sentiment favorable. Thinking of the buying public, Page suggested to Lee that any slurs of the military would hurt book sales. Yet it was apparently too late to save the sales of the book.[15]

Further, as the reviews came in, the indelible and belated perception of Lee as silly and long-winded became widespread. *The Nation* commented that Lee's belief "in collective miracles is his forte and his foible. It is his particular half-truth, and it leads him to represent the general complacency and inertia of America, our mere laziness, as a regeneration principle for a stricken world." From England, where the book was also badly received, the *Times Literary Supplement* commented that Lee seemed unaware that "he is talking very like a German professor."[16]

It was Randolph Bourne, however, who sounded the literary death knell of Gerald Lee in a review published in the *New Republic*. Having read widely on the subject of crowd psychology by 1916, Bourne was obviously intrigued with some of Lee's ideas but ultimately found *We* shallow. It was more a journal of Lee's daily thoughts than a well-constructed book, he observed. "A good book could be made of the idea that a civilization of expressiveness, irony, candor, intelligence, would banish war and all the virus of social conflict," but Lee chose to smother his idea in "mushiness." Bourne proceeded to denounce Lee's utopian vision of America as a happy consumer culture under the leadership of inspired millionaires such as Henry Ford. In retrospect, Bourne penned an epitaph for the age of the advertised automobile within which we still live.

[It] seems to be Main Street, Northampton, on Sunday afternoon, with one Ford after another rolling by brimming over with the happy faces of children, the sun and skies beaming down an indomitable optimism on us all. In the distance would be seen the factory with the "inspired millionaire" paying humanity five dollars a day, as convict and saint together, in loyal cheer, turned out the ceaseless stream of cars to bear humanity into its endless joy ride. Peace would come not by building facades on peace temples but through inspired advertisers making the people stop, look and listen.

Lee, Bourne charged, "reek[ed] with benevolence"; his criticism of such luminaries as Bernard Shaw, Andrew Carnegie, and Theodore Roosevelt "must be founded on a secret rivalry in patronizing America, rather than a real spiritual antithesis." Lee was a "finicky, desperately popular yet well groomed literary Billy Sunday." Devastatingly, Bourne continued by noting that Lee had left his literary endeavors on the mountaintop and wrote ads that readers liked, altering his philosophy in the process. "He found that most Americans were businessmen and had business thoughts and business ideals. The profession of advertising was the art of expressing business men's ideals for them." It must have been interesting, Bourne observed contemptuously, to come down from the mountain and lunch with corporate presidents and publicity agents. "Mere literature was pallid and remote in comparison with this contact with real men and real things. His heart opened up and he embraced his age."[17]

Bourne had effectively sealed the fate of Lee's popularity, a feat which others soon recognized. John Burroughs, for example, after reading Bourne's comments, wrote a friend that "it is excellent and paints Lee truly. I could not have done a thing like that. I cannot read Lee seriously because he does not seem to write seriously; his shop is all show window where his verbal monkeys do their tiresome tricks."[18]

Walter Lippmann had grown exceedingly critical of Lee by 1914. He commented to Van Wyck Brooks that Lee had sold "like a novel," making "every self-righteous businessman feel like Julius Caesar and St. George rolled into one . . . But I think Lee is a toady and a flatterer and a great self deceiving fraud." Then in *The Stakes of Diplomacy* (1915) Lippmann sought to distance himself from broad abstractions related to collective behavior. "The moment you assume that there is a collective soul, a collective heart, and a collective mind, you are falling into . . . the error of treating a nation as an individual, rather than as a group of people." The nation, in literal terms, has no eyes, ears, or mouth and its will is "compounded of many wills." Lippmann saw through the illusion that equated spokesmanship with collective will, an illusion which Lee and postwar European fascists both sought to exploit. But Lippmann did not question the need for a public guided by journalistic experts, a theme reinforced by his wartime experiences.[19]

Attacks on Lee's popular crowd psychology and inspirationalism—sometimes without naming him—also came from psychologists and social scientists. Lee had always been able to deny the validity of critical appraisals of his own work by asserting that the critic did not understand human nature as well as he did. Nonetheless it was becoming impossible for him to remain a viable cultural therapist, prophet, or spokesman of the public if professional psychologists successfully condemned his intuitive methodology. For example, Hugo Munsterberg, a professor of psychology at Harvard, a correspondent of Lee's, and a man who vied with Lee on the best-seller lists in 1913, wrote an article in the *Atlantic Monthly* criticizing the "naive psychology" that was being disseminated throughout the country. "We psychologists do not take our revenge by thinking badly of the naive psychology of the poets and of the man in the street . . . [W]e have seen that their so-called psychology is made up essentially of picturesque metaphors, or of moral advice, of love and malice, and that we have to sift big volumes before we strike a bit of psychological truth; even then how often it has shown itself haphazard and accidental, vague and distorted." The statistics of the psychological laboratory were certainly less picturesque, but they had the advantage of achieving results that were verifiable; science had clearly replaced religion as the definer of the human psyche. Munsterberg added that mankind did not have the "right to deceive itself with the half true naive psychology of the amateur, when our world is so full of social problems which will be solved only if the aptitudes and the workings of the mind are clearly recognized and traced."[20]

Graham Wallas, Lippmann's close friend, called for getting "rid of the verbal ambiguities which are due merely to the employment of collective terms." He found nothing "more annoying or useless" than the misapplication of ambiguous meaning. By the mid 1920s the prominent philosopher John Dewey commented angrily in his book *The Public and Its Problems* that "men do not run together and join in a larger mass as do drops of quicksilver." Not crowd instincts but patterns of learned behavior were at the core of men's propensity to act in collectivities. While the simplistic characterizations of crowds continued to be issued by many intellectuals, the categories of behavior were slowly becoming more closely scrutinized by some. Agreeing that more empirically based conceptions involving the management of public opinion were needed, a writer for *Printer's Ink* wrote in June 1916: "The old conception of the advertising man as a genius who got results by the flash of inspiration has pretty largely passed into the limbo of forgotten things. It has given place to a more substantial, though less romantic, conception of the advertising man as one who is responsible for certain definite results which can be measured in concrete terms." Lee was caught between these two newer callings—professional advertising and psychology—with his notions about heroes and beautiful crowds.[21]

A number of novelists, poets, and newspaper columnists heightened their alternative political visions of the crowd. Carl Sandburg criticized the connection made by Lee and others, of the people as a primitive mob seeking only to follow demagogues or wealthy leaders. Ernest Poole's novel *The Harbor* (1915) pictured workers in New York harbor gathering to protest their conditions in terms distinctly at odds with Lee's vision. The crowd was beginning to "question, think and plan." This crowd did not need commercialized heroes or efficiency experts to find fulfillment. For Poole, the "crowd spoke its will through many voices, through men who . . . had simply been parts of the crowd, and the crowd had made them rise and speak." This working-class crowd was able to reason.[22]

Ironically, World War I provided the conditions in which the bifurcated nature of the crowd metaphor manifested itself anew: a deferential public whose attention was being engineered by experts became juxtaposed against the perception of the public as moblike. Exhorted by preachers, managed by professional wordsmiths, and governed by Progressive idealists and businessmen, the United States seemed to blossom as an obedient crowd all fixated on the same goals. Of course the reality of American unity was far more problematic, but hyperpatriots could see only loyalty or treason.

Lee's Progressive vision of a beautiful crowdlike public led by inspired millionaires, attention engineers, and poetic leaders seemed fulfilled by the war. During the spring of 1917 inspired millionaires like Bernard Baruch and William Gibbs McAdoo took charge of industrial production, while prowar preachers, such as Rev. Newell D. Hillis, spread atrocity stories and virulent propaganda against German "barbarians." In April journalist George Creel was asked by President Wilson to manage the Committee on Public Information. Creel was the former editor of Charles Ferguson's abortive *Newsbook,* with whom Lee had been associated in 1908. He presided over hundreds of ad men, journalists, and historians who feverishly sought to rewrite history and channel the thoughts of millions of Americans in favor of Wilson's war for democratic ideals. This effort in mass persuasion, unprecedented in American history, was backed by repressive legislation against free speech, by local pressure groups, and by mobs of violent citizens who grew highly intolerant of dissent. War heightened the prewar trend that saw the compulsive organization of the political emotions and social behavior of the American people. Numerous liberals and socialists joined the war effort and remained mute at the widespread repression of dissent. The war, William Leuchtenberg has written, "offered an outlet for the messianic zeal of the Progressive era without jeopardizing the structure of American society."[23]

In April, after Wilson called for American entry into the war, Lee remained unattached to any war organization but soon produced several ads for the Liberty Bond campaigns. His ads utilized religious imagery combined with romantic fantasies, gross exaggerations of historical and social reality, and the personalization of collectivities—all aimed at creating psychological pressure on people to buy bonds. A full-page ad which was published in the *New Haven Journal-Courier* exhibited another religious image when Lee wrote: "I see Saint Francis in the street! He might be anybody. He might be selling Liberty Bonds. He would have bought Liberty Bonds."[24]

An important break for Lee came in 1918 when two of his articles appeared in Cyrus Curtis's *Saturday Evening Post,* one of the most widely circulated magazines in the country. At least among advertisers, one of the articles evoked "countrywide discussion and considerable protest" for proposing what Lee called "superadvertising" while castigating the dullness of most ads. Dredging up his elitist romantic assumptions, Lee claimed that the visionary men in the advertising profession should be "swung free in it and be given by their clients and by the public and by all of us—by the people they advertise to—the right of way." Ads should not be created by committees, "fussed with by clients and worried over by board of directors." Nervous about the onset of the bureaucratization of propaganda, Lee demanded that ads be written in the first person in order for them to be effective and true.[25]

Printer's Ink, however, thought the former parson's ideas were silly, roasting him "to a brown crisp." Lee's attack on the copywriters for the Liberty Loan campaign ought not to be taken seriously, one writer in *Printer's Ink* said, because the true test was the thirty one million people who subscribed to the three loan drives. A third critic simply observed that "Haste makes waste and we are in a hurry."[26]

Advertiser Ernest Elmo Calkins defended Lee, asserting that "discussion of advertising does not affect the value of the advertising. Discussion is publicity." A more exultant defender of Lee's vision was *Chicago Advertising,* which commented: "Super-advertising it is, and nothing short of it, which will expand a reckless, wasteful, profit-chasing, pleasure-seeking people into a nation of world saviors. Super-ads there will be from now on because the world will need them. Men and women to write them will appear just as the great men and women of the past have appeared—when needed. With nations as with men—great words and great works come forth through great sacrifices. Out of the roaring furnaces of this war will pour forth the golden stream of a super race." Even those advertisers who were critical of Lee tried to confirm their endeavors as agencies of public education and social reform.[27]

As Lee had earlier advocated, advertising and publicity were selling more than products. They were also selling political ideas and social styles of behavior. "Today advertising educates people regarding political situations, industrial crises, social development," the elderly ad man A. J. Ayer told a banquet audience in April 1919. He felt that the recent Liberty Loan ads pointed the way "toward the field of its great usefulness in the extension of goodwill advertising for private commercial business, as well as for the more efficient service of the community at large." Propaganda had become a legitimate tool to use against the enemies of capitalism. The businessmen, St. Elmo Lewis wrote, "should organize quickly that ideal propaganda that shall fight the socialistic, morbid . . . ideas which are neither good sense, sound judgement, nor safe politics. He must fight that thing with an entirely new conception and make the people see it, and with efficiency in selling and advertising, the ideal of real values will be acceptable, and you will have a public whose habit of mind fights with you and not against you."[28]

Lee would have agreed. Like a drowning man gasping for air, he kept conjuring up new schemes of personal fulfillment through attention engineering and architectural grandeur. He contacted scores of leading men to promote the idea of building a "Superman Inn" or "Commonwealth Hotel," for example, which neatly symbolized the continuity of his elitist assumptions about the control of the public mind. His inn was a semiprivate club, to be erected in New York, where America's leaders could congregate and formulate ideals with which to manage the country. Like a palace for the National Civic Federation, the inn would have as its object to "mobilize the leading constructive imaginations of this country into a compact organization in New York to save leadership or imagination for democracy and the world and to make mob rule or Bolshevik methods impossible to America." This was to be the headquarters for a national "anti-class war campaign." The fear of the contagious quality of socialism or mob rule needed to be stopped. Leading men would "loom up in America, great towering citadels of freedom and the powers of the people—loom up like national strikes. [They would] combine to express and serve the people," and attract national attention because of their collective status. "The hotel would be famous all day, all night, all the year [and] crowds would stand and look at [it] like a cathedral."[29]

Lee devised his hotel scheme with construction magnate W. J. Hoggson, another of his wealthy patrons. A number of influential people were contacted by letters informing them that they had been selected to become members of the hotel. They, in turn, were asked to choose others with the right "temperament." It was, as Lee conceived it, a self-selected pyramid containing leaders of imagination. The ideal member was the dollar-a-year men who "flocked up to the nation to win the war." The nation needed its imaginative men concentrated in one place to more effectively deal with the "desperate and complex problems of peace." Lee was trying to perpetuate the wartime crisis atmosphere and centralize the control of America by business, circumventing instead of abolishing Congress and the federal bureaucracy.[30]

The overlapping language Lee used for years in describing civil architecture and church architecture betrayed his search for "sacred space" in which civil religion became tied to business values. Symbolizing technological achievement as well as moral grandeur, a therapeutic retreat as well as a cultural nerve center, Lee's great inn was also to function like an enlarged public face, possessing personality and the ability to influence crowds, a way to read public opinion, a sketch of people's inner values.[31]

The idea for the Superman Inn had come to Lee as he was walking down Victory Way during a loan drive in New York. He fantasized having "a whole country all fitted up the way the Victory Way was— loud-speaking telephone receivers hanging low over ten thousand cities . . . each crowd all alone as it were in its own city by itself, but knowing of the other ten thousand crowds." He would begin saying from up on Mount Tom "in a low dignified tone to the congregation of cities (I used to be a parson and I naturally think of them as a congregation) 'I am starting a hotel for big men in New York. Each city proceed to pick out, please, the ten best men you have, the men who make you proudest of yourself the way Ole Hansen makes Seattle proud, and send their names and addresses." Clearly a prevision of the influence of radio, this statement possesses all the elements of Lee's metaphorical obsessions: he fantasized gaining the attention of all the crowds and separated congregations of the nation by having them all wired up to listen to a single electronic source. His use of Ole Hansen, who had just become well known for his antilabor activities as mayor of Seattle, also reveals Lee's attraction to the hyperpatriotism then affecting the nation.[32]

What is so astounding about the inn scheme is not the novelty of its formulation but its reception. One might think, especially after Lee had been so discredited by advertisers and literary critics, that his idea would be totally ignored. Yet William Gibbs McAdoo, former treasury secretary and director general of the railroads, wrote that he would be "very happy to see if there is not some way in which I can further your desires." Feminist Charlotte Perkins Gilman was "proud and glad to be named as a possible helper in this big good work" and suggested several other names. Others expressed skepticism but wished Lee well in his venture. Former president Theodore Roosevelt, for instance, wrote: "I think any idea of the type mentioned is good if it could be put across. The difficulty is that it requires endless time and patience and you could not depend on the functioning of such a body because the individual members would not be able to leave the communities from which they come in order to congregate sufficiently often to conceive and execute policies."[33]

The failure of the hotel scheme was foretold most succinctly by a New York town planner, Perry MacNeille, who praised Lee for his "almost childlike confidence in men." Nevertheless, MacNeille was bothered by the thought that "the whole plan of promotion is not childlike in straightforwardness and simplicity, but is so complicated and intricate that even astute minds find it difficult to follow its structure." He wondered whether it was a commercial or a patriotic enterprise, recognizing that its "virtues belong on one side of the fence or on the other, but are not common to both sides." What MacNeille had put his finger on was Lee's inability to separate business from religion or patriotism; they all sought to secure people's attention.[34]

The projected function of the Superman Inn represents the unrequited yearnings of many American leaders for a managed, though formally democratic, public. Lee's scheme—as impractical as it was—was one manifestation illustrating how the intellectual residue from the war might confuse "sacred spaces" with commercial opportunities. That those sacred spaces and forms of attention continued to become more secularized was neither a conspiracy nor an accident; the construction of sports stadiums, movie palaces, radio networks, and the growth of advertising agencies during the twenties all helped reinforce the prevalent view of the public as analogous to a politically quiescent crowd, out for a good time, attracted by personality, sensation, and spectacle.

By 1919 middle class anxiety was extended from its wartime context and refocused on the politicization of disorder: several million unsettled troops came home from Europe just as strikes erupted around the nation; American troops marched into Russian streets trying to thwart the Bolshevik Revolution while the Communist party of the United States was formed in New York; ugly race riots scarred a number of cities; the country grew cynical about Wilsonian calls for democracy while Wilson himself became more rigid and shrill in the face of Republican attacks. It was another dramatic period in American history like the 1890s—a time when the hegemony of corporate leaders that Lee had helped rationalize was being ruthlessly reinforced throughout the culture.

The changing language and iconography related to the public fed that hegemony. Younger intellectuals grew disgusted at the moblike character of the American middle class. Back in 1916, John Macy, writing in *The Masses,* exhibited the plasticity—and the antidemocratic direction—toward which the language of collective behavior was headed. The connotations surrounding mobs had widened from their simplistic associations with the lower class; they were increasingly "seen to be any assemblage of persons, of any class, united by any idea good or bad," he wrote. Everyone was a potential participant in mob activity. "We belong to college mobs, class mobs, professional mobs, strike mobs, political party mobs, military mobs, even national mobs." Macy's comment reveals the continuing power of ambiguity related to the crowd metaphor.[35]

Honed from the romantic republican conceptions of crowds in the Gilded Age (whose formulators had largely died by 1920), the idea of a crowd mind burgeoned as a characteristic of all sorts of groups and socialization processes. Everett Dean Martin of New York's People's Institute used Freudian psychology in his book *The Behavior of Crowds* (1920) in explaining that "if you are to get anywhere in this progressive age you must be vulgar, . . . a 100% crowd man." Martin agreed with Graham Wallas's criticism of Le Bon for foolishly relying on vivid descriptions of French Revolution mobs for universal laws of crowd psychology. The "old intellectualism" had seen the "true mental life primarily a knowledge affair," Martin added, whereas now the crowd connoted a classless state of mind. In reviewing Martin's book, H. L. Mencken commented that "all the old restraints upon the swinishness of men in the mass are fading away, and the world is gradually coming to be run on principles borrowed from the communal ethics and politics of wolves and hyenas—nay, of rabbits and polecats." Democracy had become nothing but a series of crowds, a theme Mencken repeated endlessly. At once derisive of all forms of collective behavior, Mencken's characterizations informed a style of humor that continued to disparage the "booboisie" and philistines throughout the 1920s. Lee, of course, had surfaced many of these perceptions as early as 1896, albeit with a tone far removed from Mencken's.[36]

Younger liberal and socialist intellectuals, notably Van Wyck Brooks and Waldo Frank, reacted against the moblike culture, linking it to the material success that had co-opted the visions of many poets and reformers of Lee's generation. "Romanticism had given birth to a verbal fatty degeneration that revealed the degeneration of the life it sprang from," Brooks later wrote. The old phrases such as "quest for beauty" seemed false and hollow by wartime. The Emersonian and Puritan traditions had become passé, while a few writers still valued Whitman's idealism and his bold affront to social convention. Waldo Frank, in *Our America* (1919), characterized Emerson as "pale and shredded and remote beside the immediacy" of Whitman's prose in *Democratic Vistas*. America was in the midst of dark days, Frank wrote, as newspaper syndicates dispensed news wholesale and universities stifled dissenting professors. "Whitman and his sons cry for their multitudes to be born anew: and the American powers take every step to preserve them in a state of ignorance, flatulence, complacency which shall approximate the Herd." To be stamped a pale copy of Whitman or an heir of the Puritans—as Lee had been—was clearly to be out of fashion.[37]

Even though Lee was seldom used as a reference by the 1920s, the derogatory view of the public as moblike had become a convention of political perceptions that supported the cultural utility of modern managerial elites. Secretary of Commerce Herbert Hoover, in *American Individualism* (1922), affirmed that "man in the mass does not think but only feels . . . The mob functions only in the world of emotion . . . Popular desires are no criteria to the real need; they can be determined only by deliberate consideration, by education, by constructive leadership." Walter Lippmann's highly praised book *Public Opinion,* using notions about crowds derived from Le Bon and Everett Dean Martin, called for trained experts to dispense news in order to channel opinion to the herdlike public. By 1928 public relations man Edward Bernays authoritatively claimed that the invisible government of those who were manipulating the organized opinions and habits of the masses was a "logical result of the way in which our democratic society is organized." Few questioned the increasing devaluation of language that attended the denigration of the public. Service, André Siegfried wrote, had become an "indispensable password of those who wish to justify their profits."[38]

The crowd-market as emotional beast had become a series of entities capable of rendering vast financial rewards upon those who could appear to master it. It was an age of the *Reader's Digest* and Emile Coué, an age of consumption, condensed experiences, and car racing. The young had little time or interest to ingest the older values expounded by Samuel Smiles or Henry Ward Beecher, as they bobbed their hair and broke older taboos against dancing and sex. Historian Eugene Leach writes that "during the 1920s, American theorists redefined as virtues crowd attributes that had been commonly treated as scourges a decade earlier. Now the crowd's primitivism, its lack of culture and stable structure, became a promise of its manageability; now the crowd's volatility was reinterpreted as its capacity for rapid adaptation to new environments." A host of entertainers, advertisers, and business evangelists exploited the notion of the public as moblike. It was a convenient shorthand device for obviating moral or religious qualms about aiming emotional appeals at the lowest common denominator of public appeal. Even Jesus had become an attractive hero to vast crowds in a deMille film and a crowd psychologist and organization man in Bruce Barton's best-selling biography, *The Man Nobody Knows*. Not only an incipient inspired millionaire and attention engineer, Jesus legitimized the impenitent control of crowds; he was a man who would have fit into modern corporate life in a flash.[39]

By 1920 Lee clearly sensed that his role as a prophet of advertising was over as he switched his interests into a new field, this time a field related to mind-body coordination. Ignored by an anxious public, he turned his own attention inward. The shift from a focus on the social body to the human body was far from a unique postwar reaction by many disillusioned Progressives. Herbert Croly, for example, had been frustrated in reconceptualizing any sort of "class concert" in the postwar years. By the mid 1920s he emphasized mind control techniques and the revitalization of local clergy as cultural redeemers.[40]

Many of the tired themes Lee reiterated for years reappeared in his 1920 inspirational tract entitled *The Ghost in the White House.* In it one can also sense Lee's inward shift. Doubtless projecting his own obsessions, he warned that the White House was "haunted by a vague, helpless abstraction, a kind of ghost of a nation, called the people." Lee sought to perpetuate the aura of national crisis in order to retain the social unity and conformity that the war had bred. Not surprisingly, Lee advocated the candidacy of the great engineer Herbert Hoover to the presidency and spoke in Freudian terms about binding workers together in a national effort at cooperation. The American public was characterized as banal and repetitious, mirroring the processes of mass production with which it lived. "A very large part of even quite intelligent conversation has no origination in [the public] and is just made up of phonograph records," he asserted. Few people over thirty years of age listened to any criticism, possessing minds that "cannot really be budged." After acknowledging that he was "weary and sad about the word propaganda" because of its overuse by uninspired practitioners, Lee confessed, "I have written many hundred pages of what I believe about reformers—about people who are trying to get other people's attention, and about advertising, but the brunt of what I believe now is that most people if they would stop trying to get other people's attention and try to get their own, would do more good."[41]

By the early twenties Lee, along with his wife and daughter Geraldine, began to do just that. They parlayed their interest in psychology into developing a series of "invisible exercises" aiding personal efficiency and helping people to accomplish such rudimentary functions as walking properly. "What a splendid word 'psychology' is to impress people with their sins," Lee wrote his wife in 1924. Balance and coordination were qualities which needed to be reinvigorated, actually reinvented, for modern times, he believed.[42]

He eventually published three books explaining his various therapies: *Invisible Exercise, Rest Working: A Study in Relaxed Concentration,* and *Recreating Oneself.* The sales of all three books were low, although prominent people remained associated with his endeavors. The Lees moved to New York and lived there from 1922 to 1930 as they practiced their therapy on such people as Mrs. Thomas Edison, economist Irving Fischer, William Allen White, Ray Stannard Baker, and other academic, literary, or wealthy clients. Filene's store in Boston hired the Lees to administer their technique to its employees. On one occasion the Lees sponsored a "Poise Party." Ironically, one patient was Van Wyck Brooks, apparently in a suicidal state, who spent part of the summer of 1928 at Monhegan Island under the care of the man he had savaged in his 1916 essay "The Precipitent."[43]

By the early 1930s Lee's mission had led him to try to control the world's emotions resulting from the effects of the Depression. But his series of verbal tricks had grown tiresome, as John Burroughs and William James had foretold. "If I were appointed dictator to the whole world and placed in charge of forty nations," Lee mused in 1933, "I would at once proceed to deal with each nation and its various prejudices—its emotional unbalances—as if it were a trained seal or an about to be trained seal. It would not be given enough to eat, until it could properly balance its organs on its nose."[44]

Although coming from a progressive Republican tradition, Lee was enthralled by how Franklin Roosevelt's personality had become such a crucial element in his public appeal. The public's admiration for Roosevelt's personal triumph over infantile paralysis, Lee wrote to Wilson's old confidant and adviser, Colonel Edward House, was "the most baffling thing for his enemies to deal with. It cuts under all his difficulties and [was] the short cut to faith." "My feeling is that the best way to avoid a detour in National Recovery is through the mass-emotion response of our people to the personality of Franklin Roosevelt. They cannot, millions of them at a time—debate and understand his policies . . . either the short range ones or the long range ones but they can understand him—the man himself and not have to wait for details." The public's ability to grasp political reality was discounted.[45]

Lee felt his notions about crowds and heroes, about business leaders and mutualism, were vindicated by Roosevelt's presidency. He wrote Charles Ferguson in 1934 that "the things I was believing in Crowds 20 years ago—the synthesis of the employer, the laborer and the consumer—is being (God bless the Depression) shouted on the house tops now. The Depression is making millions see every day right before our eyes the things about socializing industry that thousands saw then."[46]

The last decades of Lee's life found him sad over his inability to

Gerald and Jennette Lee at their fireside. Lee wrote: "A great man is a kind of crowd fireplace."

gain the renown he had hoped would be his. Sometimes he projected his failure onto others; seldom did he find fault with himself. "Perhaps I always had too much expectation," he asserted to Walter Lippmann in 1925 while introducing one of his books. "I do admit that I feel that when most people believe and act on what I have been saying, most of the prejudice we now combat will be exchanged for a new and better set." Lee had doubtless become an embarrassing reminder to some of the naive idealism of an earlier era. To Roger Babson in 1937, Lee wrote, "I am obviously a very unsettling and unacceptable person for you to have for a friend."[47]

Earlier Gerald acknowledged a parting of the ways to Ivy Lee that reveals that his individualistic brand of the visionary was dead. Ivy had achieved great success by the early twenties as his talents as a public relations counsel were sold for a high price. Gerald noted how Ivy was becoming a millionaire from "helping millionaires to think," then asked mournfully, "Where is Ivy Lee's success? I do not know. I only know that it is placed somewhere I can't see it . . . I

Gerald Lee tending his
garden in Northampton.

used to feel that the kind of man I was had something to do with Ivy
Lee and could commune in a way with what was going on in him."
He admitted to feeling "in all this success like a ghost, or like a bird
fluttering through a rolling mill . . . [A]ll I do now is to faintly haunt
him—haunt him and the clack of his huge machine with the stillness
and light outside." The peaceful, natural outside world beyond the
factory remained Gerald Lee's refuge. By 1934, however, Ivy had
begun working for I. G. Farben and briefly consulted with Hitler and
Goebbels. The ethical boundaries of attention engineering were
being stretched even further. Although their friendship had clearly
dissipated, Ivy did pen one final note to Gerald shortly before his
own death, in which he affirmed that he was "still interested in
everything you are doing, and still believe in your powers of prophetic vision." Yet prophecy was not in vogue in 1934, nor, one
suspects, did Ivy Lee really believe in such prophets anymore.[48]

Gerald's loneliness grew until his death. As he continued to feel
ever since his Sharon sermon in 1891, the heart of America's problem lay in the lost power of the clergy. In *Heathen Rage,* his 1931
diatribe against professionalization and specialization, he be-
moaned the loneliness and helplessness which he felt characterized

the average contemporary clergyman, a man entrapped in the "impossible profession." Most people seemed to consider the parson as a "spray of goodness for the town," he wrote, barely touching the lives of his congregation. "He becomes a wistful generalization . . . It is a very lonely, almost ghostlike life in a town—being just a generalization." His jealousy for the growing power of professions which rivaled the minister was obvious.

> If the minister, as supposed spiritual expert in his community, knows God the way the chemist in town knows chemistry for other people, the way the lawyer knows the law for them, the way the physician knows their bodies for them, he would soon find himself occupying a very different place in the life of the community from the place he is usually found occupying now. His relation to the life about him would have a challenging reality in it, a keenness, a grip of companionableness upon the hearts of men, which would make him incomparably the town's most intimately known, most used and most indispensable man . . . He would live a flocked-through, lived in life. The town, as one might say, would inhabit him.

Lee never solved the problem of the lost authority of the Puritan parson.[49]

As the Great Depression grew in scope, of course, many intellectuals asked probing questions about American ideals and the reigning economic policies. Lee, characteristically, was not among the soul searchers. His pattern of belief was largely set, adaptable to different circumstances. Lincoln Steffens, in a letter to Lee in 1931, noticed that there had been little change in the way Lee approached the world during their twenty-year acquaintance. From his self-imposed exile in California, Steffens wrote Lee about *Heathen Rage*, fondly remembering earlier conversations they had had and wondering:

> Don't you know that it is not your sliver of Right, but the excuse to preach it that is all you need to be happy? Why, I could feel your happiness all through those delicious pages. And it's all right with me. I am down on happiness; I want to beat it up whenever I see Happiness. I know that happiness, pleasure, any sign of enjoyment is a sure sign of error if not of sin. But in your case, in the person of any rival author I enjoy happiness because it is evidence that he will not slip over into the truth that I proclaim: that the truth is that we are all wrong about

everything and that my distinction is that I am the only preacher that knows that he (and the others) are all wrong.

Attracted to the example of a society like the Soviet Union that was able to transform its entire social structure instead of being mired in petty reforms as was the case in the United States, Steffens was led to a "passive vigil for the destruction of the old America," Otis Graham has written, "and the coming of a new order." Not Lee.[50]

Lee must have been a bizarre figure to most Northampton residents as he walked the streets in these last years. One longtime resident recalled seeing Lee seeming to "float" down an icy road. Others recalled erratic behavior as he practiced his theory of tension release while walking down the street. Tall and emaciated, frequently dabbing his nose with a large handkerchief that he kept in his sleeve, with long disorderly hair and a black cape he wore on all occasions except on hot summer days, Lee had developed himself into an original character, a man who must have stood out in a crowd.[51]

In 1940, when Lee was seventy-eight years old, two years from death, and almost penniless, the Northampton Chamber of Commerce asked for suggestions for publicity to stimulate tourism and aid the financial condition of the city. Responding in a small pamphlet, Lee began by tying memories of social cohesion during the Great War to a biblical reference. "Everybody, like the animals entering the Ark, could be seen in 1916 piling right in to get the war over and done with, each after his kind in his own way." Those were the days when people acted in glorious concert, he felt. He wrote that he had recently gone home, gotten into bed, but had remained in a lonely house without "a thread of companionship leading to something . . . just me—mere me and a mere universe." "In the loneliness of my body—and the loneliness of my mind I reached out . . . I sought to gather Northampton round me out of the night, out of the years . . . I wanted, I must have people! With my eyes fastened on the infinite abyss of darkness I wanted people—streets of people—I peopled myself inside."[52]

Gerald Lee died on 3 April 1944. He had tried to describe the metaphorical structure behind modern existence to others as a religion of the crowd; an interpreter of public opinion and a prophet of

Gerald Lee in his later years.

the present age of attention engineering, Lee wanted to show what the face of a truly modern personality would look like, a face that would entrance leaders and transform the public mind; he wanted to elevate the aspirations of Americans into higher forms of cooperation and individual fulfillment. But from an early age he ensnared himself, through literature, in an ambiguous dynamic involving crowds, machines, wealth, and national identity. His compulsive quest for the heroic personality ultimately acted to obscure, distort, and dangerously simplify the social reality of American forms of collective behavior. His misunderstanding of American history and political economy, his disdain for the public, and his ignorance about the real lives of working people all helped produce a naively romantic but deeply cynical view of the world. Lee can act as a warning about the misuse of language and about the pitfalls in constructing new ideals of social cohesion and political justice in a postmodern age.

Democracy and the Age of
Attention Engineering

It is advertising that has been the death of words.
The word "Personal" now on an envelope means "impersonal;"
"Important," "unimportant."
"The finest," "The Best," "The Purest"—what do they mean now?
Something somebody wants to sell.
We are a nation of word-killers: hero, veteran, tragedy.—
Watch the great words go down.

Edna St. Vincent Millay, "Conversation at Midnight"

The life and writings of Gerald Stanley Lee confirm Richard Sennett's comment that "modern images of crowds have consequences for modern ideas of community." Like many academic and popular social philosophers at the turn of the century, Lee expressed unbounded hope for a revitalized definition of elitism achieved through a nationalistic progressive faith. His faith, however, was formulated by what Robert Wiebe has called "the rhetoric of antithetical absolutes." A picture of class conflict, urban chaos, faceless anonymity, godless socialism, quixotic fads, and an immigrant siege of American institutions was counterposed against the nostalgia for a bucolic valley town with a village green, a white church steeple, and an uncomplicated aura of consensus and purity. As Lee's writings show, this dualistic view had significant consequences for the emerging "professions" of advertising and public relations as well as in the relentless use of techniques of mass persuasion throughout a wide variety of social institutions, from churches and schools to the public health movement, from industry to politics.[1]

Like many other Progressives, Lee lived with an unconscious contradiction regarding his perception of the public. He associated himself with the rising power of public opinion while concurrently seeking both to legitimate and exploit the capacity to control it. His prewar stature testifies to the trend of organizing the public mind as a central concern of many reformers and conservatives well before the creation of the wartime Creel Committee. In 1914 social psychologist Robert Park claimed that "publicity has come to be a recognized form of social control, and advertising—'social advertising'—has become a profession with an elaborate technique supported by a body of special knowledge."[2]

Living from the Civil War to World War II, Lee shaped his identity in a transitional period between eras with sharply different concepts of mass persuasion, between the more genteel tradition of the Victorian world and the era of the media expert. With the passage of half a century, it is easier to appreciate the role that Lee played as a representative of the native American optimism which attended the advent of the age of attention engineering. At times, Lee's banal blandishments, convoluted logic, and egotistical fantasies betray both a childish playfulness as well as an Olympian condescension toward his audiences. But there was a serious core to his ideas, a core that resonated, to a significant degree, with the hopes of many people in the Progressive Era.

In his effort to extend a mythical unanimity of the past into the machine-made world of the twentieth century, Lee looked back on the nineteenth century as "moment mad," a century "that turned all eternity upside down in the present tense," a century that read about itself "incessantly [and was] dizzied with its own sunrises and its own sunsets." He struggled to find a scheme to freeze a frame of time, to create modern Days of Humiliation, and force all Americans to follow their greater prophets. To control the attention of a dispersed yet interdependent public, who all read the same newspapers and magazines, or all watched a moving picture as if they were in the same theater, or had true leaders gathered under his tutelage in the Superman Hotel—this, Lee felt, was the first step toward the restoration of the lost consensus, common purpose, and containable patterns of behavior of early New England. His quest to define the modern heroic personality illustrate disturbing tendencies that were later muffled under the more scientific jargon of those successors who sought to discover and manage public opinion.[3]

Alongside his naively optimistic and expectant modernism, Lee's simplistic rhetoric about individualism, cooperation, and nature also manifests the moralistic and coercive nationalism willingly promoted by middle class spokesmen. These vaguely wrought expressions were bound up with an ideology promoting a romanticized view of work and a belief in a boundless consumerism that few critics could clearly comprehend at the time, much less effectively counteract. Part of the strength of this emerging ideology emanated from the illusions of mutualism, the uses made of the public as a crowdlike entity.

In literature, journalism, social theory, popular culture, business, and political life, the denigration of the ideal of the public man has continued since the years of Lee's prominence. The ideology which extols the functional value of appealing to the lowest common denominator of public appeal has suffused the mass media as well as its governmental regulators. The former chairman of the Federal Communications Commission stated that the United States has "passed the point where reliance on the marketplace is merely a regulatory trend. It has become a social imperative, a commercial imperative, and a constitutional imperative." With a civil-religious aura, Commissioner Fowler aptly expressed the old assumption, given such momentary force by Lee, that the heart of any definition of the will and needs of the American public can best be found through the voice of the dollars it spends.[4]

Americans remain the victims of loose language and fallacious ideas and images about the relationship between collective behavior and the marketplace. Correctly drawn (upon occasion) or not (which is the norm), notions about crowds surround our social lives, have a profound impact on our political and economic consciousness, and our interactions with other people. Images of ourselves as members of crowds or as separated from them go to the heart of our self-esteem, our cultural identity, or even the therapies, social models, and political personalities we choose to follow in "finding" ourselves as individuals. The patterns that these ideas and images about crowds have taken in the minds of men and women of all different classes, sexes, and ages as well as those with varied ethnic or educational backgrounds should be more rigorously explored. Perhaps by concentrating on such imagery and the diverse human reality with which it intersects, we may help vitalize the belief that this country is more than a simple economic marketplace in which citizens are seen as consumers of packaged goods and salable experiences. Perhaps we may come to see that the "public interest is not the plural of self-interest," as one television critic has recently stated, and that the historically determined patterns taken by images of crowds have strongly affected the public's definition of itself and the self-interest of its individual members. While the terms of collective behavior are "permeated with varying degrees of value or political biases" and can "never be freed from such biases," as sociologist Robert Park long ago warned, it nonetheless remains an important task to try to define their scope and derivation.[5]

If the central quest for our time is to survive our technological achievements and create a coherent and humane social order within an interdependent world, then Lee's recurrent picture of the relationship between heroic personalities and crowds can serve as a warning against the misuse of ambiguous terminology about collective behavior. Human souls are not revealed on a moving picture screen; one individual cannot function as the spokesman for the true inner lives of other human beings; nor can anyone embody a community, city, or nation. Yet so many of us still seem resigned to parceling out our interests to a myriad of hired spokesmen, achieving little lasting gratification by identifying with the manufactured celebrities that frantically patronize us.

NOTES

Introduction. *Advertising and the Contours of a Preaching Mentality*

1. Coolidge is quoted in Ashley Thorndike, ed., *Modern Eloquence,* ed. Ashley Thorndike, 15 vols. (New York, 1928), 4: 130.
2. Ibid. See the reaction to Coolidge's speech in "The U.S.A. as an Advertising Achievement," *Literary Digest,* November 13, 1926, p. 15.
3. See Quentin Schultze, "An Honorable Place: The Quest for Professional Advertising Education, 1900–1917," *Business History Review* 56 (Spring 1982): 16–32; Michael McMahon, "An American Courtship: Psychologists and American Advertising Theory in the Progressive Era," *American Studies* 13 (Fall 1972): 5–16.
4. For background see Donald Meyer, *The Positive Thinkers* (New York, 1980); Richard Weiss, *The American Idea of Success* (New York, 1971).
5. Walter Lippmann, *Drift and Mastery* (New York, 1914), p. 51.
6. Van Wyck Brooks, *America's Coming of Age* (New York, 1958), p. 72.
7. See George Fredrickson, *The Inner Civil War* (New York, 1965), p. 9. On the notion of the preaching mentality see Leo Spitzer, "Advertising Explained as Popular Art," in *Essays on English and American Literature,* ed. Anna Hatcher (Princeton, 1962), p. 274. I am grateful to the late Warren Susman for informing me of Spitzer's essay and for his comments and encouragement related to my study of Lee and the crowd metaphor.
8. Charles Stelzle, *The Principles of Church Advertising,* as quoted in Christian Reisner, *Church Publicity: The Modern Way to Compel Them to Come In* (New York, 1913), p. 19. See also R. Jackson Wilson, *In Quest of Community* (New York, 1968), p. 38; Daniel Walker

Howe, "American Victorianism as a Culture," *American Quarterly* 27 (1975): 521.

9. Raymond Williams, "Advertising the Magic System," in *Problems in Materialism and Culture* (London, 1980), pp. 184, 191, 193; Daniel Rogers, "In Search of Progressivism," *Reviews in American History* 10 (December 1982): 125.

10. William James to W. S. Parker, June 1900. This postcard is located in the Gerald Lee Collection at the Forbes Library, Northampton, Mass. For contemporary analysis of the media in this regard see Neil Postman, *Amusing Ourselves to Death* (New York, 1986).

1. The Crowd Metaphor in Industrializing America

1. Gerald Stanley Lee, "Making the Crowd Beautiful," *Atlantic Monthly* 87 (1901): 248. Hereafter Gerald Stanley Lee's name will be shortened to GSL.

2. For background see Warren Susman, "Personality and the Making of Twentieth-Century Culture," in *New Directions in American Intellectual History*, ed. John Higham and Paul Conkin, (Baltimore, 1979), pp. 198–222; Jackson Lears, *No Place of Grace* (New York, 1982); William Graebner, *The Engineering of Consent* (Madison, Wis., 1987); John G. Sproat, *The Best Men* (New York, 1968), chap. 8; Benjamin Ginsberg, *The Captive Public: How Mass Opinion Promotes State Power* (New York, 1986); Frederic Cople Jaher, *Doubters and Dissenters* (Glen Coe, N.Y., 1964).

3. Charles Horton Cooley, *Social Organization* (New York, 1909), pp. 195, 303; John Macy, "Mobs," *The Masses* 8 (May 1916); G. T. W. Patrick, "The Psychology of Crazes," *Popular Science Monthly* 57 (1900): 285–94; Boris Sidis, *The Psychology of Suggestion* (New York, 1898); Walter D. Scott, *The Psychology of Public Speaking* (New York, 1906), chap. 12; James Mark Baldwin, *Social and Ethical Interpretation of Mental Development* (New York, 1906), pp. 244–55; Josiah Royce, *Race Questions, Provincialism, and Other American Problems* (Freeport, N.Y., 1967 [1908]), pp. 80–96. See also R. Jackson Wilson, *In Quest of Community* (New York, 1968), pp. 159–64.

4. Murray Edelman, *Politics as Symbolic Action: Mass Arousal and Quiescence* (New York, 1971), p. 83. See also Elias Canetti, *Crowds and Power* (New York, 1963); Hugh Dalzell Duncan, *Communication and Social Order* (New York, 1962), p. 190.

5. Salvador Giner, *Mass Society* (New York, 1976), p. 6. See also Richard

Sennett, *The Fall of Public Man* (New York, 1977), pp. 3–4, and his edited volume *The Psychology of Society* (New York, 1977); P. A. Brunt, "The Roman Mob," in *Studies in Ancient Society,* ed. M. I. Finley (London, 1974), pp. 74–102; M. I. Finley, *Democracy Ancient and Modern* (New Brunswick, 1985), chap. 1; Grant Brantlinger, *Bread and Circuses: Theories of Mass Culture as Social Decay* (Ithaca, 1983), chaps. 1, 2.

6. Giner, *Mass Society,* chap. 3. The shorthand designation "mob" finally became used by the eighteenth century, much to the horror of literary purists like Swift, according to Raymond William, *Keywords* (New York, 1976), p. 158–63. See also George Rude, *Ideology and Popular Protest* (New York, 1980), pp. 41–67, 81–93; Keith Thomas, *Man and the Natural World* (New York, 1983), pp. 41–50; Fernand Braudel, *Capitalism and Material Life 1400–1800* (New York, 1973), p. 34; Christopher Hill on "the many headed monster" in *Change and Continuity in Seventeenth Century England* (Cambridge, Mass., 1974), pp. 182–83. For a recent summary see Suzanne Desan, "Crowds, Community, and Ritual in the Work of E. P. Thompson and Natalie Davis," in *The New Cultural History,* ed. Lynn Hunt (Berkeley, 1989), pp. 47–71. For recent views of the eighteenth-century American context see Edward Countryman, *The American Revolution* (New York, 1985), chap. 3, and William Pencak, "Samuel Adams and Shays' Rebellion," *New England Quarterly* 62 (1989): 63–74.

7. The best overview of the term *masses* in the nineteenth century focusing on England is found in Asa Briggs, "The Language of Mass and Masses," in *The Collected Essays of Asa Briggs,* 2 vols. (Chicago, 1985), 1: 34–54. See also George Rude, *The Crowd in History* (New York, 1964); Eric Hobsbawm, *The Age of Empire, 1875–1914* (New York, 1987), chap. 4; Robert J. Holton, "The Crowd in History: Some Problems of Theory and Method," *Social History* 3 (May 1978): 219–33.

8. Abraham Lincoln, "Lyceum Address," in *The Collected Works of Abraham Lincoln,* ed. Roy P. Basler et al., 9 vols. (New Brunswick, N.J., 1953–55), 1: 108–15. See also George Forgie, *Patricide in the House Divided* (New York, 1979), chap. 2; Paul C. Nagel, *One Nation Divisible: The Union in American Thought* (New York, 1964), chap. 7; Fred Somkin, *Unquiet Eagle* (Ithaca, 1967), pp. 39–46; "Mobs," *New England Magazine* 7 (December 1834): 471–77; James Fenimore Cooper, *The American Democrat* (Baltimore, 1969 [1838]), p. 130. See also Alexis de Toqueville, *Democracy in America* (New York, 1945), vol. 2, bk. 4; Sean Wilentz, *Chants Democratic* (New

York, 1984); Paul Gilje, *The Reign of Mobocracy* (Chapel Hill, 1988); Michael Feldberg, *The Turbulent Era* (New York, 1980); David Grimsted, "Rioting in Its Jacksonian Setting," *American Historical Review* 77 (1972): 361-97.

9. Hugh Peters, "The Theory and Regulation of Public Sentiment," An Address before Columbia Alumni, October 5, 1842, pp. 11, 46, 39. (A copy can be found in the New York Public Library.) See also Daniel Walker Howe, *The Political Culture of American Whigs* (Chicago, 1979), p. 53. For analysis of the crowd in American literature in this period see Nicolaus Mills, *The Crowd in American Literature* (Baton Rouge, 1986), chap. 2.

10. Charles Dickens, *Barnaby Rudge* (New York, 1973), p. 414; *Chicago Times*, 29 July 1877. See also Paul Stigart and Peter Widdowson, "Barnaby Rudge: A Historical Novel?" *Literature and History*, no. 2 (November 1975): 36.

11. Stephen Skowronek, *Building a New American State: The Expansion of National Administrative Capacities, 1877-1920* (New York, 1982), chap. 4; Joseph Ecclesine, *A Compendium of the Laws and Decisions Relating to Mobs, Riots, Invasion, Civil Commotion, Insurrection, &c., as Affecting Fire Insurance Companies* (New York, 1863); Eugene Leach, "Riot Duty: Managing Class Conflict in the Streets, 1877-1919," a paper delivered at the 1989 meeting of the Organization of American Historians in St. Louis, Mo.; Susan Davis, *Parades and Power* (Philadelphia, 1986); Robert Reinders, "Militia and Public Order in Nineteenth-Century America," *Journal of American Studies* 11 (April 1977).

12. Several months after the Haymarket bombing and the subsequent police riots, the *New York Times* defined respectability as "that vast class of honest, industrious men and women who already have savings or who strive for them, who have the strongest interest in the present peace and order of society, and who know that their future and that of their children depend on the firm enforcement of the law." The *New York Times* quote is reprinted in *Public Opinion*, 15 July 1886, p. 84. The best overview of the subject remains Paul Boyer, *Urban Masses and Moral Order* (Cambridge, 1978), pt. 3. See also Steven Mintz, *A Prison of Expectations* (New York, 1982); Richard Sennett, "Violence and Family Life in Chicago," in *Nineteenth-Century Cities*, ed. Stephen Thernstrom and Richard Sennett (New Haven, 1969); Susanna Barrows, *Distorting Mirrors: Visions of the Crowd in Late Nineteenth-Century France* (New Haven, 1981), chap. 2. On the growing professionalization of language see JoAnne Brown, "Professional Lan-

guage: Words That Succeed," *Radical History Review* 34 (1986): 33–51.

13. Jane Addams, *Democracy and Social Ethics* (Cambridge, 1964 [1907]), pp. 174–75. See also Walter Lippmann, *Public Opinion* (New York, 1922), p. 222; Victor Turner, *Drama, Fields, and Metaphors* (Ithaca, N.Y., 1974), pp. 29, 37–39.

14. The term "nurseries of crime" was made by the Rev. O. P. Hoyt, "The Influence of Public Opinion: An Address Delivered at Potsdam, N.Y., July 4, 1827" (NYPL); Joaquin Miller, *The Destruction of Gotham* (New York, 1886), p. 12 (see also pp. 7, 130, 172–76); George W. James, *Chicago's Dark Places: Investigations by a Corps of Specially Appointed Commissioners* (Chicago, 1891), pp. 80, 63. See also Adrienne Siegel, *The Image of the American City in Popular Literature, 1820–1870* (Port Washington, N.Y., 1981), p. 21.

15. See Henry Ward Beecher, *New York Times*, 23 July 1877, as quoted in Leon Litwak, *American Labor* (Englewood Cliffs, N.J., 1962), p. 56; Josiah Strong, *Our Country* (Cambridge, Mass., 1963), p. 176. See "The Commune in America," *New York Daily Graphic*, 15 January 1874.

16. Herbert Gutman, "Class Status and Community Power in Nineteenth-Century American Cities," in *Work, Culture, and Society in Industrializing America* (New York, 1976); Roy Rosenzweig, *Eight Hours for What We Will* (Cambridge, 1985); Davis, *Parades and Power*; Mary Ryan, "The American Parade: Representations of the Nineteenth-Century Social Order," in Hunt, *The New Cultural History*, pp. 11–53.

17. Raymond Williams, *Culture and Society* (New York, 1983), p. 300.

18. Edward A. Ross, for example, had read Carlyle's *History of the French Revolution* six times and found that *Sartor Resartus* "rang in [his] heart like Cathedral bells." Edward Ross, *Seventy Years of It* (New York, 1936), p. 21. Gerald Lee found Carlyle's picture of the French Revolution "a spiritual play, a series of pictures of faces . . . It is dynamic [and] dramatic—great abstractions playing magnificently over great concretes." GSL, *The Lost Art of Reading* (New York, 1903), p. 372. Lee read, or reread the book in April 1890. The best recent biography of Carlyle is Philip Rosenberg, *The Seventh Hero: Thomas Carlyle and the Theory of Radical Activism* (Cambridge, Mass., 1974). See p. 36.

19. Rosenberg, *The Seventh Hero*, p. 99; Thomas Carlyle is quoted from Eric Bentley, *A Century of Hero Worship* (Boston, 1957), p. 76. Rosenberg states that Carlyle's *French Revolution* showed an obses-

sion with "the gestural aspects of how men conduct themselves" (pp. 69–70).

20. John Fiske, *The Critical Period of American History* (Boston, 1888), pp. 55–57. On the controversy over erecting a statue to the victims of the 1770 Boston Massacre, see *Massachusetts Historical Society Proceedings*, 2d ser., vol. 3 (1886–87): 313–18; Franklin J. Moses, "Mob or Martyr? Crispus Attucks and the Boston Massacre," *Bostonian* 1 (1894–95): 641–45. See also Edward Bellamy's novel *The Duke of Stockbridge* (Cambridge, 1962 [1901]) about Shays' Rebellion and the comments by Harry Henderson in *Versions of the Past* (New York, 1974), pp. 198–204. See also Joel T. Headley, *The Great Riots of New York* (New York, 1883).

21. Annie Cary Morris, "Glimpses at the Diaries of Gouverneur Morris," *Scribner's Magazine* 1 (1887): 93–106, 199–210; E. B. Washburn, "Reminiscences of the Siege and Commune of Paris," *Scribner's Magazine* 1 (1887): 2–21, 161–83, 289–307, 446–67.

22. Daniel Aaron, *Men of Good Hope: A Story of American Progressives* (New York, 1951), p. 11; Robert Linscott, ed., *The Journals of Ralph Waldo Emerson* (New York, 1960), pp. 159, 81. Larzar Ziff, *Literary Democracy: The Declaration of Cultural Independence in America* (New York, 1981), p. 27. See also Wilson, *In Quest of Community*, p. 9.

23. Henry Maine, *Popular Government* (London, 1918 [1885]), p. 23–25; Francis Lieber, *On Civil Liberty and Self-Government* (3rd ed.; Philadelphia, 1883), pp. 407, 123. See also E. L. Godkin to F. L. Olmsted, 25 Dec. 1864, as quoted in H. Wayne Morgan, ed., *The Gilded Age* (Syracuse, 1970), p. 65; Stow Persons, *The Decline of American Gentility* (New York, 1973), pp. 144–56.

24. Elisha Mulford, *The Nation: The Foundations of Civil Order and Political Life in the United States* (Boston, 1883), pp. 9, 17, 19, 50. See also Mark Neely, Jr., "Romanticism, Nationalism, and the New Economics: Elisha Mulford and the Organic Theory of the State," *American Quarterly* 29 (1977): 404–21; Howard Mumford Jones, *The Age of Energy* (New York, 1971), p. 35–37; George Fredrickson, *The Inner Civil War* (New York, 1965), chaps. 9, 14. See also James Bryce, *The American Commonwealth*, 2 vols. (New York, 1908), 2: 267, 374, 362.

25. Matthew Arnold, "Numbers; or the Majority and the Remnant," in *Discourses in America* (New York, 1894), pp. 68, 71. See also E. L. Godkin, "The Growth and Expression of Public Opinion," *Atlantic*

Monthly 81 (1898): 1–15; W. S. Lilly, "The Shibboleth of Public Opinion," *Forum* 10 (November 1890): 256–63.

26. Swing is quoted in the *Chicago Inter Ocean,* May 10, 1886, p. 1. See Henry David, *The Haymarket Affair* (New York, 1936); Paul Avrich, *The Haymarket Tragedy* (Princeton, 1984); Almont Lindsay, *The Pullman Strike* (Chicago, 1943); Carlos Schwantes, *Coxey's Army* (Lincoln, Neb., 1985); Jaher, *Doubters and Dissenters,* chaps. 1, 2.

27. Ignatius Donnelly, *Caesar's Column* (Cambridge, 1960), p. 37.

28. Josiah Strong, *The New Era* (New York, 1893), pp. 312, and chap. 7; Charles Sheldon, *In His Steps* (Old Tappan, N.J., 1963), p. 53. See Paul Boyer's article *"In His Steps:* A Reappraisal," *American Quarterly* 23 (1971): 70, and Henry F. May, *Protestant Churches and Industrial America* (New York, 1967); Dominick Cavallo, *Muscles and Morals* (Philadelphia, 1981); David Glassberg, "Restoring a 'Forgotten Childhood': American Play and the Progressive Era's Elizabethan Past," *American Quarterly* 32 (1980): 351–68; David Shi, *The Simple Life* (New York, 1985), pp. 206–14; J. Adams Puffer, *The Boy and His Gang* (Boston, 1912).

29. Howard Hurwitz, *Theodore Roosevelt and Labor* (New York, 1943), p. 179; Edmund Morris, *The Rise of Theodore Roosevelt* (New York, 1979), p. 552; Michael McGerr, *The Decline of Popular Politics: The American North, 1865–1928* (New York, 1986), chap. 7; Richard Jensen, *Winning the Midwest* (Chicago, 1971), chap. 6.

30. *Nation* 66 (May 5, 1898): 336. An international copyright law, enacted in 1893, provided greater financial rewards to budding writers. See also Jean B. Quandt, *From the Small Town to the Great Community* (New Brunswick, N.J., 1970), p. 31; Michael Schudson, *Discovering the News* (New York, 1978), p. 64.

31. Stephen Crane, *The Red Badge of Courage* (New York, 1976), p. 30; Jay Martin, *Harvests of Change: American Literature 1865–1920* (Englewood Cliffs, N.J., 1967), p. 63. See also Edward Bellamy, *Looking Backward* (New York, 1960), pp. 182, 212, and Mary E. W. Freeman's story "A Village Singer," in *The American Tradition in Literature,* ed. Sculley Bradley et al., 2 vols. (New York, 1962), 2: 527–38; Arthur Mann, *Yankee Reformers in the Urban Age: Social Reform in Boston, 1880–1900* (New York, 1954).

32. Bliss Perry, *The American Mind* (Boston, 1912), p. 100; George L. Clark, *Notions of a Country Parson* (Boston, 1910), p. 38. See also (Ernest Howard), "The Decay of the New England Churches," *Nation* 43 (November 4, 1886): 367–68. On the patriotic impulse in this era

see Wallace Davies, *Patriotism on Parade* (Cambridge, 1955); William B. Rhoads, *The Colonial Revival*, 2 vols. (New York, 1977).

33. Theodore Roosevelt and Henry Cabot Lodge, *Hero Tales of American History* (New York, 1895); Theodore Greene, *America's Heroes* (New York, 1970), chap. 4.

34. Elbert Hubbard, "Heart to Heart Talks with Grown-Ups by the Pastor of His Flock," *Philistine* 8 (March 1899): 109–16. See also Charles Horton Cooley, *Social Organization* (New York, 1909), pp. 152–53. Nathaniel Shaler, *The Citizen* (New York, 1904), p. 151. On Hubbard see Richard M. Huber, *The American Idea of Success* (New York, 1971), chap. 6. On the Spanish-American War see David Axtell, " 'Heroes of the Engine Room': American 'Civilization' and the War with Spain," *American Quarterly* 36 (1984): 492.

35. William Dean Howells, *A Traveller from Altruria* (New York, 1957), p. 107. See Cecilia Tichi, *Shifting Gears* (Chapel Hill, 1987), chap. 3; Mary Moss, "Machine-Made Human Beings," *Atlantic Monthly* 94 (1904): 264–68; Mills, *The Crowd in American Literature*, chap. 3.

36. On Whitman's funeral see Charles B. Willard, *Whitman's American Fame* (Providence, 1950), chap. 2. On his influence see, for example, *The Autobiography of William Allen White* (New York, 1946), p. 195; Robert Crunden, *Ministers of Reform* (New York, 1982), pp. 98–99; Ann Massa, *Vachel Lindsay: Fieldworker for the American Dream* (Bloomington, Ind., 1970), pp. 242–45; Van Wyck Brooks, *America's Coming of Age* (Garden City, N.Y., 1958), pp. 57–75.

37. Ralph Barton Perry, *The Life of William James* (New York, 1948), Briefer Version, pp. 226–28, 248–49.

38. Fred Mathews, *Quest for an American Sociology: Robert E. Park and the Chicago School* (Montreal, 1977), pp. 31–33. James's address can be found in John McDermott, ed., *The Writings of William James* (New York, 1968), pp. 638–39. See Ziff, *Literary Democracy*, pp. 244–45, and "Whitman and the Crowd," *Critical Inquiry* 10 (June 1984): 579–91; Leo Braudy, *The Frenzy of Renown* (New York, 1986), pp. 464–67.

39. Carey McWilliams, *The Idea of Fraternity in America* (Berkeley, 1973), p. 410. See also Philip Fisher, "Democratic Social Space: Whitman, Melville, and the Promise of American Transparency," *Representations* 24 Fall (1988): 60–101.

40. Walt Whitman, "Democratic Vistas," reprinted in *The Works of Walt Whitman*, 2 vols. (New York, 1968), 2: 228.

41. Gay Wilson Allen, *Walt Whitman as Man, Poet, and Legend* (Carbondale, Ill., 1961), pp. 101–34; Willard, *Whitman's American Fame*,

chaps. 2, 3. For contemporary critical views see W. B. Harte, "Walt Whitman's Democracy," *New England Magazine*, n.s., 6 (1892): 722, and Barrett Wendell, *A Literary History of America* (New York, 1900), pp. 465–79.

42. Sennett, *The Fall of Public Man*, p. 151.

43. For background on social theorists in the mid to late nineteenth century see Robert Nye, *The Origins of Crowd Psychology: Gustave Le Bon and the Crisis of Mass Democracy in the Third Republic* (Beverly Hills, 1975); Thomas Bender, *Community and Social Change in America* (Baltimore, 1978), chap. 12; Wilson, *In Quest of Community;* Thomas Haskell, *The Emergence of Professional Social Science* (New York, 1977); Howe, *The Political Culture of the American Whigs*, p. 52.

44. Gustave Le Bon, *The Crowd* (New York, 1960 [1896]), p. 31. See also James Gilbert, *From Work to Salvation* (Baltimore, 1977), p. 32; Lionel Trilling, *Sincerity and Authenticity* (Cambridge, Mass., 1972), p. 100; Justin Kaplan, *Mr. Clemens and Mark Twain* (New York, 1966), p. 341.

45. Edward Ross, *Social Psychology* (New York, 1908), pp. 63, 83. Ross's article on "The Mob Mind," first published in 1897 in *The Popular Science Monthly,* was the seed for much of his later work. He followed the lead of Gabriel Tarde in France, and tried to distinguish between the crowd and the public. The literature that illustrates the crowd as a metaphorical reference in the Progressive Era is large and significant. See, for example, Clayton Hamilton, "The Psychology of Theater Audiences," *Forum* 39 (October 1907): 234–48; Scott, *The Psychology of Public Speaking*, chap. 12; Charles Ferguson, *The Religion of Democracy* (New York, 1900), pp. 166, 98, 104, 87; Frederick Davenport, *Primitive Traits in Religious Revivals* (New York, 1905), pp. 314–15.

46. See Wilson, *In Quest of Community;* Eugene Leach, "Mob, Audience, Market: Crowd Psychology in America, 1890–1930," a paper delivered at the Popular Culture Association Convention, 16 April 1982; John Dewey, "The Need for Social Psychology," *Psychological Review* 24 (July 1917): 266–77.

47. On amusement parks and changing forms of entertainment see John Kasson, *Amusing the Million: Coney Island at the Turn of the Century* (New York, 1978); Guy De Bord, *Society of Spectacle* (Detroit, 1970); Rosenzweig, *Eight Hours for What We Will*. On urban commercial culture and crowds see Alan Trachtenberg, *The Incorporation of America* (New York, 1982), chap. 5; Susan Porter Benson, "Palace of

Consumption and Machine for Selling: The American Department Store, 1880–1940," *Radical History Review* 21 (1979): 197–221; Neil Harris, *Humbug! The Art of P. T. Barnum* (Boston, 1973).

48. For moralistic "reformers" view of the emerging arenas of modern crowds see Richard Edwards, *Christianity and Amusements* (New York, 1919); Jane Addams, *The Spirit of Youth and the City Streets* (New York, 1908).

49. Michael Davis, *Psychological Interpretations of Society* (New York, 1904), p. 61. Warren Susman writes that "the social role demanded of all in the new culture of personality was that of a performer. Every American was to become a performing self." His argument is persuasive but the determinants of the "culture of personality" need to be pushed back a decade or more in time. Susman, "Personality and the Making of Twentieth-Century Culture," p. 220.

50. Herbert Croly, *Progressive Democracy* (New York, 1914), p. 226.

51. Henry Adams, *The Education of Henry Adams* (New York, 1931 [1918]), p. 489. See also Moses Ostrogorsk, *Democracy and the Party System in the United States* (New York, 1902), p. 410.

52. Gerald Stanley Lee, *Crowds: A Moving Picture of Democracy* (Garden City, N.Y., 1913), p. 551.

2. The Lost Frontier of a Puritan Parson

1. GSL, *About an Old New England Church* (Sharon, Conn., 1891), pp. 72, 11, 29.

2. On GSL's genealogical background see Charles F. Warner, *Representative Families of Northampton*, 9 vols. (Northampton, Mass., 1917), 2: 241–45 (hereafter cited as Warner, *Northampton Families*). See also *Who Was Who in America, 1897–1942* (Chicago, 1943), p. 717; William R. Cutter, *Genealogical and Personal Memoirs Relating to the Families of the State of Massachusetts*, 4 vols. (New York, 1910), 1: 181.

3. The status anxiety of preachers is examined in Richard Hofstadter's book, *The Age of Reform* (New York, 1955), pp. 150–52.

4. On the genteel tradition see John Tomisch, *A Genteel Endeavor: American Culture and Politics in the Gilded Age* (Stanford, 1971). The best analysis of antimodernism is Jackson Lears's *No Place of Grace* (New York, 1982). See also David Macleod, *Building Character in the American Boy* (Madison, 1984); Shi, *The Simple Life;* Robert Crunden, *Ministers of Reform* (New York, 1982). On Puritanism see

Warren Susman, "Uses of the Puritan Past," in *Culture as History* (New York, 1984), pp. 39–49; Richard E. Cauger, "The Concept of the Puritan in American Literary Criticism, 1890–1932" (Ph.D. diss., Northwestern University, 1964), pp. 1–36.

5. Warner, *Northampton Families*, pp. 241–42.

6. Ibid.; U.S. Department of Commerce, Bureau of the Census, *United States Census of Population: 1880*, Ohio (hereafter referred to as *U.S. Census*). The Lee family wealth listed in the 1880 census is a mere $800.

7. GSL, *About an Old New England Church*, pp. 18, 19, 20, 21, 14, 32–33, 80, 35, 81, 89. The young parson's remarks were soon published as a book that drew favorable remarks from such New England luminaries as Oliver Wendell Holmes, George William Curtis, and Charles Dudley Warner.

8. GSL, *The Lost Art of Reading* (New York, 1903), p. 298.

9. Larzar Ziff, *Puritanism in America* (New York, 1973), p. 6. "What made a pastor" in the late colonial times, historian Harry Stout has observed, "was not simply the preaching of the word but a direct, authoritarian identification with a specific flock." Harry Stout, "Religion, Communication, and the Revolution," *William and Mary Quarterly* 34 (October 1977): 526. See also Donald Scott, *From Office to Profession: The New England Ministry, 1750–1850* (Philadelphia, 1978), pp. 7, 16; Lee W. Huebner, "The Discovery of Propaganda: Changing Attitudes toward Public Communication in America, 1900–1930" (Ph.D. diss., Harvard University, 1968), p. 89.

10. Perry Miller, *Errand into the Wilderness* (New York, 1956), pp. 202–3; Horace Bushnell, *God in Christ* (Hartford, Conn., 1849), p. 38; as quoted in Barbara Cross, *Horace Bushnell: Minister to a Changing America* (Chicago, 1958), p. 107. On the declining literary talents of New England in the late nineteenth century see Barrett Wendell, *A Literary History of America* (New York, 1900), pp. 436–46.

11. Scott, *From Office to Profession*, p. 154. On disestablishment see Samuel C. Pearson, "From Church to Denomination: American Congregationalism in the Nineteenth Century," *Church History* 38 (1969): 68; Conrad Cherry, "Nature and the Republic: The New Haven Theology," *New England Quarterly* 51 (1978): 521.

12. Henry Ward Beecher, "The Study of Human Nature," *Popular Science Monthly* 1 (1872): 327–28, 330, as quoted in Thomas Haskell, *The Emergence of Professional Social Science* (New York, 1977), p. 83. See also Robert Cross, ed., *The Church and the City* (New York, 1967),

pp. 169, 180. As a young man GSL apparently saw Beecher speak and read Lyman Abbott's biography, *Henry Ward Beecher: A Sketch of His Career* (Hartford, 1887).

13. Sarah Orne Jewett, *The Country of the Pointed Firs* (Boston, 1896). See Larzar Ziff, *The American 1890s: Life and Times of a Lost Generation* (New York, 1966), p. 214; John Brinkerhoff, *American Space* (New York, 1972), pp. 87–136; William McLoughlin, *The Meaning of Henry Ward Beecher* (New York, 1970), p. 140; GSL, *Mt. Tom* 1 (August 1905): 81. A complete collection of this journal, edited and largely written by GSL from 1905 to 1918 is located in the Smith College Library.

14. GSL to Chris Lee, March 1884. This letter is located in the Gerald Lee collection of the Forbes Library, Northampton, Massachusetts, hereafter referred to as GSL-FL; *U.S. Census, 1880, 1890, 1900, 1910.* See also Hal S. Barron, "Rediscovering the Majority: The New Rural History of the Nineteenth-Century North," *Historical Methods* 19 (Fall 1986): 141–52; Van Wyck Brooks, *New England Summer* (New York, 1940), p. 330; Jay Martin, *Harvests of Change: American Literature 1865–1920* (Englewood Cliffs, N.J., 1967), p. 136.

15. GSL, "In Behalf of Boys," *Springfield Republican*, 20 January 1891. See Lears, *No Place of Grace,* p. 146; Shi, *The Simple Life,* chap. 8; Dominick Cavallo, *Muscles and Morals* (Philadelphia, 1981).

16. GSL, "New York City," n.d. (GSL-FL). It is probably dated May 1890, when Lee was attending a school to improve his public speaking.

17. Ibid.

18. Richard P. Harmon, "Tradition and Change in the Gilded Age: A Political History of Massachusetts, 1878–1912" (Ph.D. diss., Columbia University, 1966), esp. pp. 380, 18; Richard M. Abrams, *Conservatism in a Progressive Era: Massachusetts Politics, 1900–1912* (Cambridge, Mass., 1964), p. 28, for census data. Jack Tager, "Massachusetts and the Age of Economic Revolution," in *Massachusetts in the Gilded Age,* ed. Jack Tager and John Ifkovic (Amherst, Mass., 1985), pp. 17–18; Carl Siracusa, *A Mechanical People: Perceptions of the Industrial Order in Massachusetts, 1810–1880* (Middletown, Conn., 1979); Michael Frisch, *Town into City: Springfield, Massachusetts, and the Meaning of Community, 1840–1880* (Cambridge, Mass., 1972). On nativism, see Barbara Miller Solomon, *Ancestors and Immigrants* (Chicago, 1956). On Northampton see John F. Manfredi, "Immigration to Northampton," in Tercentenary History Committee, *The Northampton Book* (Northampton, 1954), pp. 331–36.

19. GSL, "Dry Goods and Notions," No. 7 (September–October 1886)

(GSL-FL). The dream suggests the scope of Lee's fears. The ground shook under his feet; fences "seemed possessed with an evil spirit"; everybody he met was "drunk and wobbled all over the sidewalk"; the "telegraph poles were bowing indiscriminately to things in general." Even the town clock was suspect; a "clock that couldn't keep any steadier than that," he wrote, "was too drunk to tell the time right anyway."

20. Ibid.

21. Lee's view of women as somehow existing alien to and apart from the frontier experience was widely mirrored in the popular literature of the day as well as in many of the historical studies then being conducted.

22. GSL, "A Boy's Joys and Sorrows," *Greenfield Gazette and Courier*, 6 June 1903 (GSL-FL). See also GSL, *Crowds: A Moving Picture of Democracy* (Garden City, N.Y., 1913), p. 13.

23. GSL, "A Boy's Joys and Sorrows."

24. Oberlin theology emphasized free will in seeking salvation and "the possibility of moral progress," according to historian John Barnard in his *From Evangelicalism to Progressivism at Oberlin College* (Columbus, Ohio, 1969), pp. 50, 57, 62.

25. GSL, "Does Our Railroad System Need Legislation against Government Ownership," Oberlin, 26 June 1878; "The History and Character of John B. Gough," 28 February 1881 (GSL-FL).

26. GSL, "The Romish Church in America," 11 June 1881 (GSL-FL).

27. GSL, "General Quotations, No. 1," p. 35 (GSL-FL). Haskell, *The Emergence of Professional Social Science*. See also Sacvan Bercovitch, "Emerson the Prophet: Romanticism, Puritanism, and Auto-American-Biography," in *Emerson: Prophecy, Metamorphosis, and Influence*, ed. David Levin (New York, 1975), pp. 6–7; Steven Mintz, *A Prison of Expectations* (New York, 1982), p. 5.

28. GSL, "Personal Thoughtful Notebook, No. 1," 30 July 1884 (GSL-FL). See also GSL, "Sketch Class at Yale," n.d. (GSL-FL).

29. GSL, "Men Moving Finis," vol. 1, August 1885; GSL to the editor of the *North American Review* 170 (13 January 1900); "Personal Thoughtful Book No. 1" (5 September, [no year]) (GSL-FL). See also John Zelie, "Gerald Stanley Lee: A Growing Writer Whom Western Massachusetts Claims," *Springfield Sunday Union*, 8 August 1897, p. 10. GSL, "Sketch Class at Yale" (GSL-FL).

30. GSL, *The Critic* 31 (17 July 1897): 36–37; GSL, Review of Charles Hall's *Qualifications for Ministerial Power*, in *The Critic* 27 (26 October 1895): 262; GSL, Review of David Greer's *The Preacher and His*

Place, in *The Critic* 28 (6 June 1896): 404; GSL, "Intellectual Life," p. 12, November 1, 1890 (GSL-FL). He later admitted that he never graduated from Yale because he had become entranced with literature. *The Critic* 27 (26 October 1895): 262.

    At Yale, Lee fell under the influence of William R. Harper and Samuel Harris, the latter a theologian with a penchant for quoting Wordsworth, Whittier, Browning, and Goethe. Harris also nurtured Lee's notion of Anglo-Saxon superiority. See Samuel Harris, *The Kingdom of Christ on Earth* (Andover, 1874), p. 255; Roland Bainton, *Yale and the Ministry* (New York, 1957), pp. 173, 178.

31. "I think metaphorically," Lee related in his diary on 10 March 1885. Four years later, on a cold February Monday, while he was in charge of his first parish in Princeton, Minnesota, he related that he had been "trying to entertain myself by conjuring up metaphors and tracing out analogies," but felt that others could not appreciate them. GSL, "Personal Thoughtful Book, No. 1"; "Anything," p. 2b, 19 February 1889 (GSL-FL).

32. GSL, "General Thoughtful Book"; GSL, "On Science," n.d. (GSL-FL); GSL, *The Lost Art,* p. 74. See also Catharine Albanese, "The Kinetic Revolution: New Transformation in the Language of the Transcendentalists," *New England Quarterly* 48 (1975): 319–41; Donald Meyer, *The Positive Thinkers* (New York, 1980), chaps. 2, 5; Thomas Haskell, *The Emergence of Professional Social Science* (Urbana, 1977), p. 250. Raymond Williams, *Culture and Society, 1780–1950* (New York, 1958), Pt. 2. On the battle over the Great Man Theory in the 1880s see William James, "Great Men, Great Thoughts, and Their Environment," *Atlantic Monthly* 46 (1880): 441–59; John Fiske, "Sociology and Hero Worship," in *The Writings of John Fiske,* 23 vols. (Cambridge, Mass., 1902), 9: 158–83.

33. GSL, "Carlyle," n.d. (GSL-FL).

34. GSL, "Carlyle Has Immortal Faults," n.d. (GSL-FL). GSL, "Thomas Carlyle," *The Critic* 27 (30 November 1895): 359. See Philip Rosenberg, *The Seventh Hero: Thomas Carlyle and the Theory of Radical Activism* (Cambridge, Mass., 1974), p. 126; Hugh D. Duncan, *Communication and Social Order* (New York, 1962), pp. 193–94.

35. The quote, referring to Franklin Giddings, Jane Addams, and Charles Cooley is from Jean Quandt's *From the Small Town to the Great Community* (New Brunswick, N.J., 1970), p. 13.

36. Ann Douglas, *The Feminization of American Culture* (New York, 1977), p. 20; GSL, "General Quotations No. 6," p. 54. See also McLoughlin, *The Meaning of Henry Ward Beecher,* p. 143; John

Kasson, *Civilizing the Machine* (New York, 1976), p. 116; Emerson, *The Complete Works of Ralph Waldo Emerson*, 12 vols. (New York, 1903), vol. 4, "Uses of Great Men," p. 25; Robert Linscott, ed., *The Journals of Ralph Waldo Emerson* (New York, 1960), p. 347.

37. GSL, "The Uses of Extraordinary Men," *Independent*, 20 August 1891 (GSL-FL); GSL, "Qualifications for Ministerial Power," *The Critic* 27 (26 October 1895): 262; GSL, "A List of My Books," n.d. (GSL-FL).

38. GSL, "Personal Thoughtful Book, No. 1"—hereafter referred to as PTB; "Notebook No. 20," 19 December 1887; PTB No. 2, 5 August 1889 (GSL- FL).

39. GSL, "General Thoughtful Book, No. 2" (March 1885), p. 24 (GSL-FL).

40. GSL, "The Printing Press and Personality," *New World* 8 (1899): 315. "A Paper Civilization" was the title Lee used for this piece of a proposed book, "The View from Olympus."

41. Ibid.; GSL, Review of Ezra Byington's *The Puritan in England and New England* (Boston, 1896), in *The Critic* (GSL-FL); GSL, "The Dominance of the Crowd," *Atlantic Monthly* 86 (1900): 759.

3. "Parson of the World"

1. Unlabeled clipping, 9 March 1896 (GSL-FL).
2. Ibid.
3. GSL, *The Shadow Christ* (New York, 1896), p. 66.
4. GSL, *The Lost Art of Reading* (New York, 1903), p. 53; Randolph Bourne, "Very Long and Sunny," *New Republic* 7 (15 July 1916): 282.
5. GSL, "Stray Leaves," n.d., pp. 2–3 (GSL-FL). See also GSL, "Thomas Carlyle," *The Critic* 27 (30 November 1895): 359. Lee's fascination with language and mass persuasion was shared by many of his contemporaries, from William Jennings Bryan to Woodrow Wilson.
6. GSL, *Lost Art*, pp. 64, 371–72. On Walt Whitman and photography see Miles Orvell, *The Real Thing: Imitation and Authenticity in American Culture, 1880–1940* (Chapel Hill, 1989), chap. 1. See also GSL, *Lost Art*, p. 410; "Personal Thoughtful Book, No. 1" (7 June 188?); "Men Moving Finis, Vol. 1" (29 August 1885) (GSL-FL).
7. "Mrs. Barker," n.d., but undoubtedly in 1888 or early 1889 (GSL-FL). He wrote that "it is really Will that men most worship in this world and it is Will that runs the interests of men." See also GSL, "The Priest Who Passed on the Other Side," (17 November 1888), p. 3 (GSL-FL). The 1890 census of Princeton noted 816 people. See "Princeton" (12

May 1889), p. 4. Lee failed to get another pulpit in Duluth because he preached a bad trial sermon and returned east by August for a family wedding. This was doubtlessly very humiliating for him. See GSL to the Rev. J. H. Morley, 14 May 1889 (GSL- FL).

8. GSL, "Fragment on Preaching" (3 September 1890); GSL, "My Preaching" (11 December 1890); GSL, "Preaching" (12 January 1890) (GSL-FL).

9. GSL, n.t., n.d.; GSL, "Preaching" (12 January 1890) (GSL-FL).

10. GSL, "New York City" (1890); GSL, "New York City" (May 1890) (GSL-FL); GSL, n.t. (5 June 1890) (GSL-FL). According to one of the few biographical articles written about Lee, he was spending this time reading and writing, having his first important contact with editors. See Charles F. Warner, *Representative Families of Northampton*, 2 vols. (Northampton, 1917), 1: 246.

11. GSL to Mr. F. C. Jones, 15 October 1890; GSL to his Sharon, Conn., congregation, 6 April 1892 (GSL-FL).

12. *Springfield Republican*, 24 May 1892 (GSL-FL). See also William McLoughlin, *The Meaning of Henry Ward Beecher* (New York, 1970), p. 148; Charles G. Finney, *Lectures on Revivals* (Cambridge, Mass., 1960); Daniel Calhoun, *The Intelligence of a People* (Princeton, 1973), pp. 17, 256–90; James G. Findlay, Jr., *Dwight Moody: American Evangelist, 1837–1899* (Chicago, 1969), chap. 4; Sandra Sizer, "Politics and Apolitical Religion: The Great Urban Revivals of the Late Nineteenth Century," *Church History* 48 (1979): 96. Lee Huebner notes that "preachers of religion, particularly the revivalists, represented one of the few areas in which any theory of mass persuasion had been advanced before the twentieth century." "The Discovery of Propaganda, Changing Attitudes toward Public Communication in America, 1900–1930" (Ph.D. diss., Harvard University, 1968), p. 96.

13. GSL, "Qualifications for Ministerial Power," *The Critic* 27 (26 October 1895): 262; GSL, "Literature and the Modern Pulpit," *The Critic* 30 (2 January 1897): 1–2.

14. *Springfield Republican*, 9 March 1896 (GSL-FL).

15. GSL, n.t. (1 April 1896) (GSL-FL).

16. GSL, *The Shadow Christ*, pp. vii, 13, 72–73, 79–80. See also Carlyle's chapter on "The Everlasting Yeah" in *Sartor Resartus* (London, 1834); Ernest Cassirer, *The Myth of the State* (New Haven, 1946), p. 195; Arthur Mann, *Yankee Reformers in the Urban Age: Social Reform in Boston, 1880–1900* (New York, 1954), p. 89.

17. Ferenc Morton Szasz, *The Divided Mind of Protestant America, 1880–1930* (University, Ala., 1982), p. 22; Margaret Deland, *John*

Wards, Preacher (New York, 1888). On Harold Frederic see Larzar Ziff, *The American 1890s: Life and Times of a Lost Generation* (New York, 1966), p. 216.

18. GSL, *The Shadow Christ*, pp. 61, 43, 118; GSL, "The Use of Extraordinary Men," *Independent*, 20 April 1891.

19. GSL, *The Shadow Christ*, pp. 118, 63–64, 125, 44. GSL, "Prophets of the Christian Faith," *The Critic* 29 (16 January 1897): 36.

20. (GSL-FL); GSL to Ferguson, 1896 (GSL-FL).

21. GSL to Upton Sinclair, 16 July 1903 (GSL-FL). Jennette Lee's papers are located in the Smith College Library. According to Julia Taylor, who lived with the Lees in the 1930s, they were "serene and gentle people . . . proud and aloof about ordinary considerations." Letter to the author, 11 October 1981.

22. GSL to Samuel and Emma Lee, 26 April 1893 and 7 August 1901 (GSL-FL). See GSL to Emma Lee, 15 October 1899. Apparently Samuel Lee's religious beliefs had little ecumenical flavor to them. See Charles G. Fairman, "College-Trained Immigrants: A Study of Americans in the Making," *New England Magazine*, n.s., 42 (July 1910): 584.

23. GSL to President Seelye, 20 January 1896; GSL to Charles Ferguson, 9 November 1897 (GSL-FL). Among the many writers that the Lees entertained in Northampton over the years were Bertrand Russell, Lincoln Steffens, and Frederick Howe. See also GSL to Dr. E. Winchester Donald, 8 January 1898 (GSL-FL); GSL to W. R. Harper, 27 October 1898 (GSL-FL).

24. *The Northampton Book* (Northampton, 1954), p. 237.

25. GSL, *The Critic* 38 (7 March 1896): 157; GSL, *Lost Art*, p. 317. GSL, "Harriet Beecher Stowe," *The Critic* 30 (24 April 1897): 281–83; GSL, *Lost Art*, p. 398. See John Tomisch, *A Genteel Endeavor: American Culture and Politics in the Gilded Age* (Stanford, 1971).

26. GSL, "Journalism as a Basis for Literature," *Atlantic Monthly* 85 (1900): 232–34. Kipling was a raging literary success in the United States by the late 1890s, "the object of one of the great literary 'crazes' of the nineties," according to Frank Luther Mott in *Golden Multitudes* (New York, 1947), p. 184.

27. GSL, n.d.—printed article, possibly printed in the *Boston Evening Transcript* (GSL-FL).

28. GSL, "The Sex-Conscious School in Fiction," *New World* 9 (March 1900): 77–84; GSL, "The Prevalence of Parsons," *The Book Buyer* 14 (n.d.): 373. GSL, "Mr. Howells on the Platform," *The Critic* 35 (November 1899): 1029–30.

29. Charles Ferguson, *The Religion of Democracy* (New York, 1900), pp.

9, 51, 87, 113, 163. For background on the religious excitement in these years see Robert T. Handy, *A Christian Nation: Protestant Hopes and Historical Realities* (New York, 1971), pp. 115–39; Henry May, *Protestant Churches and Industrial America* (New York, 1967), pp. 112–234. Robert Handy sees 1897–99 as the focal point of the new religious movement, while Peter Frederick in *Knights of the Golden Rule: The Intellectual as Christian Social Reformer in the 1890s* (Lexington, Ky., 1976) writes that these dates are too restrictive. Frederick also asserts that George Herron was the "charismatic leader of the movement" (p. 26). GSL wrote to Upton Sinclair in 1903 that he had a "very much marked copy [of Herron's] *Larger Christ*," 29 July 1903 (GSL-FL).

30. Charles Ferguson, *The University Militant* (New York, 1904), pp. 111, 88, 67, 157–59. See also GSL to Charles Ferguson, 19 April 1900 and 17 November 1900 (GSL-FL). It should be emphasized that neither Ferguson nor Lee was interested in creating highly profitable enterprises. Lee wrote to his friend in 1903 that "there are plenty of magazines with money and it has been the death of them. What is wanted—to start a magazine nowadays is brains, moral courage and unpurchasableness—willingness to be rich or poor according to circumstances." GSL to CHF, 23 May 1903 (GSL-FL).

31. Ferguson, *The University Militant*, p. 158.

32. GSL to Ferguson, 7 February 1908, Box 3 (GSL-FL); George Creel, *Rebel at Large* (New York, 1950), p. 72.

33. GSL, "The Church of the Strong Men," *Outlook* 79 (4 February 1905): 336–41.

34. Ibid.; Henry Adams, *The Education of Henry Adams* (New York, 1931 [1918]); Henry Adams, *Mont Saint Michel and Chartres* (New York, 1913).

35. GSL, "Some Experiences of a Church Goer," *Outlook* 80 (29 July 1905): 820–24.

36. Ibid.

4. Psychic Currents

1. GSL, "The Dominance of the Crowd," *Atlantic Monthly* 86 (1900): 755, 761. Much of this article was included in Lee's later best-selling book *Crowds* (Garden City, N.Y., 1913). GSL, *Crowds*, p. 159.

2. GSL, "The Dominance of the Crowd," p. 761.

3. Frances Perkins is quoted in Marshall Berman, *All That Is Solid Melts into Air* (New York, 1988), p. 304.

4. On the legacy of romanticism see Leon Bramson, *The Political Context of Sociology* (Princeton, 1961), p. 30; Jean Quandt, *From the Small Town to the Great Community* (New Brunswick, N.J., 1970).

5. GSL, "Intellectual Life," 16 April 1890, p. 4 (GSL-FL). See also Elias Canetti, *Crowds and Power* (New York, 1963), p. 15.

6. See Marshall Berman on "The Heroism of Modern Life," in *All That Is Solid Melts into Air,* pp. 142–48; Stephen Kern, *The Culture of Time and Space, 1880–1918* (Cambridge, Mass., 1983), pp. 221–22; Jan Romein, *The Watershed of Two Eras: Europe in 1900* (Middletown, Conn., 1978), chaps. 3, 5.

7. GSL, "New York City," 8 May 1890, p. 1 (GSL-FL). GSL, *The Lost Art of Reading* (New York, 1903), p. 386. GSL, "Paris," 16 May 1892 (GSL-FL). For perspective on this see Frederick Cople Jaher, *Doubters and Dissenters* (Glen Coe, N.Y., 1964), chaps. 1–3.

8. GSL, *Mt. Tom* 1 (November 1905): 185–86; GSL, *Mt. Tom* 1 (September 1905): 12, 13. GSL, *The Lost Art,* pp. 38, 379.

9. I am indebted to Janine Perry and Margaret Bush for insight into the work of Jennette Lee.

10. Jennette Lee, *Kate Wetherill* (New York, 1900), pp. 12–13, 92; *The Pillar of Salt* (New York, 1901), p. 83; *A Taste of Apples* (New York, 1913), pp. 71, 115.

11. GSL, "A Plea for the Individual," 25 December 1884 (GSL-FL).

12. GSL, "Anything," Written shortly before 30 March 1890 (GSL-FL).

13. *The Complete Works of Ralph Waldo Emerson,* 12 vols., (New York, 1903) 5: 117, 186; George Fredrickson, *The Inner Civil War* (New York, 1965), pp. 177–78; R. Jackson Wilson, *In Quest of Community* (New York, 1968), p. 13.

14. See Stephen J. Gould, *Mismeasure of Man* (New York, 1981), pp. 104–5; Patrick Brantlinger, *Bread and Circuses: Theories of Mass Culture as Social Decay* (Ithaca, 1983), chaps. 4, 5; Eileen Boris, *Art and Labor: Ruskin, Morris, and the Craftsman Ideal in America* (Philadelphia, 1986); Benjamin Lippincott, *Victorian Critics of Democracy* (New York, 1964), pp. 93–134.

15. GSL, "Making the Crowd Beautiful," *Atlantic Monthly* 87 (1901): 251; Gustave Le Bon, *The Crowd* (New York, 1960) p. 37. See also Roger Geiger, "Democracy and the Crowd: The Social History of an Idea in France and Italty, 1890–1914," *Societas* 7 (Winter 1977): 47–71.

16. GSL to Arthur Page, 3 December 1912 (GSL-FL).

17. George H. Mead, Review of Le Bon's *The Psychology of Socialism,* *American Journal of Sociology* 5 (1899): 404–12; William James,

Review of Le Bon's *The Crowd, Psychological Review* 4 (1897): 313–16; Elting Morrison, ed., *The Letters of Theodore Roosevelt,* 8 vols. (Cambridge, Mass. 1951), 1:535; "The Morality of Crowds," *Nation* 66 (17 March 1898): 281; Robert Church, "The Economists Study Society," in *The Social Sciences at Harvard, 1860–1920,* ed. Paul Buck (Cambridge, 1965), p. 60.

18. Newell Dwight Hillis, "An Outlook upon the Agrarian Propaganda in the West," *Review of Reviews* 14 (September 1896): 304–5; Lloyd Bryce, "The Political Menace of the Discontented," *Atlantic Monthly* 78 (1896): 450. See also Lloyd Bryce, "A Study in Campaign Audiences," *North American Review* 164 (1897): 82–91; "The Anarchist Platform," *Puck,* 30 September 1896, and "Bryan as an 'Attraction,'" *Puck,* 14 October 1896.

19. GSL, "General Thoughtful Book, No. 2," p. 10 (GSL-FL); GSL, *The Lost Art,* p. 412; GSL, "Hullabaloo," *The Critic* 29 (22 August 1896): 113–14. For the legacy of fear that the campaign of 1896 represented in several intellectual leaders see Walter Lippmann, *Drift and Mastery* (New York, 1914), p. 135; H. L. Mencken, "Heretics," *American Mercury* 3 (October 1924): 202; *The Autobiography of William Allen White* (New York, 1946), p. 279.

20. GSL, "Hullabaloo."

21. Ibid.

22. Ibid.

23. Ibid.

24. GSL, "The Printing Press and Personality," *New World* 8 (1899): 318–19.

25. GSL, "Journalism as a Basis for Literature," *Atlantic Monthly* 85 (1900): 236–37. Edward Ross, *Social Psychology* (New York, 1908), pp. 63, 83. See also Clayton Hamilton, "The Psychology of Theater Audiences," *Forum* 39 (October 1907): 234–48; Walter Dill Scott, *The Psychology of Public Speaking* (New York, 1906), chap. 12.

26. GSL, *The Lost Art,* p. 242, 298. The sales of *Lost Art* were minimal.

27. Ibid., pp. 372, 193–94, 374, 22, 10.

28. Ibid., pp. 49–51, 54.

29. Henry Dwight Sedgwick, *The New American Type and Other Essays* (New York, 1908), p. 49; Arthur Hadley, *Undercurrents in American Politics* (New Haven, 1915), pp. 164–65; "The Mob Spirit," *The Chautauquan* 38 (September 1903): 12; Theodore Roosevelt, *The New Nationalism* (Englewood Cliffs, N.J., 1961), pp. 101–2.

30. GSL, "A Plea for the Individual" (GSL-FL).

31. James Gilbert, *Work without Salvation* (Baltimore, 1977), p. 66; GSL, "The Philadelphia Exposition" (September 1878) (GSL-FL). For another reaction to the exposition see John Kasson, *Civilizing the Machine* (New York, 1976), pp. 162–63.

32. GSL, "General Thoughtful" Book, No. 3 (begun 20 February 1886); GSL, "A Plea for the Individual" (GSL-FL). On the parallel influence of mesmerism and "mental telegraphy" see Robert Darnton, *Mesmerism* (New York, 1968), pp. 144–59. On engineers as cultural heroes see Cecilia Tichi, *Shifting Gears* (Chapel Hill, 1987); Elizabeth Ammons, "The Engineer as Cultural Hero," *American Quarterly* 38 (Winter 1986): 746–60; Miles Orvell, *The Real Thing: Imitation and Authenticity in American Culture, 1880–1940* (Chapel Hill, 1989), pp. 171–72. See also Robert Park, *The Crowd and the Public* (Chicago, 1972), p. 22.

33. Clara Barras, *Life and Letters of John Burroughs*, 2 vols. (Boston, 1925), 1:364; 2:34.

34. GSL, "An Order for the Next Poet," *Putnam's Monthly* 1 (1907): 698–702.

35. Ibid.

36. GSL, "Journalism as a Basis for Literature," *Atlantic Monthly* 85 (1900): 236–37.

37. GSL, "The Poetry of the Machine Age," *Atlantic Monthly* 85 (1900): 762; GSL, *Voice of the Machines*, (Northampton, Mass., 1906) pp. 31, 19, 24–25. James Gilbert, in *Work without Salvation*, has found such views to have been widespread at the time. See pp. viii, 47.

38. Richard Burton, *The Bellman* (GSL-FL); George Hodges to GSL, 28 March 1907; Edwin Markham to GSL, 14 March 1907 (GSL-FL).

39. W. H. Mallock to GSL, 17 February 1907; Havelock Ellis to GSL, 6 January 1908 (GSL-FL).

40. William James to W. B. Parker, 22 June 1900; GSL to William James, 21 February 1907; William James to GSL, 27 April 1907 (GSL-FL).

41. GSL to Frank Sanborn, 21 February 1907 (GSL-FL). *Mt. Tom* 9 (October–November 1916): 155. See also *The Bellman*, 20 June 1908.

42. GSL, "The Poetry of the Machine Age," p. 761. See also Canetti, *Crowds and Power*, pp. 42–47, for a cross-cultural view of images of flocking.

43. GSL, *Lost Art*, pp. 184, 437, 439.

44. GSL, *Crowds*, p. 21.

45. Walter Shepard, "Public Opinion," *American Journal of Sociology* 15

(1909): 33; Gabriel Tarde, "The Public and the Crowd," in *Gabriel Tarde: On Communication and Social Influence,* ed. Terry N. Clark (Chicago, 1969), p. 277.

5. *"Redeemer of Wealth"*

1. GSL, *Inspired Millionaires* (New York, 1908), pp. 258, 161.
2. GSL to Andrew Carnegie, n.d.; James Bertram, secretary to Andrew Carnegie, to GSL, 21 April 1908 (GSL-FL). See Alun Munslow, "Andrew Carnegie and the Discourse of Cultural Hegemony," *Journal of American Studies* 22 (1988): 213–24. See also H. S. Miller, Secretary to Thomas Edison, to GSL, 18 February 1909 (GSL-FL).
3. For analysis about corporate strategies that appealed to the public, see Roland Marchand, "Creating the Corporate Soul: The Origins of Corporate Image Advertising in America," a paper delivered at the April 1980 convention of the Organization of American Historians.
4. George Gilder, *The Spirit of Enterprise* (New York, 1984), p. 19. See also Martin Gottlieb, "An 80's Folk Hero," *New York Times,* 3 July 1986.
5. Mark Sullivan, *Our Times,* 6 vols. (New York, 1930), 4: 89. See also Warren Susman, "Personality and the Making of Twentieth-Century Culture," in *New Directions in American Intellectual History,* ed. John Higham and Paul Conkin (Baltimore, 1979), pp. 198–222; Andrew Carnegie, *Personality in Business* (New York, 1911), pp. 31–32; W. J. Ghent, *Our Benevolent Feudalism* (New York, 1902), p. 124. The role of business ideology in this era can be traced in Robert Wiebe, *Businessmen and Reform* (Chicago, 1963); Edward C. Kirkland, *Dream and Thought in the Business Community* (Chicago, 1956); Peter Frederick, *Knights of the Golden Rule: The Intellectual as Christian Social Reformer in the 1890s* (Lexington, Ky., 1976), pp. 242–43; Joseph Wall, *Andrew Carnegie* (New York, 1970), pp. 806–15, 894.
6. Maxwell Bloomfield, *Alarms and Diversions: The American Mind through American Magazines, 1900–1914* (The Hague, 1967). On the muckrakers, see David Chalmers, "The Muckrakers and the Growth of Corporate Power: A Study in Constructive Journalism," *American Journal of Economics and Sociology* 18 (April 1959): 295–311; Stanley K. Schultz, "The Morality of Politics: The Muckrakers Vision of Democracy," *Journal of American History* 52 (1965): 527–47. For background on the political climate in which business oper-

ated see Richard McCormick, "The Discovery That Business Corrupts Politics," *American Historical Review* 86 (1981): 247–74.

7. Otis Graham, *The Great Campaigns* (Englewood Cliffs, N.J., 1970), p. 282; William Jewett Tucker, *Public Mindedness* (Concord, N.H., 1910), p. 348; Herbert Croly, *Marcus Alonzo Hanna: His Life and Work* (Hamden, Conn., 1965 [1912]), pp. 166–67; Carl Hovey, *The Life of J. P. Morgan: A Biography* (New York, 1911). See also Lincoln Steffens, *The Upbuilders* (Seattle, Wash., 1968), p. vii; GSL to Lincoln Steffens, 4 December 1909, Steffens Collection, Columbia University; Charles Forcey, *Crossroads of Liberalism* (New York, 1961), pp. 142–44; William Allen White, *A Certain Rich Man* (New York, 1910).

8. Wiebe, *Businessmen and Reform*, passim; Alfred Kazin, *On Native Grounds* (New York, 1970), p. 94; Edward M. House, *Philip Dru, Administrator* (New York, 1912); Theodore Dreiser, *The Titan* (New York, 1914); Jack London, *The Iron Heel* (New York, 1907).

9. Henry L. Higginson, "A Word to the Rich," *Atlantic Monthly* 107 (1911): 306, 309; "Wealth and Idealism," *Nation* 92 (9 March 1911): 237–38.

10. William Gibbs McAdoo, "The Soul of the Corporation," *World's Work* 23 (March 1912): 579–92; C. M. Keys, "The New Spirit of Business," *World's Work* (1912): 418; Louis Brandeis, "Business—A Profession," as quoted in *Modern Eloquence,* ed. Ashley Thorndike, 15 vols. (New York, 1928), 4:79–86. See also William Gibbs McAdoo, *Crowded Years: The Reminiscences of William G. McAdoo* (Boston, 1931), pp. 104–5; John J. Broesamle, *William Gibbs McAdoo: A Passion for Change 1863–1917* (Port Washington, N.Y., 1973), chap. 2. On McAdoo's "the public be pleased" policy also see Walter Lippmann, *Drift and Mastery* (New York, 1914), p. 31. On Perkins see "Giving the Corporation a Soul," *Current Literature* 51 (October 1911): 460–62; George Perkins, *The Modern Corporation* (New York, 1908); Robert Crunden, *Ministers of Reform* (New York, 1982), p. 206. On the popularity of the concept of public service see David Kennedy, *Over Here* (New York, 1980), pp. 153–54.

11. On the Rotarians see Lewis Atherton, *Main Street on the Middle Border* (Bloomington, Ind., 1954), p. 247; Stewart C. McFarland, "Rotarianism, A Flower of the New Consciousness," *Rotarian* 3 (1913): 59–60, as cited in Henry May, *The End of American Innocence* (Chicago, 1959), p. 131.

12. Lippmann, *Drift and Mastery*, pp. 23–24, 43, 50–51.

13. The creation of the Chicago Civic Federation can be traced in Graham

Taylor's *Pioneering on Social Frontiers* (Chicago, 1930), chap. 4;
Albion Small, "The Civic Federation of Chicago: A Study in Social
Dynamics," *American Journal of Sociology* 1 (1895): 79–103. See
also David Paul Nord, *Newspapers and New Politics: Midwestern
Municipal Reform, 1890–1899* (Ann Arbor, Mich., 1981), chap. 5;
James Weinstein, *The Corporate Ideal in the Liberal State* (Boston,
1968).

14. Arthur Mann, "British Social Thought and American Reform of the
Progressive Era," *Mississippi Valley Historical Review* 42 (March
1956): 672–92.

15. Samuel Lee, "Men of Wealth and Institutions of Learning," *New
Englander and Yale Review* 209 (June 1888): 393, 402–5, 409, 420.
On Samuel Lee's activities on social work see Report of Samuel H. Lee,
Secretary before the Hartford Convention, "College Student Work,"
September 1890 (Springfield, Mass., 1890).

16. Samuel Lee, "Man of Wealth, pp. 383, 420; William McLoughlin, *The
Meaning of Henry Ward Beecher* (New York, 1970), p. 151.

17. Thomas Carlyle, *Past and Present* (London, 1843), as quoted in *The
Norton Anthology of English Literature,* ed. M. H. Abrams et al., 2
vols. (New York, 1979), 2: 1027. See also Ivan Melada, *The Captain
of Industry in English Fiction, 1821–1871* (Albuquerque, N.M.,
1970).

18. Ruskin is quoted in Frederick, *Knights of the Golden Rule,* p. 12. See
also Roger B. Stein, *John Ruskin and Aesthetic Thought in America,
1840–1900* (Cambridge, Mass., 1967); Scott Nearing, *Poverty and
Riches* (Philadelphia, 1916), pp. 25–28; Alta Saunders and Herbert
Creek, *The Literature of Business* (New York, 1928), pp. 47–53;
Jackson Lears, *No Place of Grace* (New York, 1982), chap. 2.

19. Raymond Williams, *Culture and Society, 1780–1950* (New York,
1958), p. 163. On Rudyard Kipling see Herbert Sussman, *Victorians
and the Machine: The Literary Response* (Cambridge, Mass., 1968),
pp. 200–212.

20. William Mallock, *Aristocracy and Evolution* (New York, 1898), pp.
xiii, 93–95; Michael Davis, *Psychological Interpretations of Society*
(New York, 1904), pp. 244–45; Benjamin Lehman, *Carlyle's Theory
of the Hero* (Chapel Hill, N.C., 1928), p. 182; Frederick, *Knights of
the Golden Rule,* p. 12.

21. Mallock, *Aristocracy and Evolution,* p. 128, 252, 349, 146, 168, 215,
282, 274–75. On his view of specialists see pp. 284, 343–44. For a
critique of Mallock see Thorstein Veblen's comments in *The Portable
Veblen,* ed. Max Lerner (New York, 1948), p. 543. See also George

Bernard Shaw, *Socialism and Superior Brains* (London, 1909), pp. 7–9, 28–29, 36.

22. See George Mowry, *The Era of Theodore Roosevelt* (New York, 1958), p. 223; David Shannon, *The Socialist Party of America* (New York, 1955), pp. 26–33; Ray Ginger, *Eugene V. Debs: A Biography* (New York, 1962), pp. 279–302; McCormick, "The Discovery That Business Corrupts Politics," 247–74.

23. Charles Ferguson, "Wanted: Cities with a Sane Ideal," *National Magazine* 24 (1906): 177; Theodore Roosevelt, *The New Nationalism* (Englewood Cliffs, N.J., 1961), p. 34; Frederick T. Martin, *The Passing of the Idle Rich* (New York, 1911), pp. 156–61.

24. GSL, "Two Books on an Island," *Putnam's Monthly* 3 (1908): 615; Olaf Hansen, ed., *The Radical Will: Randolph Bourne Selected Writings 1911–1918* (New York, 1977), p. 295.

25. GSL, *Inspired Millionaires* p. 123–24.

26. Ibid., pp. 127–29. On the impact of the 1902 strike, see Wiebe, *Businessmen and Reform*, pp. 159–61. On Ivy Lee, see Ray Hiebert, *Courtier to the Crowd: The Story of Ivy Lee and the Development of Public Relations* (Ames, Iowa, 1966), chap. 5.

27. GSL, *Mt. Tom* 1 (December 1905): 213–18; GSL, *Mt. Tom* 8 (February–March 1908): 117–18, 120. New York governor and later Supreme Court justice Charles Evans Hughes was a reader of at least some of Lee's books. In one letter, Hughes wrote that "repeatedly, late at night, I have dismissed the cares of the day and soothed myself with your philosophy." C. E. Hughes to GSL, 27 July 1907 (GSL-FL). On Roosevelt see George Juergens, *News from the White House* (Chicago, 1981), chap. 1; Lee Huebner, "The Discovery of Propaganda: Changing Attitudes toward Public Communication in America, 1900–1930" (Ph.D. diss., Harvard University, 1968), p. 109.

28. Richard Abrams, *Conservatism in the Progressive Era: Massachusetts Politics, 1900–1912* (Cambridge, Mass., 1964), p. 105. See also Michael Hennessy, *Twenty-Five Years of Massachusetts Politics* (Boston, 1917), pp. 128–32.

29. GSL, *Inspired Millionaires*, pp. 107–10.

30. Wiebe, *Businessmen and Reform*, p. 68; *The Autobiography of William Allen White* (New York, 1946), p. 39. On the effects of the Panic of 1907, see also Charles Edward Russell, *Business: The Heart of the Nation* (New York, 1911), p. 124; Bloomfield, *Alarms and Diversions*, pp. 63–64; Robert Wiebe, *The Search for Order, 1877–1920* (New York, 1968), p. 201.

31. GSL, *Inspired Millionaires*, pp. 71, 99, 191, 221, 71, 99, 191. See also

Daniel Rogers, *The Work Ethic in Industrializing America* (Chicago, 1978), chap. 3.

32. GSL, *Inspired Millionaires*, pp. 62–63, 67.

33. GSL, *Crowds: A Moving Picture of Democracy* (Garden City, N.Y., 1913), p. 453; GSL to Eugene Debs, 1 December 1909; GSL to Upton Sinclair, 29 July 1903 (GSL-FL).

34. Robert Hunter to GSL, 9 July 1908 (GSL-FL); GSL, *Inspired Millionaires*, p. 18. See also David Shi, *The Simple Life* (New York, 1985), pp. 165, 180.

35. GSL, *Inspired Millionaires*, pp. 19–20.

36. Eileen Boris, *Art and Labor: Ruskin, Morris, and the Craftsman Ideal in America* (Philadelphia, 1986), chap. 8.

37. GSL, *Inspired Millionaires*, pp. 291, 91, 86, 77.

38. Ibid., pp. 70–71, 74. On theorists' interest in the consumer, see Daniel Horowitz, "Consumption and Its Discontents: Simon N. Patten, Thorstein Veblen, and George Gunton," *Journal of American History* 67 (1980): 301–17.

39. See GSL, "Is Ford an Inspired Millionaire?" *Harper's Weekly* 58 (14 March 1914): 9–11; GSL, *Crowds*, p. 495; GSL, *Inspired Millionaires*, pp. 21, 180, 163, 99, 173, 155, 211–12, 241, 238.

40. Ibid., pp. 266, 275, 284–85, 290, 307.

41. Louis Brandeis to GSL, 2 November 1908; Alfred Stieglitz to GSL, 24 March 1910; Louis Sullivan to GSL, 27 November 1908; William Allen White to GSL, 10 January 1910 (GSL-FL); Lincoln Steffens to GSL, 27 July 1909; Steffens to GSL, 13 May 1910. Walter Lippmann to GSL, 10 March 1910. See also Lippmann's letter to GSL of 26 August 1913, in which he wrote, "I have been reading you for years" (GSL-FL). See also Justin Kaplan, *Lincoln Steffens: A Biography* (New York, 1974), pp. 170–71.

42. GSL to Samuel and Emma Lee, 29 July 1911 (GSL-FL). Apparently Samuel Lee was quite upset about his son's use of Jesus as merely a great man. Samuel Lee to GSL, 24 September 1910 (GSL-FL). Other letters of Gerald's to his parents from 1909 to 1913 recount his visits to famous people of the day such as Victoria Woodhall, Lord Grey, and Israel Zangwell. See GSL to his parents, 7 September 1909; 23 January 1912; 20 July 1913; 7 September 1913 (GSL-FL).

43. GSL to Lyman Gage, 2 October 1909; GSL to John Graham Brooks, 8 January 1910. See also GSL to H. G. Wells, 30 August 1911; H. G. Wells to GSL, 7 September 1911, and n.d. (GSL-FL). For the few newspaper reviews of *Inspired Millionaires* see *New York Times*, 20 June 1908; *Outlook* 89 (18 July 1908): 623.

44. Ralph Easley to GSL, 28 June 1908. On the National Civic Federation see Weinstein, *The Corporate Ideal in the Liberal State*, pp. 3–41. See also L. Clark Seelye to GSL, 6 January 1910; J. R. Newberry to GSL, 12 August 1909; Edward Acheson to GSL, 7 December 1909; C. W. Post to GSL, 17 February 1909; GSL to C. W. Post, 29 November 1909 (GSL-FL).

45. John Moody is quoted in *Mt. Tom* 4 (October–November 1909): 108–15; GSL, *Mt. Tom* 4 (October–November 1909): 116, 117. In *The Triumph of Conservatism* (Chicago, 1963), Gabriel Kolko writes that Moody probably had "more factual insights into the workings of business than any of his contemporaries" (p. 15). Weakly defending his ideas in *Mt. Tom,* Lee responded to Moody that the inspired millionaire did not necessarily have to have a million dollars but was the man "who was worth it. The inspired millioniare is the man who . . . creates values . . . and he will do this with the money or without it, as happens to be convenient." Ibid.

46. G. Lowes Dickinson to GSL, 30 December 1908 (GSL-FL).

47. Ibid.

48. Dickinson's letter was reprinted in *Inspired Millionaires,* pp. 309–20; GSL, *Crowds,* p. 232. All told there were four editions of *Inspired Millionaires.* For other responses to the book see Edward Ross to GSL, 18 January 1910; Edward Ross, *Sin and Society* (New York, 1907); Washington Gladden to GSL, 28 November 1909; George Hodges to GSL, 1 December 1909; Rudyard Kipling to GSL, 28 September 1908; Lord Grey to GSL, 30 April 1912; George Herron to GSL, 7 October 1909 (GSL-FL). Two years later, Herron wrote Lee that "some of the things you have written have impressed me as the writing of no other American has done . . . Heaven knows there is needing of altar-fires! The old altars are all ashes . . . The world is approaching a universal catastrophe. Maybe there will be a telescoping of civilization. There is no force in the privileged world, either intellectual, or spiritual or financial, that can withstand the catastrophe. The sole hope lies in the awakening of the soul of labor itself. If this fails, I am positive that the world will fall back into the melting-pot, for who knows how long. We must not suppose that because we have a lot of iron stretched round the world, that therefore another catastrophe of civilization is impossible. In three months of confusion every channel of communication can become obsolete, and the wheels of the world a scrap-heap. It is also true, and upon this truth I build my hope, that a great shock to civilization may precipitate the soul of the new man." George Herron to Lee, 12 October 1911 (GSL-FL).

49. GSL, *Inspired Millionaires,* pp. 332–33, 324; GSL to Dickinson, 11 July 1909 (GSL-FL).
50. Lee corresponded with Joseph Fels, who provided financial assistance in distributing hundreds of copies of the book to influential businessmen in England and the United States. Fels eventually tired of Lee. Lee's book gained favorable attention from a number of prominent Jews. See Isador Singer, "A Jewish Opportunity," *New York Sun,* 6 October 1908, 6. GSL to Isador Singer, 7 October 1908; Singer to GSL, 9 October 1908; Edward Filene to GSL, 6 October 1908 (GSL-FL); GSL, "Is Ford an Inspired Millionaire?" pp. 9–11. See also Sullivan, *Our Times,* 4: 51; David Lewis, *The Public Image of Henry Ford* (Detroit, 1976), chaps. 1, 2.
51. Clyde Griffen, "The Protestant Ethos," in *The Development of an American Culture,* ed. Stanley Coben and Lorman Ratner (Englewood Cliffs, N.J., 1970), p. 149.

6. Righteous Crowds and Moving-Picture Minds

1. On the management of public opinion in the Progressive Era see George Juergens, *News from the White House* (Chicago, 1981); Michael Schudson, *Discovering the News* (New York, 1978), chaps. 3, 4; Lee Huebner, "The Discovery of Propaganda: Changing Attitudes toward Public Communications in America, 1900–1930" (Ph.D. Diss., Harvard University, 1968); Alan Raucher, *Public Relations and Business, 1900–1929* (Baltimore, 1968); Don Kirschner, "Publicity Properly Applied: The Selling of Expertise in America, 1900–1929," *American Studies* 19 (Spring 1978): 65–78; Michael McGerr, *The Decline of Popular Politics: The American North, 1865–1928* (New York, 1986), chap. 6; Sally Griffith, *Home Town News: William Allen White and the Emporia Gazette* (New York, 1989). Contemporary treatments can be found in E. L. Godkin, "The Growth and Expression of Public Opinion," *Atlantic Monthly* 81 (1898): 1–15; William Kittle, "The Making of Public Opinion," *Arena* 41 (July 1909): 433–50; George Kibbe Turner, "Manufacturing Public Opinion," *McClure's* 39 (July 1912): 316–27; W. J. Ghent, *Our Benevolent Feudalism* (New York, 1902), chap. 7. On consumerism see Neil Harris, "The Drama of Consumer Desire," in *Yankee Enterprise,* ed. Otto Mayr and Robert C. Post (Washington, 1981). For a broad overview of the changing modes of perception and communication see Donald Lowe, *History of Perception* (Chicago, 1982); Stephen Kern, *The Culture of Time and Space, 1880–1918* (Cambridge, Mass., 1983).

On advertising see Daniel Pope, *The Making of Modern Advertising* (New York, 1983); Jackson Lears "Some Versions of Fantasy: Toward a Cultural History of American Advertising, 1880–1920," *Prospects* 9 (1984): 349–05; Otis Pease, *The Responsibilities of American Advertising* (New Haven, Conn., 1958).

2. For background on the rise of public relations see Ray Hiebert, *Courtier to the Crowd: The Story of Ivy Lee and the Development of Public Relations* (Ames, Iowa, 1966); Richard Tedlow, *Keeping the Corporate Image: Public Relations and Business, 1900–1950* (Greenwich, Conn., 1979); Roland Marchand, "Creating the Corporate Soul: The Origins of Corporate Image Advertising in America," a paper presented at the April 1980 convention of the Organization of American Historians.

3. GSL to Theodore Roosevelt, 6 June 1913 (GSL-FL).

4. For a sampling of other exuberant proponents of advertising see "The Romance of the Advertising Page," *Current Opinion* 56 (January 1914): 68–72; MacGregor Jenkins, "Human Nature and Advertising," *Atlantic Monthly* 94 (1904): 393–401; Elbert Hubbard, *The Book of Business* (East Aurora, N.Y., 1913), pp. 95–99; Edward L. Thorndike, "Psychology and Advertising," *Scientific American*, 16 September 1911, pp. 250–51; Walter Dill Scott, "The Psychology of Advertising," *Atlantic Monthly* 93 (1904): 29–36; Elizabeth C. Billings, "A Revolution in Advertising," *Atlantic Monthly* 110 (1912): 782–85.

5. Arthur Hadley, *Undercurrents in American Politics* (New Haven, 1915), pp. 164–65. William Allen White, "The Leaven in the National Lump," *American Magazine* 68 (May 1909): 63–70; William Jennings Bryan, "Advertising and Politics," *Agricultural Advertising* 18 (April 1908): 594–96.

6. See William Graebner, *The Engineering of Consent* (Madison, Wis., 1987); Murray Edelman, *Politics as Symbolic Action: Mass Arousal and Quiescence* (New York, 1971) and *Political Language: Words That Succeed and Policies That Fail* (New York, 1974).

7. GSL, *Crowds* (Garden City, N.Y., 1913), p. 146.

8. Ibid., p. 70.

9. Ibid., pp. 139–41. See also Henry Adams, *Mont Saint Michel and Chartres* (Garden City, N.Y., 1933). For an analysis of the development of urban space, see William R. Taylor, "The Launching of a Commercial Culture in New York," paper delivered at "Accumulation and Display" Conference, University of Delaware and the Winterthur Museum, November 8, 1986.

10. GSL, *Crowds,* pp. 130, 137–41. See also GSL, "Advertising Goodness," *Everbody's* 28 (February 1913): 147–58; Susan Porter Benson, "Palace of Consumption and Machine for Selling: The American Department Store, 1880–1940," *Radical History Review* 21 (1979): 199.

11. GSL, *Crowds,* p. 80. On Progressive journalists see David Chalmers, "The Muckrakers and the Growth of Corporate Power: A Study in Constructive Journalism," *American Journal of Economics and Sociology* 18 (April 1959): 295–311; Stanley K. Schultz, "The Morality of Politics: The Muckrakers' Vision of Democracy," *Journal of American History* 52 (December 1965): 527–47.

12. Lary May, *Sceening Out the Past: The Birth of Mass Culture and the Motion Picture Industry* (Chicago, 1980), p. 59.

13. Ibid., p. 15. See also GSL, "Machine Trainers," *Atlantic Monthly* 111 (1913): 198–207.

14. Quentin Schultze, "Advertising, Science, and Professionalism, 1885–1917" (Ph.D. diss., University of Illinois at Urbana-Champaign, 1978), p. 12; George Coleman, ed., *Democracy in the Making: Ford Hall and the Open Forum Movement* (Boston, 1915), p. 218. See also Walter Rauschenbusch, "George W. Coleman," *American Magazine* 72 (1911): 183–84.

15. Seymour Eaton, "Sermons on Advertising" (New York, 1907), n.p. (This pamphlet is located in the J. Walter Thompson Collection at Perkins Library, Duke University.) "Altruism in Advertising" (Chicago, 1911), pp. 23–25. For general background consult Stephen Fox, *The Mirror Makers* (New York, 1985), chaps. 1, 2.

16. GSL, "Intellectual Life," Booknotes, p. 2; GSL, "Preaching," n.d. (GSL-FL).

17. Frank Presbrey, *The History of Advertising* (Garden City, N.Y., 1929), p. 302; Neil Harris, *Humbug: The Art of P. T. Barnum* (Boston, 1973); *Chicago Tribune,* May 2, 1886, p. 2; William Dean Howells, *The Rise of Silas Lapham* (New York, 1963), p. 95.

18. On Gladden's resignation see: Henry May, *Protestant Churches and Industrial America* (New York, 1967), p. 171; Jacob Dorn, *Washington Gladden: Prophet of the Social Gospel* (Columbus, Ohio, 1967), p. 58. On Beecher see Burton Bledstein, *The Culture of Professionalism* (New York, 1976), p. 52; *Nation,* 20 May 1875, 343, as quoted in Edward Kirkland, *Industry Comes of Age* (Chicago, 1961), p. 275. On politics see McGerr, *The Decline of Popular Politics,* chap. 7.

19. Neil Borden, *The Economic Effects of Advertising* (Chicago, 1942);

New York Sun, n.d., as quoted in Presbrey, *History of Advertising*, p. 350.

20. John Powers, "Advertising," *Annals of the American Academy of Political and Social Science* 22 (1903): 473; Ernest Calkins and Ralph Holden, *Modern Advertising* (New York, 1905), p. 6; Huebner, "The Discovery of Propaganda," pp. 106–7; see also Pope, *The Making of Modern Advertising*, pp. 87–88.

21. GSL, *The Critic* 29 (20 November 1897).

22. Ibid. Copy in GSL-FL.

23. GSL, "The Lords of Attention: A Study of Publicity in America," pp. 10–12, 14–16 (GSL-FL).

24. Ibid.

25. Ibid.

26. Charles Ferguson, "The Genius of Business," *National Magazine* 18 (1903): 248–53, 584–86, 714–16; GSL, *Mt. Tom* 1 (November 1905): n.p.; *Mt. Tom* 1 (August, 1905): n.p.

27. Walter Dill Scott, *The Theory of Advertising* (Boston, 1904) and *The Psychology of Advertising* (Boston, 1908); Eugene Leach, "Mob, Audience, Market: Crowd Psychology in America, 1890–1930," a paper delivered at Popular Culture Association Convention, April 16, 1982, p. 13; Huebner, "The Discovery of Propaganda," pp. 79–80.

28. GSL to John Powers, 5 October 1909 (GSL-FL).

29. GSL to James Kehler, 26 August 1909 (GSL-FL). See also Kehler to Lee, 4 September 1909.

30. James Kehler to GSL, 9 November 1909 (GSL-FL).

31. GSL to James Kehler, 13 April 1910 (GSL-FL). This is handwritten so that it is possible that it was not sent, or that it was revised.

32. GSL, "Lords of Attention," pp. 18–19, 24–26.

33. Ibid., p. 28.

34. GSL, n.t., n.d. (probably 1889–92) (GSL-FL); GSL, *Crowds*, p. 167. See also GSL, *The Lost Art of Reading* (New York, 1903), p. 410; GSL, "Making the Crowd Beautiful," *Atlantic Monthly* 87 (1901): 251.

35. GSL, *The Shadow Christ* (New York, 1896), pp. 9, 61, 43, 118; GSL, "Making the Crowd Beautiful," pp. 247, 250.

36. GSL, *Crowds*, pp. 324–25.

37. Ibid., p. 170. See F. W. Taylor's letter to GSL, 16 June 1911 (GSL-FL).

38. GSL to Lincoln Steffens, 3 January 1910, located in the Steffens Collection at Columbia University. See also GSL, *We* (Garden City, N.Y., 1916), p. 24; GSL, *Crowds*, p. 300–301. On the rising star system see May, *Screening out the Past*, chap. 5.

39. Calkins and Holden, *Modern Advertising,* p. 3; GSL, *Crowds,* p. 339. See also Theodore Greene, *America's Heroes* (New York, 1970), p. 114.

40. GSL, *Crowds,* p. 358; GSL, "The Machine Trainers," *Atlantic Monthly* 111 (1913): 200–207. See also *Crowds,* pp. 245, 150.

41. GSL, *Crowds,* pp. 524, 503, 460.

42. Ibid., p. 460; GSL, "Lords of Attention," pp. 34, 31, 39; GSL, *Crowds,* p. 552. See Harris, *Humbug,* p. 57.

43. GSL, *Crowds,* pp. 460–65, 369, 121, 486.

44. Ibid., p. 553.

45. Ibid., p. 224.

46. Ibid., pp. 146–47.

47. GSL to Theodore Roosevelt, 6 June 1913 (GSL-FL).

48. On the popularity of *Crowds* see "The Book Mart," in *The Bookman* 38 (September 1913): 87–96; (October 1913): 208–16; (November 1913): 328–36; (December 1913): 448–56; (January 1914): 576–84. In November, *Crowds* was the best-selling nonfiction book in Chicago, Dallas, Detroit, Baltimore, New York, Los Angeles, and Minneapolis. See also "The Bane of the Crowd," *Current Opinion* 55 (August 1913): 115.

49. GSL, *The Lost Art,* p. 107.

50. Charles F. Taylor, pastor of Greenwich, Conn., Congregational Church, as noted in W. J. Hoggson to GSL, 6 June 1914; A. E. Keigwin of West End Presbyterian Church, as noted in Henrietta Porter to GSL, 5 January 1914. GSL to Bishop of Oxford, 14 June 1912 (GSL-FL).

51. *New Statesman,* 9 August 1913 (GSL-FL). *Newark Evening News,* 5 July 1913; *Brooklyn Eagle,* 21 June 1913; *Springfield Republican,* 4 August 1913. See also *Nation* 97 (21 August 1913): 170; *St. Louis Post Dispatch,* 6 December 1914.

   For other reaction by the British press see *Yorkshire Observer,* 5 November 1913; *English Review,* 11 August 1913; *Justice,* 16 August 1913; *The New Age,* 3 July 1913. Clippings of these and other reviews are in the Lee Collection at the Forbes Library.

52. *The Independent* 75 (24 July 1913): 211; Wallace Rice, *The Dial* 55 (16 August 1913): 116; Charles Shinn, *San Francisco Star,* 5 July 1913; Floyd Dell, *Chicago Evening Post,* n.d. (GSL-FL).

53. Hamlin Garland to GSL, 3 August 1913; Jack London to James Kehler, 9 June 1913 (copy) (GSL-FL); Jack London, *The Iron Heel* (New York, 1957), pp. 113, 119, 142, passim; Jack London, *Martin Eden* (New York, 1908), p. 372. London, of course, had a strong interest in animal packs. See his *The Call of the Wild* (New York,

1931), p. 82. Economist Scott Neering wrote that he was going to buy *Crowds* because he wanted to "read it again . . . You have good stuff there and a big idea." SN to GSL, 7 September 1913. On Frank Lloyd Wright, see *Miami Herald*, 1 April 1984. On Whitman's impact on Wright see Peter Abernathy, "The Expatriate's Dream of Home," *American Studies* 18 (Fall 1977): 45–53.

54. Edward Filene to GSL, 11 December 1913; GSL to ?, 8 December 1913 (GSL-FL).

55. On the New York Telephone Co., see James Kehler to GSL, 8 January 1914 (GSL-FL); J. Berg Esenwein and Dale Carnegie, *The Art of Public Speaking* (Springfield, Mass., 1915), pp. 308, 312.

56. On advertisers' understandable enthusiasm toward Lee's ideas see F. V. Martin to GSL, 29 September 1913; Oscar Binner to GSL, 20 October 1913; Oliver Gales to GSL, 9 June 1913 and 13 June 1913, and Gales to Kehler, 13 June 1913 (GSL-FL) for a small sample. Ivy Lee began his correspondence with second cousin Gerald on 8 February 1913. Ivy's positive view of Gerald was reinforced by his minister father who advocated positions from *Crowds* in his sermons at St. John's Methodist Episcopal Church in St. Louis. See 8 June 1913 letter from Ivy with enclosure. See also Ivy Lee to GSL, 22 April 1914 (GSL-FL). On Ivy Lee, see Huebner, "The Discovery of Propaganda," 29–30; Hiebert, *Courtier to the Crowd*, pp. 72–73; Raucher, *Public Relations and Business*, pp. 119–23.

57. Ivy Lee, *Human Nature and Railroads* (Philadelphia, 1915), pp. 14, 18–19. See also GSL, *We*, p. 236.

58. Percy Mackaye, *The Civic Theater in Relation to the Redemption of Leisure* (New York, 1912).

59. Nicholas Vachel Lindsay, *The Art of the Moving Pictures* (New York, 1922), pp. 78, 23, 94–95, 163–64, 177. See also Elias Canetti, *Crowds and Power* (New York, 1963), pp. 42–47, 75–90. Warren Susman writes that "films are not only a mass medium, they also represent one of the major ways in which a mass society can examine itself as a mass. There was from the start of serious motion pictures an intimate relationship between it and the portraying of the role of the crowds." Quoted from "Personality and the Making of Twentieth Century Culture," in *New Directions in American Intellectual History*, ed. John Higham and Paul Conkin (Baltimore, 1979), p. 222.

60. "Futurist Manifesto" as reprinted in *Mt. Tom* 7 (August–September 1914): 117–29; Carra is quoted in Alfred Barr, ed., *Masters of Modern Art* (New York, 1958), pp. 98–99. On Nathanael West and James Ensor, see Jay Martin, *Nathanael West: The Art of His Life* (New

York, 1970), pp. 302–11. *The Day of the Locust* (New York, 1962) can be seen to be a later writer's answer to Lee's optimism. The horror of alienated people inhabiting modern crowds is highlighted in a scene at the end of the novel in which movie fans have little to occupy their time except to idolize celebrities.

61. H. L. Mencken, "Marie Corelli's Sparring Partner," *The Smart Set,* n.d., pp. 159–60 (GSL-FL).

62. Van Wyck Brooks, *America's Coming of Age* (Garden City, N.Y., 1958), pp. 64–73.

63. Ibid., pp. 71–72.

64. James Hoopes, *Van Wyck Brooks: In Search of American Culture* (Amherst, Mass., 1977), p. 102.

65. Walter Lippmann, *Drift and Mastery* (New York, 1914), pp. 50–53.

66. Lincoln Steffens to GSL, 30 July 1913 (GSL-FL); John Dos Passos, *The 42nd Parallel* (Boston, 1963), pp. 225, 244; Upton Sinclair, *The Brass Check* (Pasadena, Calif., 1919), p. 48.

67. GSL, *Crowds,* pp. 167, 189. See also Roger Babson, *Religion and Business* (New York, 1921), p. 34. On Bruce Barton see Donald Meyer, *The Positive Thinkers* (New York, 1980), pp. 177–80; Leo Ribuffo, "Jesus Christ as Business Statesman: Bruce Barton and the Selling of Corporate Capitalism," *American Quarterly* 33 (1981): 207–31.

7. "The Soul of Advertising Is the Soul of America"

1. GSL, *We* (Garden City, N.Y., 1916), p. 668.

2. *Springfield Republican,* "The Insanity of the Crowd," 4 December 1915; Wilfred Trotter, *Instincts of the Herd in Peace and War* (London, 1915). See also Gilbert Murray, "Herd Instinct and the War," *Atlantic Monthly* 115 (1915): 830–39. On the impact of the war more generally see David Kennedy, *Over Here* (New York, 1980), chap. 4. On the impact of the European war on American thought see Charles Forcey, *Crossroads of Liberalism* (New York, 1961), pp. 221–72; Christopher Lasch, *The New Radicalism in America, 1889–1963* (New York, 1965), pp. 181–224; J. A. Thompson, "American Progressive Publicists and the First World War, 1914–1917," *Journal of American History* 58 (1973): 363–83.

3. *New York Evening Post,* 30 November 1915; G. K. Chesterton is quoted in *Mt. Tom* 9 (February–March 1916): 47. On liberal pacifists from whom Lee distanced himself after the entry of the United States into the war, see Charles Chatfield, "World War I and the Liberal

Pacifist in the U.S.," *American Historical Review* 75 (1970): 1920–37.

4. GSL, *We,* p. 4, 401, 184.

5. Ibid., p. 220, 188–89.

6. Ibid., p. 215. See also pp. 242–43. For background on consumerism see Daniel Horowitz, *The Morality of Consumption: Attitudes toward the Consumer Society in America, 1875–1940* (Baltimore, 1985).

7. GSL, *We,* pp. 219–21, 106. On Ford and Americanization, see Stephen Meyer, "Adapting the Immigrant to the Line: Americanization in the Ford Factory, 1914–1921," *Journal of Social History* 14 (Fall 1980): 67–82.

8. Ibid., p. 309. The star system in the movie industry may well have been an important reference in Lee's mind in this regard. See Lary May, *Screening out the Past* (New York, 1980), chap. 5; Leo Braudy, *The Frenzy of Renown* (New York, 1986), chap. 5.

9. GSL to Ivy Lee, 28 March 1916. See also GSL to Ivy Lee, 30 April 1915; Ivy Lee to GSL, 11 May 1915. On Ivy Lee and the Ludlow aftermath, see Herbert J. Seligman, "A Skilled Publicity Man," *The Masses* 6 (August 1915): 14; Ray Hiebert, *Courtier to the Crowd: The Story of Ivy Lee and the Development of Public Relations* (Ames, Iowa, 1966), chaps. 11, 12.

10. GSL to Ivy Lee, 28 March 1916 (GSL-FL). One sadly ironic example of Lee's desperation and overly active fantasy life occurred after he had purchased his first automobile in 1915; appropriately enough it was a Ford. He proceeded to hit and kill a boy, Michael Buonoconti, on 17 October 1915. At the subsequent trial for this offense, he testified that he had seen "an apparition in the air" immediately following the accident. See *Hampshire Gazette,* 18 October, 20 November, 3 December 1915, 5, 7, 14 January 1916. Lee was acquitted in court.

11. GSL to Ivy Lee, 28 March 1916 (GSL-FL).

12. GSL, n.d., typewritten "notes from diary," p. 2 (GSL-FL). For sales figures on *We* see Box 14 (GSL-FL). Lee made $526.00 in royalties for *We.*

13. Ibid.

14. GSL, *Crowds: A Moving Picture of Democracy* (Garden City, N.Y., 1913), pp. 179, 189; GSL to G. K. Chesterton, 30 March 1916.

15. Arthur Page to GSL, 17 July 1916 (GSL-FL).

16. *Nation* 102 (8 June 1916): 625; *Times Literary Supplement,* 10 August 1916, p. 379 (GSL-FL).

17. Randolph Bourne, "Very Long and Sunny," *New Republic* 7 (15 July 1916): 282–83.

18. Clara Barras, *Life and Letters of John Burroughs*, 2 vols. (Boston, 1925) 2:233.

19. Walter Lippmann, *The Stakes of Diplomacy* (New York, 1915), pp. 27–78. See also D. Steven Blum, *Walter Lippmann: Cosmopolitanism in the Century of Total War* (Ithaca, 1984), chap. 2. WL to Van Wyck Brooks, 15 February 1914, in *Public Philosophy: Selected Letters of Walter Lippmann,* ed. John Blum (New York, 1985), p. 17.

20. Hugo Munsterberg, "Naive Psychology," *Atlantic Monthly* 112 (1913): 812. See also Munsterberg's letter to GSL of 5 April 1916 expressing anger at Lee's attack on him (Box 7 GSL-FL).

21. Graham Wallas, *The Great Society* (Lincoln, Neb., 1967), pp. 133–34; John Dewey, *The Public and Its Problems* (New York, 1927), p. 10. See also Robert Bannister, *Sociology and Scientism: The American Quest for Objectivity, 1880–1940* (Chapel Hill, 1987), chaps. 8, 9; Edward Purcell, *The Crisis of Democratic Theory* (Lexington, Ky., 1973), p. 25; Floyd Allport, *Social Psychology* (Boston, 1924), p. 295, and "Behavior and Experiment in Social Scientists," *American Journal of Abnormal Psychology* 14 (December 1919): 297–98; Robert Park and Ernest Burgess, *Introduction to the Science of Sociology* (Chicago, 1924), p. 868; W. Brooke Graves, ed., *Readings in Public Opinion* (New York, 1928), p. xxiv. *Printer's Ink,* 29 June 1916, p. 195. See also Charles Gardner, *Psychology and Preaching* (New York, 1919), chaps. 1, 2, 11, 12.

22. Ernest Poole, *The Harbor* (New York, 1915), p. 315. See also Carl Sandburg's poem "I Am the People, the Mob," which can be found in Mark Schorer et al., *The Literature of America,* 2 vols. (New York, 1971), 2:389.

23. George Creel, *How We Advertised America* (New York, 1920), pp. 158–59. William Leuchtenburg, *The Perils of Prosperity* (Chicago, 1958), p. 45. On the role of churches during the war see Robert T. Handy, *A Christian Nation: Protestant Hopes and Historical Realities* (New York, 1971), pp. 151–54; Ray Abrams, *Preachers Present Arms* (Scottdale, Pa., 1969), chaps. 5, 12. See also R. Jackson Wilson, *In Quest of Community* (New York, 1968), pp. 84–85, 138–41, 169–70; Henry May, *The End of American Innocence* (Chicago, 1959), pp. 361–98. For background on the CPI see Stephen Vaughn, *Holding Fast the Inner Lines: Democracy, Nationalism, and the Committee on Public Information* (Chapel Hill, N.C., 1980). For the impact of the war on public relations see Lee Huebner, "The Discovery of Propa-

ganda: Changing Attitudes toward Public Communications in America, 1900–1930" (Ph.D. diss., Harvard University, 1968), chap. 3.

24. N.t., n.d.; *New Haven Courier*, 2 May 1918, p. 1; see also the *Evening Sun*, 10 May 1919, p. 9 (GSL-FL).

25. *Bi-Monthly Chicago Advertiser* 4 (1 November 1918): n.p.; GSL, "SuperAdvertising," *Saturday Evening Post* 191 (28 September 1918): 4, 71.

26. *Printer's Ink* 108 (3 October 1918): 122–23; Charles Austin Bates, *Printer's Ink*, (n.d., [1918]): 18 (GSL-FL).

27. Elmo Calkins, *Printer's Ink* (1918): 82; *Chicago Advertising* (1918): 11 (GSL-FL). See J. Walter Thompson archives located in the Perkins Library, Duke University.

28. A. J. Ayer, 4 April 1919, as quoted in Ralph Hower, *The History of an Advertising Agency* (Cambridge, Mass., 1949), p. 110; St. Elmo Lewis, "Propaganda as a Modern Part of Advertising," *Advertising and Selling* 28 (June 1918): 11.

29. GSL, *The House with Twenty-Seven Gardens* (Northampton, Mass., 1919), pp. 82–83, 86.

30. Ibid., pp. 91, 35.

31. See also William McLoughlin, *The Meaning of Henry Ward Beecher* (New York, 1970), p. 147; Jackson Lears, "Some Versions of Fantasy: Toward a Cultural History of American Advertising, 1880–1930," *Prospects* 9 (1984): 356, 359. The idea of a sacred space as a facet of fascism in Nazi Germany is explored in George Mosse, *The Nationalization of the Masses* (New York, 1975), pp. 67–68.

32. GSL, *House*, pp. 15–16. On Ole Hansen and hyperpatriotism see Robert Murray, *The Red Scare* (New York, 1955), pp. 62–72.

33. William G. McAdoo to GSL, 20 August 1919; Charlotte Perkins Gilman to GSL, 27 October 1919 (GSL-FL); Theodore Roosevelt to GSL, 7 July 1919; Ida Tarbell to GSL, 5 August 1919; George Bellows to GSL, n.d.; Bellows recommended Childe Hassam, Robert Henri, John Sloan, William Glackens, and the directors of the Chicago Art Institute as well as Max Eastman for Lee's hotel; Harrison Emerson to GSL, 28 October 1919. See also Herman Hagedorn, Jr., to GSL, 2 August 1919; John G. Brooks to GSL, 20 January 1920. Brooks wrote that "you fly too high for me but you do fly."

34. Perry MacNeille to GSL, 23 October 1919 (GSL-FL). The distribution of the profits of the hotel and the commissions to the construction company behind the project seemed unclear, although no evidence exists to indicate that Lee himself wanted to become wealthy from it.

35. John Macy, "Mobs," *The Masses* 8 (May 1916): 16.

36. Everett Dean Martin, *The Behavior of Crowds* (New York, 1920), p. 8, 17; H. L. Mencken, "The Anatomy of Ochlocracy" (February 1921), as reprinted in Carl Bode, *H. L. Mencken* (Carbondale, 1969), p. 151. Mencken's view of mass culture had been influenced by Nietzsche more than by Carlyle or Emerson. See also William Graebner, *The Engineering of Consent* (Madison, Wis., 1987), chap. 2.

37. Van Wyck Brooks, *New England: Indian Summer, 1865–1915* (New York, 1940), p. 498; Waldo Frank, *Our America* (New York, 1919), pp. 205, 206, 210; Van Wyck Brooks, *The Ordeal of Mark Twain* (New York, 1920), p. 71. See also Van Wyck Brooks, "On Creating a Usable Past," *Dial* 44 (11 April 1918): 341; Thomas Bender, *New York Intellect* (New York, 1987), pp. 241–50; see Frederick J. Hoffman, *The Twenties: American Writing in the Postwar Decade* (New York, 1962), pp. 149–51, 261–62.

38. Herbert Hoover, *American Individualism* (Garden City, N.Y., 1922), p. 25; Walter Lippmann, *Public Opinion* (New York, 1922); E. L. Bernays, *Propaganda* (New York, 1928), p. 11. André Siegfried, *America Comes of Age* (New York, 1927), p. 178.

39. Eugene Leach, "Mastering the Crowd: Collective Behavior and Mass Society in American Social Thought, 1917–1939," *American Studies* 27 (Spring 1986): 105; Bruce Barton, *The Man Nobody Knows* (New York, 1925), pp. 31. See also Roland Marchand, *Advertising the American Dream* (Berkeley, Calif., 1986); Warren Susman, "Piety, Profits, and Play: The 1920s," in *Men, Women, and Issues in American History,* ed. Howard Quint and Milton Cantor (Homewood, Ill., 1980). For recent research that shows patterns of mass culture less prevalent than widely believed see Lizbeth Cohen, "Encountering Mass Culture at the Grassroots: The Experience of Chicago Workers in the 1920s," *American Quarterly* 41 (1989): 6–33.

40. For the shift inward by other Progressives see also Forcey, *Crossroads of Liberalism,* p. 305; Robert Crunden, *From Self to Society* (Englewood Cliffs, N.J., 1972), p. 33. Sidney Kaplan, "Social Engineers as Saviors: Effects of World War I on Some American Liberals," *Journal of the History of Ideas* 18 (June 1956): 365.

41. Gerald Lee, *The Ghost in the White House* (New York, 1920), pp. 28–29, 12, 156, 158, 203–11.

42. GSL to Jennette Lee, 10 March 1924, Jennette Lee Papers, Sophia Smith Collection, Smith College Library. "Doing Invisible Exercises with Gerald Stanley Lee," *Springfield Sunday Republican,* 22 October 1922. The roots of Lee's interest in physical culture can be traced back

to the 1880s as "crusades for physical vigor swept the educated bour-
geoisie in both Europe and America" (Jackson Lears, *No Place of
Grace* [New York, 1982], p. 107). Back in 1885 Lee wrote frequent
reminders to himself to retain his physical strength. He fretted about
his constipation, endlessly enjoining himself in his diary to be calm
and gain self-balance in order to avoid greater physical deformities
and to open his bowels. "This poor body of mine [has] need of greater
efficiency," he confided. GSL, "Personal Thoughtful Book, No. 2," 10
September 1885 (GSL-FL).

43. GSL, *Invisible Exercise* (New York, 1922); GSL, *Rest Working: A
Study in Relaxed Concentration* (Northampton, Mass., 1925); GSL,
Recreating Oneself (Northampton, Mass., 1933); GSL, *Heathen Rage*
(New York, 1931); *Springfield Sunday Republican,* 22 November
1922; James Hoopes, *Van Wyck Brooks: In Search of American
Culture* (Amherst, Mass., 1977), pp. 183–84. See also GSL to Mrs.
Dwight Morrow, 22 August 1937, Box 25 (GSL-FL), and the touching
letters to GSL from Brooks, 6 December 1933 and 22 January 1934, in
which the latter relates his deep appreciation for Lee's help in over-
coming his emotional difficulties.

44. GSL, *Recreating Oneself,* pp. 374, 380.

45. GSL to Colonel E. M. House, 6 November 1933, E. M. House Papers,
Yale University Library. Franklin Roosevelt responded to a copy of
Lee's book *Recreating Oneself* by asserting that he would "be de-
lighted to read the chapters. You are right about relaxation and there is
one more thing that goes with it and that is the kind of sense of humor
that helps people from worrying." Franklin Roosevelt to GSL, 23
November 1931 (GSL-FL). A month later Roosevelt wrote the book
was "beside my bed for night reading," 17 December 1931. No claim
is being made here that Lee had a major influence on the future
president.

46. GSL to Mr. Ferguson (Charles Ferguson), 26 October 1934. See also
GSL to Henry Ford, February 1934 (GSL-FL).

47. GSL to Walter Lippmann, 18 November 1925 (Walter Lippmann
Papers, Yale University, New Haven, Conn.). GSL to Roger Babson, 8
September 1937, Box 25 (GSL-FL).

48. GSL to Ivy Lee, 12 April 1922; Ivy Lee to GSL, 15 May 1933 (GSL-
FL). On Ivy Lee's visit to Germany and visit with Hitler, see Hiebert,
Courtier to the Crowd, pp. 286–89.

49. GSL, *Heathen Rage,* p. 108.

50. Lincoln Steffens to GSL, 29 June 1931. On Steffens, see Otis Graham,
Encore for Reform: The Old Progressives and the New Deal (New

York, 1967), p. 141. See also William Allen White to GSL, 24 July 1931 (GSL-FL).

51. Alice Manning, "Gerald Lee: Strong Hampshire Influence," *Hampshire Gazette,* 16 November 1974[?].

52. GSL, "What Living in Northampton Is Like," 1940 (GSL-FL). Lee's wife was alive at the time and would survive into the early 1950s.

Conclusion. Democracy and the Age of Attention Engineering

Edna St. Vincent Millay's poem is quoted from Van Wyck Brooks, *New England: Indian Summer* (New York, 1940), p. 498.

1. Richard Sennett, *The Fall of Public Man* (New York, 1977), p. 300; Robert Wiebe, *The Search for Order, 1877–1920* (New York, 1968), p. 96.

2. Robert Park, "The City," *American Journal of Sociology* 20 (1914): 604.

3. GSL, "Journalism as a Basis for Literature," *Atlantic Monthly* 85 (1900): 236.

4. Les Brown, "Does the Public Own the Airwaves?" *Channels of Communications* 2 (April–May 1982): 21.

5. Ibid., Bill Moyers made the comment. Robert Park, *The Crowd and the Public and Other Essays,* ed. Henry Elsner (Chicago, 1972), pp. 5–6.

Index

Abrams, Richard, 101
Adams, Brooks, 83
Adams, Henry, 30, 83
Addams, Jane: on law and order, 15; GSL contrasted to, 32, 99
advertising, 3–6, 113–44, 145–49, 153, 156; seen as public education and social reform, 158, 164, 173, 174
Altgeld, John Peter, 21, 72
American Federation of Labor, 98
American International College, 34
American Social Science Association, 87
amusements, 28, 185 n.47
anarchism, 16
Arnold, Matthew, 19, 71
arts and crafts movement, 81, 97
Associated Advertising Clubs, 3
Atlantic City, 28
"attention engineers," 7, 113–33, 145
automobile as symbol of GSL's nationalistic advertising ideal, 148
Ayer, A. J., 158

Babson, Roger, 167
Baer, George, and 1902 Coal Strike, 100
Bagehot, Walter, 71
Baker, Ray Stannard, 61, 165
Baldwin, James Mark, 27
Baltimore, Associated Advertising Clubs convention in, 3
Barnum, P. T., 28, 106, 130

Barton, Bruce, 3, 144, 148, 164
Baruch, Bernard, 156
Baudelaire, Charles, 66
Beecher, Henry Ward: concerned for minister's status, 36; on parson's personality, 53; on need to educate workers, 96; makes advertising endorsement, 120; ideas outdated by 1920s, 164
behaviorism, 146
Bellamy, Edward, 23
Bennett, Arnold, 84
Bergson, Henri, 26
Bernays, Edward, 113, 150, 163
Bible, 11
Binet, Alfred, 26
Bismarck, Otto von, 141
Bok, Edward, 4
Bolsheviks, 159, 161
Boorstin, Daniel, 28
Borden, Neil, 120
Boston Massacre, 18
Boston Tea Party, 18
Bourne, Randolph: on GSL, 49; on workers' welfare, 99, 134; criticizes GSL's *We,* 153–54
Bowles, Samuel, 41
Brandeis, Louis: speaks at Brown University in 1912, 94; calls for *Inspired Millionaires* to be used at Harvard Business School, 107; Lee comments to, 134; labels *Crowds* "brilliant," 143
Brangwyn, Frank, 30

British social thought, 97–98

Brooks, John Graham, 109

Brooks, Van Wyck: sees Lee's ideal as "landmark and touchstone," 5, 45, 84, 134; on ideal of inspired millionaire, 141–42; Lippmann to, on GSL, 154; on romanticism, 163; as patron of Gerald and Jennette Lee, 166

Browne, Carl, 23

Bryan, William Jennings, 9, 21, 72–77, 101, 114

Bryce, James, 9

Buffalo Bill's Wild West Show, 23

Burke, Edmund, 13, 16

Burroughs, John, 82, 154

Bushnell, Horace, 35

business evangelists, 5, 90–112, 164, 198 n.5, 199 n.10

business organizations, 94

Byington, Ezra Hoyt, 47

Byoir, Carl, 134

Calkins, Ernest, 130, 144, 158

"captain of industry," 97

Carlyle, Thomas: GSL seen as spiritual heir of, 6, 16; view of French Revolutionary mobs, 17; compared to Emerson and Whitman, 25; impact of, on GSL, 43–44; compared to Isaiah, 54; influence of, on GSL, 69–71; on mobs, 79–80, 97, 117, 136, 141, 181 nn.18, 19

Carnegie, Andrew, 90–91, 94, 109, 133, 147, 153

Carnegie, Dale, 137

Carter, Emma C. (GSL's mother), 33

cathedrals of commerce, 116

Catholicism, GSL's fear of, 41–42, 60

Chaplin, Charlie, 149

Chautauqua, 95

Chesterton, G. K., 146–47, 152

Chicago, 16, 21, 74, 94, 120, 122

Chicago Civic Federation, 95, 199 n.13

Churchill, Winston, 93

cities, 15, 16

civic pageant movement, 138–39

civil religion, 9, 12, 13, 105, 160, 175

Civil War, legacy of, 22–23

Cleveland, 40

coal strike of 1902, 100

Coleman, George, 118–19

Committee on Public Information, 156–57

Commonwealth Hotel (Superman Inn), 159–61

communications revolution of 1890s, 21–22

Communist party of U.S., 161

Coney Island, 28

Congregational church, 31–39, 57

consumerism, consumer culture, 9, 28, 94, 112, 175, 202 n.38, 211 n.6

convention, 1896 Democratic National, 72–77

Coolidge, Calvin, 3, 105

Cooper, James Fenimore, 13

Cooper, Peter, 96

corporations, 132

Coue, Emil, 164

Coxey's Army, 23

Crane, Stephen, 21

Creel, George, 61, 156

Croly, Herbert, 29, 92–93, 99, 164

Cromer, Lord, 141

crowd, urban, 66–67

crowd metaphor: role of, in industrializing America, 8–30; GSL and, 64–89, 91, 109, 114, 139, 144, 156, 162, 170, 180 n.9, 190 n.31

"crowd principle," GSL defines, 64–66, 73, 194 n.1

crowd psychology, 9, 24, 26, 65, 66, 84, 144, 146, 153, 154, 155, 162, 178 n.3, 185 nn.43–46

Curtis, Cyrus, 157

Darwinian theory, 41, 43, 98

Daughters of American Revolution, 22

David, 53

Davis, Michael, 29

Debs, Eugene, 21, 103

Deland, Margaret, 61

Dell, Floyd, 136

deMille, Cecil, 164

democracy, 6, 11, 12, 24, 25, 67, 68, 69, 71, 74, 113, 162

democratic market society, 5, 7, 26, 175

department store, 28, 116–17

Hoover, Herbert, 163, 165
House, E. M., 93, 166
Hovery, Carl, 92
Howells, William Dean, 23, 59–60
Hubbard, Elbert, 23, 61, 104
Hunter, Robert, 103–4
Huxley, T. H., 141

Iaccoca, Lee, 91
"ideodynamism," 123–24
Ingersoll, Robert, 51
"inspired millionaires," 90–112
Insull, Samuel, 94
International Workers of the World
    (I.W.W.), 99
"invisible exercises," 165
Isaiah, 43, 54–55, 76, 148
Israel, 54, 148

James, William: comments on GSL, 6;
    on Whitman, 24–25; reads LeBon,
    27, 67, 72; on dramatic personality
    and collective soul, 82; comments on
    GSL's *Voice of the Machines*, 86–87;
    on great man theory of history, 98
Jefferson, Thomas, 133
Jesus Christ, 20, 53–55, 67, 76, 104,
    127–29, 135, 148, 152, 164
Jewett, Sarah Orne, 36
Johnson, Tom, 109

Kehler, James Howard, 125–26, 137
Keys, C. M., 94
Kiam, Victor, 91
Kingsley, Charles, 63
Kipling, Rudyard, 59, 97, 125, 136

labor and labor unions, 16, 90, 102,
    131, 132–33
Lafollette, Robert, 99
language, 6, 25, 29, 49–50, 147, 159,
    162, 163, 172, 176, 191 n.5
Leach, Eugene, 164
LeBon, Gustave, 26–27, 70–72, 74,
    76, 102, 124, 138, 146, 162, 163,
    195 n.17
Lee, Chris, 57
Lee, Emma C. (GSL's mother), 33
Lee, Gerald Stanley: family back-
    ground, 33–34, 186 n.2; in Green-

field, Mass., 36, 40; in Cleveland,
36–37, 40; in Springfield, Mass., 37;
travels to New York City, 38; resigns
from Springfield church, 48; has congregation in Princeton, Minn., 50–
51; early career as writer, 55–56;
marries Jennette Barbour Perry, 56;
has daughter, Geraldine, 56; relations of, with parents, 57–58; seeks
to contain public with Ferguson, 62;
expresses anger toward Bryan and
1896 Democratic Convention, 72–
77; on reading and print culture, 77–
80; on machine aesthetics, "psychic
currents," and poetry, 80–87; legacy
of Puritanism in ambiguous conception of crowd, 88–89; influenced by
British social thought, 97–98; importance to, of 1902 Coal Strike, 100;
attracted to T. Roosevelt, 100–101;
interested in Massachusetts governor
Douglas, 101; impact upon, of Panic
of 1907, 101–2; views workers and
idealized factory reforms, 102–3;
views Tolstoy, 104; defines organic
factory, 105–6; travels to England,
107; reaction to *Inspired Millionaires*, 109–11; ideas of, about
news, 115–16; on role of motion
pictures, 117–18; and advertising
and Progressive Movement, 118–19;
earlier attitudes of, toward advertising, 119–22; derivation of his conversion toward celebrating
advertising, 122–23; presents advertising principles in *Mt. Tom*, 123;
views of, on public's irrationality,
123–24; sees advertising as tool of
cultural redemption, 124–25; relationship with Kehler, 125–26; for-
mulates "Lords of Attention," 126;
sees Jesus as grand persuader, 127–
28; notes attraction to Taylor, 128;
on "hero habit," 129; sees T. Roosevelt as "Chancellor of People's Attention, 130–31; on labor and lawyers,
131–32; reaction to *Crowds*, 134–
38; relationship to Ivy Lee, 138; interest in, by Vachel Lindsay, 139; interest of, in Futurists Manifesto, 139;